GULL FORCE

JOAN BEAUMONT is Professor Emerita at the Strategic and Defence Studies Centre, Australian National University. She is one of Australia's pre-eminent scholars on Australian prisoners of war and is the author of *Broken Nation: Australians in the Great War*, the critically acclaimed account of Australia's experience of the First World War, which was joint winner of the Prime Minister's Literary Award for Australian History and winner of the NSW Premier's Prize for Australian History. She is also the author of *Australia's Great Depression: How a Nation Shattered by the Great War Survived the Worst Economic Crisis It Has Ever Faced* and co-editor with Allison Cadzow of *Serving Our Country: Indigenous Australians, War, Defence and Citizenship*.

Everyone who was touched by Ambon has
a crying heart which will never leave them.
So little was said and so much damage done.

— Sister of Australian soldier lost on Ambon

GULL

AUSTRALIAN POWS ON AMBON AND HAINAN, 1941-1945

FORCE

JOAN BEAUMONT

NEWSOUTH

UNSW Press acknowledges the Bedegal people, the Traditional Owners of the unceded territory on which the Randwick and Kensington campuses of UNSW are situated, and recognises the continuing connection to Country and culture. We pay our respects to Bedegal Elders past and present.

A NewSouth book

Published by
NewSouth Publishing
University of New South Wales Press Ltd
University of New South Wales
Sydney NSW 2052
AUSTRALIA
https://unsw.press/

Our authorised representative in the EU for product safety is Mare Nostrum Group B.V., Mauritskade 21D, 1091 GC Amsterdam, The Netherlands (gpsr@mare-nostrum.co.uk).

A catalogue record for this book is available from the National Library of Australia

ISBN   9781761170027 (paperback)
            9781761179235 (ebook)
            9781761178405 (ePDF)

Internal design Josephine Pajor-Markus
Cover design Peter Long
Cover image Tan Tui camp, Ambon, 22 September 1945 (Australian War Memorial, 118253)

UNSW
SYDNEY

CONTENTS

AUTHOR'S NOTE

This book is a revised edition of my *Gull Force: Survival and Leadership in Captivity, 1941–1945* (Allen & Unwin, 1988). The original text has been left largely unchanged and forms Parts I–V (Chapters 1–11) of this new edition. However, these chapters have been updated to incorporate material lodged at the Australian War Memorial since my original research in the 1980s, and feedback from members of Gull Force. Since the 1980s, too, much has been published about Australian prisoners of the Japanese and the aftermath of their captivity. The insights of these publications are reflected in the revised text.

Part VI is new to this edition. It incorporates new research about war crimes trials and the burial of Gull Force's dead on Ambon and in Japan. It also reflects the way in which our understanding of Australia's experience of war has been transformed by recent scholarship in memory studies and by the 'boom' in the national commemoration of war from about 1990 on. Both developments have generated a host of publications and media, and new rituals of commemoration and remembrance at the national and local levels. The 'memory boom' has also accorded an elevated status to Australian prisoners of war, including on Ambon and, to a lesser extent, on Hainan.

When I wrote the first edition of this book, I had the privilege of interviewing and corresponding with many survivors of Gull Force (listed in Appendix II) and some members of their families. This book could not have been written without them. Their willingness to share, with a then young female historian, memories of the past that remained powerful and sometimes traumatic was remarkable. Four decades later none of these former prisoners of war is still living. Their words and opinions have been preserved unchanged in this revised edition. They stand as a tribute to the men who were sent to defend Ambon, with no chance of success, and then endured one of the worst experiences of captivity in the national experience of war. This book also pays respect to the many hundreds of Gull Force who did not survive. Their families waited for years with no word of the men who were missing – only to learn when the war ended that they had died violent or painful deaths and were never coming home.

CITATION OF ORAL SOURCES AND RANK

In the text that follows, information attributed to individual prisoners of war, unless otherwise stated, was gained in interviews or questionnaires dating from 1982 to 1987; when a name such as 'John Smith' is cited, with no additional details, this refers to an oral history source from the 1980s.

Rank is given only for officers and non-commissioned officers. If individuals gained promotion at some later date, the rank (given in brackets) indicates the rank held at the time of capture.

ABBREVIATIONS

AASC	Australian Army Service Corps
AHQ	Army Headquarters
AIF	Australian Imperial Force
AWM	Australian War Memorial
BCOF	British Commonwealth Occupation Force (Japan)
CWGC	Commonwealth War Graves Commission
DMOP	Director of Military Operations and Plans
DVA	Department of Veterans' Affairs
HMAS	His Majesty's Australian Ship
IWGC	Imperial War Graves Commission
KNIL	*Koninklijk Nederlands Indisch Leger* or Royal Netherlands East Indies Army
NAA	National Archives of Australia
NCO	non-commissioned officer
POW	prisoner of war
PTSD	post-traumatic stress disorder
Q	quartermaster
RAN	Royal Australian Navy
RAAF	Royal Australian Air Force
USAAF	United States Army Air Force

LIST OF MAPS, FIGURES AND TABLES

PART I
INTRODUCTION

1
AN ATTEMPT TO UNDERSTAND

War has always created more victims than heroes, modern warfare particularly so. The 22 000 Australians who became prisoners of war of the Japanese in the Asia-Pacific war of 1941 to 1945 are remembered widely. This is not least because of their death toll. More than a third of the men and women captured by the Japanese did not survive captivity. They were either executed or succumbed to disease, malnutrition and forced labour over some three-and-a-half years. The number of prisoners who died in Japanese captivity was about the same as Australian losses in the wider Pacific war.[1]

Prisoners of war hold a prominent place in Australians' memory of war. However, if the prisoners of the Japanese are now remembered for their sacrifice and endurance, it was not always so. In the immediate aftermath of the Second World War, the memory of their captivity was sometimes ambiguous. The defeats and surrenders of 1942 sat uneasily within the foundational narrative of war spawned in 1915, the Anzac legend. Although this mythic narrative evolved in the late 20th century to become a post-heroic signifier of national identity, capable of incorporating even civilian security and emergency services, Anzac traditionally celebrated the fighting man. The Australian volunteer soldier was celebrated as being a natural fighter, one of the best in the world. He was deemed to be resourceful, contemptuous of formal authority and, above, all, loyal to his mates.[2] Prisoners of the Japanese made some attempt to position themselves within this narrative, but their defeat in battle and subsequent surrender suggested that they might be seen as second-class soldiers. The sympathy they received on their return to Australia meant that, so far as their families and local communities were concerned, such feelings of inferiority were unwarranted. Yet, Australia's military authorities displayed some ambiguity about the status of prisoners of war, and their relative neglect by Australian historians until the 1980s confirmed the ex-prisoners' intuition that they were outside the mainstream of the Australian experience of war. It was only when the so-called 'memory boom' of the late 20th century began to represent Australian soldiers as victims of trauma that prisoners of war were fully integrated into the national rituals of war commemoration and remembrance.[3]

Even then, the popular understanding of captivity has been partial. Prisoners of the Japanese have been more visible than any other cohort of prisoners of war, be they from the other theatres of the Second World War, the First World War or the Korean War of 1950–53.[4] This is understandable given that prisoners of the Japanese accounted for 22 000 of the total 35 000 Australians captured in the 20th century. But, even within the memory of the Asia-Pacific war, certain experiences of captivity have been given prominence over others.[5] One of the lesser known stories at the public level is the tragedy of Gull Force, a detachment of the 2nd Australian Imperial Force (AIF), consisting of the 2/21st Battalion and ancillary units. Captured on Ambon in the Netherlands East Indies (now Indonesia) in early February 1942, and interned there, and on Hainan Island, China, until the war's end, Gull Force endured an appalling captivity. The death rate, on Ambon, was over 77 per cent; only 119 of the 528 men who spent their entire internment in the camp of Tan Tui survived.[6] For the third of prisoners who were transferred to Hainan in October 1942, the toll was 32 per cent: 86 of 267 men. Only the Allied prisoners interned at Sandakan in North Borneo suffered a higher death rate than Australians on Ambon. In that case, only six of the 2500 Australian and British prisoners of war survived the death marches of 1945.[7] On the railway constructed from Thailand to Burma in 1942–43, around 21.5 per cent (2800 of an estimated 13 000 Australians) died. The worst case was F Force, who worked in the most remote regions of Thailand. In this group, around a third of the 3600 Australians died.[8]

REMEMBERING GULL FORCE

The story of Gull Force has been told before: first, in the official history of the Second World War and then in several works by survivors and historians from the 1980s on.[9] This book is a revision and updating of my own *Gull Force: Survival and Leadership in Captivity 1941–1945*, published in 1988 and reprinted in 1990 when a commercial film about the war crimes trials relating to Ambon, *Blood Oath*, was released. But despite these publications, and many years of investment in sites of memory on Ambon by veterans and their families, Gull Force's tragedy has attracted less attention than other Australian experiences of captivity. Sandakan has been featured in a dramatic gallery display in the Australian

War Memorial for some decades, while Hellfire Pass on the Thailand–Burma railway became, in the late 1990s, the site of an official Australian memorial museum.[10]

Why is this so? What is it about the national commemoration of war that continues to render Ambon and Hainan less visible? The reasons are complex, as are all the processes of memory formation that elevate one episode of the past over another in the public sphere. But the ambiguity in Gull Force's case surely arises from the unsettling elements of its experience of war and captivity. This was almost a litany of disaster from the start. Gull Force was sent by Australian military authorities in December 1941 to the remote island of Ambon as part of an ill-conceived strategy to assist the Dutch colonial forces stationed there. Like other battalion-sized forces sent to Dutch Timor and New Britain, Gull Force had no chance of effective resistance, but when its commanding officer, Lieutenant-Colonel LN (Len) Roach, predicted this in January 1942, he was summarily sacked. Australia's military leaders in Melbourne gave no consideration to evacuating Gull Force. When the Japanese attacked, on the night of 30–31 January 1942, the defenders of Ambon were overwhelmed in a matter of days. Gull Force suffered relatively few (54) battle deaths, but in the next two to three weeks, some 229 Australians, who had been assigned to defend the strategic airstrip at Laha, were massacred by the Japanese. Several small groups of Australians (52 in all) managed to escape in the weeks that followed; and, with the help of the Ambonese and a good dose of luck, made their way by island-hopping back to Australia. But the remaining 795 members of Gull Force remained prisoners of war. By the war's end, only 300 were alive.[11]

Gull Force's experience of captivity was especially challenging because of its isolation. Most Allied prisoners captured in the Asia-Pacific region moved several times during their internment in response to the demands of the Japanese for labour within their conquered territories and homeland. Prisoners were shipped or trucked from Java to Singapore, from Singapore to Burma, and from Thailand to Japan, to name only some of the more common journeys. During these travels their original formations were often broken up and they encountered prisoners from other Australian units and other armies. Gull Force, in contrast, remained a discrete force, although it was divided into two cohorts in October 1942 when one-third went to Hainan. These Australians were imprisoned with Dutch and a handful of American prisoners, but they fraternised very little outside their own national group.

Arguably, this might have been an advantage. All the literature on the sociology of prisoners of war suggests that group solidarity and social cohesion are vitally important in a situation where the struggle for survival is acute. Yet, the isolation of Gull Force became a liability. The prison camps on Ambon and Hainan were closed communities, with all the stresses of enforced intimacy of any prison life. Yes, they were free, for the most part, from the hazards that other prisoners of war experienced when moving around the region – being transported in crowded cattle trucks or being crammed into 'hell ships' that were vulnerable to Allied submarine attack – but they suffered the profound tedium of being confined in one or two locations. In the case of Hainan, this environment was depressingly unattractive.[12] The outlets for the inevitable personal and social tensions were few and the cohesion of the group came under immense strain.

To add to this, Gull Force experienced a crisis of leadership. In a case of misdirected aggression, the other ranks initially blamed their rapid defeat on their own officers, rather than the high command in far-off Melbourne that had sent them ill-equipped to Ambon. When discipline frayed, the response of the commanding officer who replaced Roach, Major WJR (Jack) Scott, was seen as autocratic and authoritarian. Then, on 15 February 1943, an Allied air attack on Tan Tui camp in Ambon killed some of the most able officers, as they rushed to extinguish a fire in a munitions dump established within the prison camp by the Japanese. Over the next two years, the surviving officers confronted disciplinary issues that threatened the collective good, such as stealing, and ultimately resorted to installing a controversial cage for interning Australian offenders. On Hainan, meanwhile, Scott, who led the part of Gull Force that left Ambon in October 1942, became alienated from the other prisoners. His solution to disciplinary breaches was to hand men over to the Japanese for punishment. When one prisoner was seriously beaten in October 1944, the ranks mutinied, establishing their own 'vigilance committee' to deal with stealing in the camp. Certain of Scott's fellow officers considered divesting him of his authority by declaring him insane.

None of this story sits easily with the values of the Anzac legend into which the men of Gull Force had been socialised. This is not to indict Gull Force. None of us has experienced the hunger, physical exhaustion, illness and mental anguish that these prisoners of war endured. We cannot condemn those who found the stresses of captivity intolerable and who acted in ways which, in retrospect, seem less than admirable.

'There but for the grace of God go I.' In such a profoundly traumatic situation, individual reputations suffered, and it is impossible, when retelling their story, to avoid disclosures that may be painful. But it is not the purpose of this history to condemn – or glorify – the Australians whose story it tells. Rather, it is an attempt to understand.

RETRIEVING GULL FORCE'S HISTORY

This history of Gull Force could not have been written without the testimonies of the men who survived the traumas on Ambon and Hainan (see Appendix II). When my original research began in 1983, it proved possible to interview 65 of the 300 men liberated in 1945. These encounters were usually face-to-face sessions lasting on average one-and-a-half to two hours. Other survivors, who were difficult to meet because of geographical distance, were sent questionnaires. Eighteen of these were returned, completed in writing or on the technology of the day, audiocassettes. Some ex-prisoners declined to be interviewed or to complete a questionnaire.

Were the memories of captivity still too painful? One of the engineers attached to Gull Force said later, 'I didn't want to know any more about Ambon. When we left Ambon we said we don't want anything that's ever going to remind us of this place again'.[13] He wrote to me when declining to complete a questionnaire: 'I have avoided reflecting on our P.O.W. experience as I found it quite upsetting, resulting in sleepless nights bad dreams etc. over fairly long periods. This has caused many things to be forgotten & others to be confused'.[14]

Some years later, many of these same men, joined in some cases by their wives, shared with me their memories of their adjustment to civilian life after their return to Australia in 1945. Some also provided their opinions on the adequacy of the compensation that they had received – or in some cases, not received – from the Australian and Japanese governments in the postwar years.[15]

Oral history thus formed a significant part of the research for this book. But my expectation that it would prove to be an empirical source, filling the gaps of the written archival record, was soon undone. I learnt what is now axiomatic in the scholarship of memory studies: that personal memory is not necessarily a precise or fixed recall of the past. Rather, memory is constantly changing, being shaped and reworked in the light of present-day situations and emotions. As Alistair Thomson put it when reflecting on his interviews with Great War veterans, we compose our memories, first, 'using the public languages and meaning of our culture': that is, we make sense of our personal experiences by employing the meanings of a public group, be it the wartime military unit, or wider public representations of the past in, say, various media, commemorative practices and rituals. How we remember the past also changes in relation to our shifting personal identity or identities. These we construct 'by telling stories either to ourselves as inner stories or day-dreams, or to other people in social situations'.[16] Oral history, then, to quote another of the leading scholars of the memory of war, Jay Winter, is a three-way conversation:

> The first party is the historian or archivist, who
> poses the questions, or encourages the subject being

interviewed to develop a point or turn to another one. The second party is the interviewee, as she is at the moment of the interview. The third, and most quicksilver presence, is the interviewee as she was at the particular point in time in the past on which the interview dwells.[17]

So it was with Gull Force veterans. In face-to-face interviews some men seemed to feel the need to recall the experience of captivity positively. This massive trauma, in which close friends died cruelly, and survivors were deprived of their youth and often their physical and emotional health, could be made comprehensible only if the good in the experience was distilled. What was the value of speaking ill of others, especially if they were dead, or voicing slanderous opinions that might return to haunt the speaker in print?

These veterans also tended, if only unconsciously, to frame their memories within the public narrative of Anzac. To quote Thomson again: 'Our memories are risky and painful if they do not fit the public myths, so we try to compose our memories to ensure that they will fit with what is publicly acceptable'.[18] Hence, despite considerable evidence that the social fabric of Gull Force was severely strained, almost shattered, in the later years of captivity, some veterans stressed that mateship was enduring, that Australians in a crisis did have special qualities of self-discipline, and that their morale did not crack.

The negative aspects of the wartime experience, in contrast, were sometimes elided. Thieving, or 'scrounging', from the Japanese was a common topic of conversation, but theft between Australian prisoners, far less so. No survivor of Ambon recalled the breakdown of health and sanitation in the last days of captivity on Ambon, in conditions that were recorded in distressing detail in the report submitted by Gull Force's dentist on his return to Australia in 1945. Some other aspects of captivity – the intimate details of disease, physical discomfort and sexuality – were kept hidden, possibly because the interviewer was a young female academic.

The interviews of the 1980s also revealed another feature of memory formation: namely, the construction within groups of a shared or collective memory. As soon as Gull Force returned home, the survivors formed a battalion association in which many (though not all) became active. Not only did this group schedule several reunions a year, but from 1967 on, they organised regular 'pilgrimages' to Ambon and mounted significant aid and development projects for the Ambonese. Initially these were gestures of gratitude to the local people who had helped the prisoners at great personal risk, but over the years they developed into a rich legacy of personal cross-cultural friendships that continues to this day, even after the original Gull Force veterans have died.

These rituals of remembrance provided the space for the telling and re-telling of stories from the war. Here the survivors could share memories that they struggled to articulate even in their own homes. Here, too, individuals came to believe that they witnessed, or personally experienced, events they actually heard about second-hand. In one instance, a veteran contacted me the day after his interview explaining that a beating that he said he had suffered at the hands of the Japanese had, in fact, been inflicted on a friend. Through constant repetition at social events, he had come to believe the experience to be his own.

Of course, oral evidence, like much evidence, can also be partial, even falsified. In the case of Ambon, the construction of a cage for detaining prisoners was spoken of openly by many interviewees, but such was its sensitivity that some officers who had been responsible for camp administration denied its existence. When confronted with the archival records of an official court of inquiry into the matter, held immediately after the prisoners' liberation (see Appendix III), they fell silent.

Hence, the interviews conducted in the 1980s (quoted with the veterans' permission and included unchanged in this revised version) are best read as evidence of what the survivors of Gull Force remembered four decades after the event, and what they chose to confide in a stranger. Quotations from interviews have been used to provide colour and emotion, and when the general accuracy of the information they contain has been confirmed by other oral accounts or contemporary written records.

It needs to be remembered, however, that documentary evidence, too, is by no means infallible, comforting though it might be to historians schooled in empiricism. In the case of Gull Force, it posed different challenges of interpretation. In the prison camps controlled by the Japanese, it was difficult to keep records. Writing materials were scarce; the Japanese punished the keeping of diaries, while resisting any attempts to record evidence of their mistreatment of their prisoners. The Australian officers managing the routine of prison camps were often forced to keep data hidden or to delay writing official reports until their return to Australia. On Hainan, for example, while officers were permitted by the Japanese to keep records of rations received, the dates of deaths and the frequency of work parties, they had to record details of Japanese atrocities in secret or consign them to memory. Not until they were liberated in September 1945 were they able put these details in writing.[19] Obviously, since they were recalling the events of the past with the intention of bringing to account the Japanese who had maltreated them, their recall was thoughtful and careful. Yet, it occurred weeks, months, even years after the event.

The same can be said for the testimony given by survivors of Gull Force in anticipation of the war crimes trials at which the Japanese were brought to account after the war. The main trial of the Ambon personnel was held in January–February 1946, and many of the sworn statements by ex-prisoners were made in the days soon after liberation, close to the event but at an emotionally charged time. But the trials of Hainan guards did not occur until January 1948. Many of the affidavits made by Gull Force for presentation to this court were given only in 1947. Fortunately, in this case and with other written records of captivity, there are often several accounts of many incidents which allow for cross-checking.

That said, almost all the evidence given at the war crimes trials was concerned with documenting Japanese atrocities. It says little about the internal group dynamics of the Australian prisoners. For insights into what might be called the sociology of prison life, diaries are a potentially fruitful source, but comparatively few men of Gull Force kept these during their captivity. Only one of any substance about life on Ambon survives. Perhaps others were destroyed in the Allied bombing raids of Ambon camp in February 1943 and August 1944.[20] Those personal records of captivity that survived, moreover, throw more light on daily struggles, such as the search for food, gardening and the rigours of work, than anything else. The memoirs that several prisoners compiled after the war are a valuable source (now lodged in the Australian War Memorial), but they lack the immediacy that a diary written during captivity would have had. No contemporary record of Gull Force matches the drama and emotional intensity of Stan Arneil's wartime diary, published in 1980 as *One Man's War*, or Sir Edward 'Weary' Dunlop's war diaries, both of which did much in the 1980s to revive popular interest in the Thailand–Burma railway.[21]

Beyond this, the historian of Gull Force faces the challenge that the reports submitted by the senior Australian officer in command of the prisoners of war – reports that would normally be definitive sources of evidence – were prejudiced when it came to documenting the behaviour of the Australian prisoners. For reasons that will emerge in the later narrative, Scott seemed intent on using his two 1946 reports to destroy the reputation of 2/21st Battalion and its former commanding officer, Roach.[22] Officers who were familiar with the events Scott described later insisted that his accounts were malicious and false in many respects. They, of course, had at stake the reputation of their unit, and by implication themselves, but their critique, which was formalised in a 1985 submission to the Australian War Memorial, was strengthened by the fact that Scott's criticisms of the 2/21st, particularly in a second unofficial report, were often based on hearsay. Many of the events he criticised happened before he took command of the battalion. It is not clear what his sources for this information were, but his opinions need to be read with caution.

The path to understanding the history of Gull Force has thus presented considerable challenges of interpretation and coverage. This book acknowledges these, and attempts to take diverse, and sometimes conflicting, opinions into account when reconstructing the narrative and assessing the behaviour of individuals. Above all, it concedes that the historian, writing decades later in the comfort of an Australian home office, can never fully understand the physical and emotional trauma and moral choices that prisoners of war faced when enduring captivity under the most profound duress.

PART II
THE ROAD TO CAPTIVITY, 1940-42

2
WAITING TO FIGHT, 1940–41

The story of Gull Force begins in Australia, since it was here that its units were raised. It was here, too, that its men formed the attitudes and values that shaped their responses to captivity. Moreover, their ability to adjust to the stresses of being prisoners of war depended to some extent upon their experience of 16 months' training in Australia.

THE ANZAC INHERITANCE

The men who made up Gull Force were overwhelmingly born in Australia in the years after 1905. They were the children of a society in which the Anzac legend had become a powerful focus for national pride and identity. Few of Gull Force would have read in full the works in which the Anzac legend had been articulated, most notably by CEW Bean, the war correspondent and official historian of the war of 1914–18. But they were familiar with its values through a range of formal and informal influences. They had heard the stories of their fathers and relatives who had served in the Great War. They had stood silently through Anzac Day rituals: the Last Post, the two minutes' silence and Binyon's elegy, 'They shall grow not old'. They had seen the memorials to the war dead installed in the main streets, public buildings, schools and churches of almost every country town and suburb. If, as many of Gull Force did, they lived in Melbourne or another capital city, they would also have visited the vast shrines of remembrance that were erected in the early 1930s, commemorating the values of patriotism, sacrifice, courage and endurance. The Returned Sailors' and Soldiers' Imperial League of Australia (later Returned and Services League, or RSL) had also kept alive the memory of the exploits of the Anzacs in the interwar years, ensuring that no one forgot the debt owed to these men. Finally, many of the men in Gull Force had previously served in the peacetime militia where the traditions of the Great War were consciously preserved and transmitted to younger generations. By the time they volunteered for overseas military service in 1940, therefore, the men who later formed Gull Force were almost certainly conscious of the tradition to which they were heirs.

This tradition, like all foundational narratives, would evolve over the decades that followed 1915, but in 1939 its essence was much as Bean depicted it.[1] Primarily, Australian diggers were thought to be natural fighters in battle whose prowess arose not from the drill, training and discipline of the military, but from the society in which they spent their youth. The Australian bush, with its good food, benign climate and active life, supposedly gave them a better physique and the qualities of independence of mind, inquisitiveness, eagerness to learn, and resourcefulness. As it happened, by 1914 the majority of Australians lived in cities and towns rather than the bush, but for Bean, as for the *Bulletin* writers who had created the powerful bush legend in the 1890s, the spirit of the bush 'set the standard of personal efficiency even in the Australian cities'.[2]

Beyond this, Bean attributed the diggers' fighting excellence to Australia's egalitarianism. As he saw it, its people 'came nearer than perhaps any other to forming one class without distinction of birth or wealth'.[3] The 1st AIF had been an unusually democratic army. To be sure, education and manners often played a role in the selection of officers, but they came from similar social backgrounds to the men they led. In many cases, they rose from the ranks on their own merits, to hold commissions within the units they had previously served. Their legitimacy as leaders and authority as officers depended not on a mindless and unquestioning respect for rank per se, but on personal qualities: intelligence, reliability, strength of will and, above all, concern for their subordinates. Competence, not formal rank, was the basis of authority in the 1st AIF.

There were, of course, qualifications. Bean conceded that promotion created a gulf between the former diggers and their mates, and the officers, when off duty, did not fraternise with their men. But these differences, Bean maintained, were like those 'between prefects or monitors of a big school and their schoolfellows'.[4] The Australian officers' messes in France were far from luxurious, and once they returned to the trenches the social distinctions between the ranks were virtually abandoned. At the front, they behaved as if all were equal. Breaches of discipline were often handled not by formal sanctions, such as fines or cancellation of leave, but by the informal methods of the mates in the bush. If a matter was in dispute, they stripped off the insignia of rank and retired behind the shed to prove who, of the officer or private, was superior. The result, so Bean maintained – and in this he was supported by another influential exponent of the Anzac legend, the Australian Corps commander in 1918, General Sir John Monash – was a wonderful understanding between the ranks, which underlay much of the AIF's effectiveness as a fighting organisation.[5]

This supposed egalitarianism within the 1st AIF, it was widely conceded, generated a cavalier attitude towards discipline. Australians serving in the First World War gained a reputation for being an undisciplined rabble, flagrant in their disrespect for military regulations and the symbols of rank, especially the saluting of officers.[6] The vast majority of disciplinary cases were minor offences, such as absence without leave, but criminal behaviour was also significant.[7] Yet in the mythic narrative of Anzac, this was seen as a strength of the AIF. The diggers' resistance to authority arose from that very individualism and capacity to exercise independent judgment that made them such effective fighters. Whatever their insubordination or breaches of discipline when on leave, in action, Bean maintained, they had an inner discipline 'firmly based on the national habit of facing facts and going straight for the objective'.[8] The success of the AIF was proof that such inner discipline was far more effective than the observance of outward forms of discipline. In Monash's words, 'individualism is the best and not the worst foundation upon which to build up collective discipline'.[9] Only when Australians were badly led would they prove to be undisciplined in battle.

Finally, at the heart of the Anzac legend was mateship between diggers. To quote a celebrated passage from Bean's official history:

[The Australian] was seldom religious in the sense in which the word is generally used. So far as he held a prevailing creed, it was … that a man should at all times and at any cost stand by his mate. This was and is the one law which the good Australian must never break.[10]

Mateship served not only as a critical form of emotional and physical support on the individual level, but it reinforced informal discipline. In battle the AIF retained its effectiveness even when the pressures conspiring to break morale were intense. To quote another of Bean's famous passages about the source of the motivation of the 1st AIF:

It lay in the mettle of the men themselves. To be the sort of man who would give way when his mates were trusting to his firmness; to be the sort of man who would fail when the line, the whole force, and the allied cause required his endurance; to have made it necessary for another unit to do his own unit's work; to live the rest of his life haunted by the knowledge that he had set his hand to a soldier's task and had lacked the grit to carry it through – that was the prospect which these men could not face. Life was very dear, but life was not worth living unless they could be true to their idea of Australian manhood.[11]

It is obvious, even from this short synthesis of the Anzac legend, that it often diverged from reality. The notion that Australia was virtually a classless society in 1914, that the diggers were very much products of a bush culture, and that the AIF's battle discipline was impeccable: all these elements in Bean's argument have been challenged by scholars taking a less mythologised view of Australia's performance in the First World War. So, too, has the claim that the AIF's officers came from identical social backgrounds to the ranks (a claim that even Bean felt obliged to qualify).[12] The nature of the AIF's mateship has also been debated. It was not an exclusively Australian trait.[13] Nor was mateship necessarily an inclusive force, providing diggers with a sense of all-embracing solidarity when confronting the external threat of danger and death. Rather, it could function in an exclusive manner, with soldiers owing loyalty primarily to members of their own small unit rather than the large military organisation of which they were part.[14]

Yet, the later critiques of Anzac and mateship, which have continued in various forms to this day, are not especially relevant here. It was the mythic narrative of the 1st AIF that seized the Australian public's imagination in the interwar years. It provided the model of the Australian soldier, and the behaviour expected of him, that the men of Gull Force carried with them to Ambon and, ultimately, the POW camp.

VOLUNTEERING AND TRAINING

The core of Gull Force was the 2/21st Battalion. This was part of the 23rd Brigade, which itself was part of the 8th Division that the Australian Government raised in May 1940, as Britain and France collapsed in the face of the German Blitzkrieg. The 2/21st was formed on 1 July 1940 and many of the men assigned to it volunteered for military service around this time. What made them join? It is impossible to know definitively. Men's motivations for fighting are rarely simple. But in the interviews conducted decades later, some veterans cited the traditions of the 1st AIF: 'My father was in the 8th Light Horse in the Middle East during the First World War, and I wanted to get into it,' said Frank Biddiscombe. Others were shocked by the fall of France and the prospect of the Nazis invading Britain. The sense of imperial loyalty and attachment to the mother country that had motivated Australians of earlier generations to fight in Sudan, South Africa and the First World War also prevailed. 'I was reading the *Herald* one night,' recalled (Lance Sergeant) Charles Crouch, 'and I saw England was going so bad, and I said, "Gee, I'd better get into that and stop those fellows"'. Mingled with this imperial sentiment was the call of patriotism. In the words of (Captain) Rod Gabriel, 'There's nothing like doing something for your country'.

We cannot discount the importance of peer pressure, too. In June 1940, 48 496 Australians volunteered for military service.[15] This was the 'rush to enlist' in the Second World War, not the first weeks after the declaration of war as had been the case in 1914. By mid-1940, according to the official historian, Gavin Long, any doubts as to whether the war would be decided without bitter fighting on land had vanished.[16] Now, the fact that 'everyone was doing it' and that a good fight was in the offing attracted men for whom more idealistic motives might have been remote. As Bill McGregor, of Irish descent, recalled, 'Where's there's a fight, the Irish are in it'. It was like going to a football match or the races.

25

Finally, some of the men of the 2/21st Battalion loved the military life. They had been in the militia in the years before the war, possibly serving with the man who was chosen to command the new 2/21st Battalion, Roach. In the first year of the war, they might have held back from transferring to the AIF in the hope that they would eventually be able to join a new battalion together. Now that opportunity had come.

It is likely the men of the 2/21st Battalion expected to serve in the Middle East, where the 6th Division and, from late 1940, the 7th Division were deployed; but, to the men's considerable frustration, the 2/21st spent some 16 months in Australia before being sent to Ambon in December 1941. The nucleus of the battalion was assembled at Trawool, near Seymour, Victoria, in July 1940.[17] After a few weeks' basic training, in conditions remembered only for the cold and rain, the unit walked to Bonegilla, near Albury. The 260-kilometre march took 11 days – reportedly the longest military manoeuvre ever undertaken in the history of Australia.[18] Hundreds of people cheered as the men marched in formation through country towns. Children lined the streets and waved flags.[19] The women's auxiliary of the Euroa RSL provided free refreshments in the soldiers' hall.[20] Photos in the press showed young men in slouch hats striding through the eucalyptus bush, fit, bronzed, jaunty and proud of their achievement. Bean would have loved it, but now the images speak only to the waste of these young men.[21]

THE COMMITMENT TO DEFEND AMBON

Five months' training at Bonegilla followed, until the 2/21st Battalion moved to Darwin in March 1941. Why Darwin, the men asked? Unknown to them, the Australian Government had made an agreement a few weeks earlier with the Dutch authorities in the Netherlands East Indies to provide troops for the defence of Ambon and Dutch Timor in the event of a Japanese attack. The security of the region to the north of Australia had been a matter of concern to the Australian chiefs of staff since October 1940, when discussions with British military leaders at Singapore revealed the woeful inadequacy of air and naval defences in the region. In February 1941, intercepted diplomatic messages suggested that Japan might be poised to expand southwards, even at the risk of war with Britain, the Netherlands and the United States. Although this scare proved premature, the Australian Government decided to retain the 8th Division in the Australian region rather than send it to the Middle East as originally planned. It also concluded that Australian air and land forces should be held in reserve for the defence of the islands to Australia's north. The February 1941 agreement with the Dutch was a consequence of this. Two battalions, the 2/21st and the 2/40th, would be assigned to Ambon and Dutch Timor respectively; a third, the 2/22nd, would go to New Britain.[22] Their code names, tellingly, were not birds of prey – vultures, hawk, osprey or the like – but rather the harmless Gull, Sparrow and Lark!

In early 1941, this strategy might have seemed rational. Given the geographical importance of the Netherlands East Indies as a barrier between Malaya and northern Australia, it was logical to do everything possible to bolster the Dutch capacity to resist. Ambon and Timor, like New Britain, had strategic airfields and harbours. Moreover, the Australian offer of aid was a political gesture to the Dutch administration in the Netherlands East Indies at a time when Vichy French authorities in Indochina were progressively succumbing to Japanese pressure.

That said, the strategy to spread the 23rd Brigade across three islands was ill-conceived and would lead to disaster in 1942. The deployment of these troops in single battalions – or so-called 'penny packets' – violated the fundamental military principle of concentration of force. It might have made some sense, if the Netherlands East Indies and New Britain were expected to be a second line of defence, sheltering behind superior British forces in Malaya and Singapore; or if the Dutch military forces had some prospect, with modest Australian support, of countering a Japanese onslaught.

However, even in early 1941 both these scenarios were improbable. The defences of Singapore were so weak that in January 1941, Prime Minister Robert Menzies went to London to lobby the British Government on the matter. As for the Dutch military capacity: it seems that Australian decision-makers had little data to give them confidence about the strength of the Netherlands East Indies military forces, which consisted of a mix of colonial officers and local troops. On the contrary, since October 1939 the Dutch authorities had been desperately exploring the possibility of securing defence supplies: modern tanks, artillery and aircraft from the United Kingdom and small arms ammunition from Australia, munitions that Australia was only partly able to provide because of its own tight supply situation.[23]

The Australian decision to assume responsibility for the defence of Ambon and Timor, therefore, was anchored less in rational calculations than in deeply held assumptions, beliefs and impressions.[24] European imperialism in the Asia-Pacific region was the permanent world order that few Australians could imagine collapsing. While Australia's leaders had gnawing doubts about the Singapore strategy, it had formed the bedrock of Australian strategic thinking for years. It required a profoundly difficult cognitive and emotional effort to imagine an alternative strategy. Beyond this, Australia's decision-makers were imbued with the biases of their deeply racist society that inhibited a rigorous analysis of Japanese military potential. As a prominent scholar of military decision-making, Norman Dixon, has observed, underestimation of your enemy is one of the hallmarks of military incompetence.[25] Australian military leaders thus concluded that the Japanese were an inferior enemy and that European power would somehow ensure that Singapore would never fall, exposing the islands to Australia's north to full-scale attack.

Logically, once the commitment to support the Dutch had been made, the 2/21st and 2/40th battalions should have been sent to Ambon and Timor to prepare. This was the view of the Australian chiefs of staff. But this was not possible politically. The British Government believed that the Dutch would accept Australian troops only if they, the British, guaranteed support in the event of a Japanese attack – a commitment that the British were not prepared to give in mid-1941. It was also feared that the Japanese would see the stationing of Australian troops in the Netherlands East Indies as a provocation. Hence, it was decided to hold the battalions in readiness in Darwin, rather than send them overseas in March 1941.

WAITING IN DARWIN

The trip from Bonegilla to Darwin was an adventure for the 2/21st Battalion. Thanks to the primitive transport system in central Australia and some floods north of Alice Springs, it took four weeks to complete the journey by rail and truck. Construction of an all-weather road across the Northern Territory, though of manifest strategic importance, did not begin until October 1941 (it was completed in July 1942). One soldier, Alan Kenwood, wrote home:

> [The train] was the most ancient thing I have ever seen … As there were no carriages, we were bundled into cattle trucks – 32 to a truck … At every station we passed we 'moo'ed and bleated like a lot of stock and raised many a grin from abos and also white spectators. In the daylight many of us climbed on to the roof of the trucks where we perched like a lot of monkeys. It was a very funny trip.[26]

The novelty of the experience and the exotic terrain compensated Gull Force for the delays, the red dust that permeated 'everything we ate, touched and breathed', and the flies and mosquitoes, which were so big that 'they could carry you off'.[27]

Darwin, however, proved frustrating.[28] This was not the posting the members of the battalion had envisaged when they enlisted for military service. They were eager to see action, not to sit idle on garrison duty in a part of Australia that, at that time, seemed scarcely threatened by Japan. As the second-in-command of the battalion (Major) Ian Macrae said later, when the rumour that they were going to Darwin spread at Bonegilla, it was treated as 'something too bad to be true'.[29] The wider strategic justification for the 23rd Brigade's being in the Northern Territory was known only to the most senior officers of the unit. So far as the troops were concerned, they were simply 'Curtin's cowboys', 'The Lost Legion' or the IAF, 'In Australia Forever'.[30]

This disaffection was fuelled when, on three occasions, drafts from the battalion were transferred to units in southern Australia that were soon to be posted overseas. The departure of these troops and their replacement with raw recruits suggested that Army Headquarters saw the 2/21st Battalion as little more than a training unit.[31] This impression was not dispelled when the RSL refused membership to the servicemen stationed in Darwin.[32]

The irritation at being 'out of the action' was not mitigated by the battalions being encamped at Winnellie, 11 kilometres south of Darwin. This was virgin scrub when the 2/21st arrived. 'There are snakes here in plenty, and we are always killing them in the camp', Kenwood wrote home.[33] Darwin itself was a frontier town with a population of fewer than six thousand. MJ (Eddie) Gilbert, later described it as 'a hole at the end of the earth'. Frank Biddiscombe's diary recorded that 'he was very disappointed in Darwin, dirty place, plenty of fights, but we had a fair amount of fun' – this despite beer being constantly in short supply.[34] The food was unexciting and nutritionally deficient. One of Gull Force's doctors, (Captain) W (Bill) Aitken, later surmised that the lack of vitamin B might have contributed to the high and early incidence of beri-beri in the prisoner-of-war camps.[35]

The climate, too, was aggravating. March to October was the dry season in the Northern Territory and the temperature rose, until by September it averaged a maximum of 32°C. When the rains came late in the year, so did the humidity. The sandflies and mosquitoes seemed to proliferate. The health of the battalion fluctuated, with skin irritations, diarrhoea, dysentery and the occasional case of dengue fever. Mail from southern Australia arrived irregularly. Outward mail was censored, even when the press seemed to be at liberty to divulge similar or even more sensitive information.[36]

Gull Force was not alone in its frustrations. In September 1941, a riot broke out among the troops based in Darwin. At the closing time for pubs, mobs surged up and down the streets, looting and smashing windows. The pickets on duty lost control and the local cinema ran slides calling out all officers. Picket reinforcements arrived in wagons that they drove through the crowds. Thirteen arrests were made; six men hospitalised.[37] Men of the 2/21st Battalion, however, were not among them.

In retrospect, the question arose as to whether these months in Darwin compromised the efficiency of the 2/21st. Scott claimed so, writing in the unofficial report that he submitted to army authorities after the war that the training and discipline of the 2/21st had suffered considerably while in Darwin. Training, he claimed, was almost entirely suspended while the battalion was required to construct the campsite at Winnellie. Such exercises as were held during the eight months in Darwin limited the breadth of experience the battalion gained. Indeed, so far as Scott was concerned, even the battalion's training at Trawool and Bonegilla had been ineffective and inadequate.[38]

Scott's report, as mentioned, needs to be treated with caution. He was not with the battalion in Darwin and his judgments about its time there were gleaned from a limited number of sources while he was a prisoner of war on Hainan. His report contained factual inaccuracies, emotive language, unwarranted generalisations, suppositions that lacked supporting evidence and inherent contradictions.[39] For instance, he condemned the battalion's training in Trawool for the lack of battalion manoeuvres and company exercises.[40] Yet the battalion had only just been formed, and many of its recruits had no military experience. They could not realistically have reached, within six weeks, the level of training that Scott demanded. As another officer of the 2/21st Battalion, (Lieutenant) Ron Green (who later served in the army, retiring with the rank of lieutenant-colonel) observed, regular army recruits in the postwar years spent 20 weeks in individual and corps training before posting to an infantry battalion where company exercises were undertaken for the first time.[41]

That said, Scott's criticisms of the 2/21st cannot be dismissed entirely. The war diary of the unit conceded that the building of the Winnellie camp and the barracks at Larrakeyah reduced its training time, even though companies were assigned to these duties on a rotational basis and building was interrupted by shortages of supply. Furthermore, the battalion was occupied in providing pickets for Darwin, and supplying troops to be held in reserve for breaking a strike, which late in 1941 paralysed the wharves of Darwin. While exercises and work on a defensive line outside Darwin continued, the battalion's training was affected by the persistent shortage of ammunition and equipment. The terrain around Darwin also meant that training was not directly relevant to the situation that eventually confronted the battalion on Ambon.[42] Ian Macrae conceded in 1996:

> The whole atmosphere of Darwin was most un-warlike, with the exception of a nucleus of people I think, but the general behaviour was not as if the country was at war. … We had a couple of exercises on the assumption that the Japs were going to land but [they] didn't leave much feeling of reality.[43]

If training was disrupted, what of the discipline of the battalion? Scott's unofficial report again depicted the 2/21st as a virtual rabble from the days in Trawool on: men throwing bottles at an officer, booing its commanding officer and other visiting dignitaries, rioting when one of their mates was disciplined, damaging trains when returning drunk from leave in Melbourne, and so on.[44] Macrae concluded, some years later, that the 'general tone and esprit de corps' of the battalion was probably never at such a level as it was at Bonegilla.[45] Other officers of the battalion did not contradict this, but at least one excused the lapses in discipline, in traditional Anzac terms, as the boisterousness and exuberance, when not in action, of otherwise efficient AIF units. In Green's view, Scott seized upon isolated incidents, giving them an exaggerated importance and the battalion as a whole an unwarranted reputation for lack of discipline.[46]

Tellingly, the regimental orders of the unit do not show a disproportionate number of disciplinary offences.[47]

Whatever the issues with discipline, they do not seem to have impacted unduly on the relationships between the ranks. Scott's account, once again, was negative, documenting tales of joking about the officers' idiosyncrasies and public chaffing of them by the ranks. But ribbing officers has always been part of the AIF culture. As Stan Arneil said in his wartime diary, 'The lower ranks of all armies regard it as a right to criticise officers and nothing will ever change that'.[48] To judge by the evidence of survivors of the 2/21st, even though there were sometimes serious breaches of discipline in Darwin, the vast majority of the unit accepted the legitimacy of their officers' authority.

ROACH THE COMMANDER

The commanding officer, Roach, seems to have particularly held the other ranks' respect and affection. He had an interesting background. He had volunteered to serve in the First World War in the first rush of patriotic fervour, on 17 August 1914, when he was only 20 years old. He fought at Gallipoli with the 5th Battalion, having a short break to rest a sprained knee. In 1916, he became a staff captain in the 2nd Infantry Brigade headquarters and was awarded the Military Cross for his role in keeping the brigade supplied during the German retreat to the Hindenburg line in early 1917. He was not, in fact, at the frontline of battle, but, according to his citation, his 'tireless energy, excellent organisation and personal supervision of the service of supplies' enabled the brigade to keep continually in touch with the enemy.[49]

Then, in early 1918, Roach left the AIF to accept a commission in the Indian Army, which was struggling to replace its officers who were being killed on the Western Front.[50] Indian troops, it was believed, fought well, but only under the leadership of Europeans. With casualties mounting, the Indian Army had tried many expedients, commissioning Britons living in India into the Indian Army Reserve of Officers, and encouraging men of the British Territorial battalions, which had gone to India from late 1914, to replace the regular battalions withdrawn to fight on Gallipoli and the Western Front. But the Indian Army kept growing and its officers kept dying. So, in 1917–18, it looked to the dominions, trying to induce Australian, Canadian and New Zealand officers, with their sense of shared imperial identity, to transfer to the Indian Army on short-service commissions.

We have no way of knowing why the Australian military authorities agreed to let Roach go, or why Roach opted to leave the AIF for a commission in the Indian Army just as the British armies were facing a major crisis on the Western Front. The dramatic German spring offensive began on 21 March, the same day that Roach proceeded to England for his interview with the Indian Army. It was a coincidence, of course, but it meant that Roach took no part in the climactic battles that the AIF fought in 1918. Possibly, Roach wished to escape the carnage in the trenches and to gain a comfortable middle-class status, as others joining the Indian Army are said to have done.[51] He might have seen this commission as a route to a more interesting military career than being a staff captain. Or possibly he responded to the call to consolidate British rule in the Middle East.

Whatever his reasons, Roach seems to have served in the 129th Baluchi Regiment during the Iraq campaign, launched to suppress the nationalist revolt in April 1920 when the principal victors of the First World War assigned a mandate for Iraq to Britain in newly conquered Mesopotamia. It is not clear what role Roach played in this nasty campaign, nor what he thought of this denial of self-determination to the Arabs and Kurds after the defeat of the Ottoman Empire. Perhaps, like one conservative Australian newspaper, he thought the intervention was justified by the need to contain Bolshevik intrigues against the British control of oil in the region.[52] Ian Macrae, giving his assessment of Roach to the author in 1986, said, 'He displayed his keenness for soldiering by serving … after the armistice; fighting Bolsheviks in Persia when most wanted to get back to Australia as quickly as possible'.[53]

On his return to Australia, Roach took up life in business but, like many returned soldiers, he kept his military links. He joined the militia, and, according to Michael Cathcart, jointly headed the intelligence section of the White Army, a Victorian anti-communist secret army in the 1920s.[54] In late 1930, he was one of a number of prominent businessmen who approached John Monash with the proposal that he assume the leadership of some kind of national movement to lead Australia during the Great Depression.[55] Roach knew he was sailing close to the wings of sedition. His letter requesting a meeting with Monash asked to see him 'PRIVATELY' to discuss 'a *very important* matter which is affecting us all and the welfare of Australia'. The matter he stressed was 'VERY URGENT'.[56] Monash, to his credit, had no truck with this, or any similar approach.

By the outbreak of the Second World War, Roach had accrued some 18 years and 295 days of militia service, some of it at the senior level. Briefly commanding officer of the 14th Battalion (the Prahran Regiment), he did not transfer to the AIF until the chance of battalion command came with the raising of the 8th Division in mid-1940.[57] He was by then 46 years old. Despite his retiring disposition, he seems to have quickly gained the respect of the men under his command. According to Macrae, he 'was always held in the highest regard by his officers ... Entirely wrapped up in the unit from the day of its formation he was unsparingly devoted to it and completely selfless in his expenditure of time and energy'. Many others interviewed in the 1980s remembered Roach positively: as 'a gentleman', a man who was a disciplinarian, yet at the same time fair, kind and approachable. He had that quality, priceless for anyone in a leadership position, of being able to remember the names of people he had met only briefly. He was known to be interested in, and willing to talk to, any man in the battalion. 'More like a headmaster than a commander of a battalion'; 'the father of our regiment'; 'our grandfather': these are the terms by which he was remembered.[58]

This positive assessment, predictably, was not shared by Scott. His unofficial report concluded that Roach was 'a failure as a battalion commander':

> The principle [sic] causes for his utter failure are shown to be due to weaknesses of character, entire failure to

make or keep up close personal contact with all ranks of his Battalion and their daily doings, and to an unjustifiable trust in weak officers and further to his inability to discern where weakness in his officers lay, and to get rid of them.

Scott further claimed that Roach did not keep a tight control on discipline, that he was ignorant of the battalion's training and that his handling of the non-commissioned officers was 'a disaster'. None of the non-commissioned officers (NCOs), Scott claimed, had had their rank confirmed, with the result that there were many men within the battalion nursing grudges and a sense of personal injustice.[59] The records of the 2/21st confirm that the NCOs were all 'acting', but none of the survivors of that rank later recalled this being an issue souring relations within the battalion. The rest of Scott's comments about Roach were so completely at variance with the recollections of all those members of the 2/21st interviewed that it seems difficult to give them much credence. In contrast, many survivors of the 2/21st believed, decades later, that if Roach been in command of Gull Force when the Japanese invaded Ambon, the force would never have gone into captivity. This is an illusion, but it was Roach, who defended his men at great personal cost in January 1942, whom the survivors of the battalion invited to lead them in the Anzac Day parades after the war. He also joined the delegation of Gull Force that attended the dedication of the Commonwealth War Graves Commission (CWGC) cemetery at Tan Tui, one of the first pilgrimages back to Ambon on 2 April 1968.[60] Scott had died more than a decade earlier, in November 1956.

GOING TO AMBON

The 2/21st Battalion's wait in Darwin ended when the Japanese attacked Pearl Harbor on 7 December 1941. The outbreak of war in the Pacific brought the agreement between the Australian and Dutch governments of February 1941 into effect, even though there were good reasons to review it. Throughout that year, the Allied global strategic position had deteriorated markedly. The initial British successes against the Italians in North Africa were reversed after the intervention of the German Afrika Korps in February–March 1941. Disastrous losses, including many personnel of the Australian 6th Division, were suffered in Greece and Crete in April and May; while in July, Japanese forces occupied French Indochina, within close range of Malaya. While Germany's attack on Russia on 22 June 1941 would ultimately be to the Allies' immense advantage, the Red Army's losses in the first months of Barbarossa were catastrophic. The British and American decision to provide the Russians with munitions, including tanks and aircraft, threatened to make resources for Singapore even scarcer. Furthermore, as 1941 progressed, British and American strategic priorities shifted away from the Pacific to the European war, with the 'Germany First' agreement in March 1941 (whereby priority would be accorded to defeating Germany if war broke out with Japan) and the deployment of US warships to escort British convoys crossing the Atlantic.

To add to this, the feasibility of sending Australians to the Netherlands East Indies looked questionable on closer examination. In May and October 1941, the commander of the 23rd Brigade, ER Lind, together with Roach and the commander of Sparrow Force, conducted reconnaissance trips to Ambon and Timor. Their subsequent reports to Army Headquarters in Melbourne recommended strongly that Gull Force would need Bren carriers and guns, anti-aircraft and anti-tank guns, and field or mountain artillery, since the Dutch artillery at Ambon seemed to be allocated to 'several alternative roles' (what these were was unstated). In July, Lind expressed his concerns directly to the Chief of the General Staff, Lieutenant-General Vernon Sturdee; in October, he complained that the amount of preparation by the Dutch was 'far from satisfactory'. He felt 'strongly that no part of our forces should be committed in either Timor or Ambon until the Dutch show by results that they attach as much importance to the well-being and safety of our troops as we ourselves do'. To send the forces without supporting artillery would be 'grossly unfair to the troops'.[61]

Despite this, the decision to commit the battalion-sized forces to support the Netherlands East Indies remained unchallenged when war with Japan broke out. The British capital ships *Prince of Wales* and *Repulse* were sunk on 10 December, shattering any notion that the Netherlands East Indies could shelter behind a British naval shield at Singapore. But the assumptions that underpinned earlier strategic thinking continued to prevail. Why? We have some insight into the thinking of the Australian Chiefs of Staff at this critical time from the appreciations they prepared for the War Cabinet on 11 and 15 December 1941.[62] The former stated that the Japanese attack on Malaya three days earlier might well be a first step in the enemy's plan for a major attack on Australia. Moreover, this attack might take the form 'of a direct move on Australia via the islands to the north and north-east', including Rabaul, Port Moresby and New Caledonia. Hence, the chiefs recommended that these areas be held with a minimum of a brigade group with anti-aircraft and coastal defences. In addition, the forces needed to meet an invasion of Australia should be raised and trained. But in the second appreciation, the Chiefs of Staff modified their view, stating that Rabaul should be left with its current garrison of one battalion group. They realised that a battalion-sized force would be too small to resist an invasion successfully, but argued that it was essential 'to maintain a forward air observation line as long as possible and to make the enemy fight for this line rather than abandon it at the first threat'.[63] The idea that the forces on Rabaul should be withdrawn was ruled out: first, because this operation was thought to be hazardous; and second, because 'it must also be borne in mind the psychological effect which a voluntary withdrawal would have on the minds of the Dutch in N.E.I.'.[64] The political importance of the island commitments thus continued to shape strategic thinking. It seems that at no stage in 1941 – or early 1942 – was this judgment ever subject to any serious analysis substantiated by intelligence about morale in the Netherlands East Indies.

The logic of leaving troops in Rabaul was assumed to apply equally to Ambon and Timor. Gull and Sparrow Forces and supporting air forces were thus despatched without any hesitation when Japan entered the war. Gull Force left Darwin on 13–14 December, three days after the sinking of the British capital ships. The operational instructions for the forces were simply 'to strengthen the existing defences of the operational bases at Ambon and Koepang'.[65]

Gull Force's means of transport were three Dutch vessels, diverted to Darwin from their normal business of inter-island trade, complete with civilian passengers and their livestock. In traditional larrikin style, some Australians quickly threw the animals overboard into Darwin harbour. Others, more reflective, lamented the loss of the much hoped-for Christmas leave with sweethearts and wives. 'Everyone was gazing over the side', James Armstrong wrote in his diary, 'taking their last look at good old Aussie, little did we know how long we would be away from it'.[66] The trip took an uneventful three days, during which the ships carrying Gull Force were protected by an escort of RAAF aircraft, the cruiser HMAS *Adelaide* and the corvette *Ballarat*. As one of the members of the 2/21st band, Don Findlay, later recounted:

> Just on dusk you'd see the old [cruiser] *Adelaide*. She'd blow off a lot of black smoke … and suddenly off she'd go. She'd disappear and we used to think, 'Gawd, where's she gone … we've got no protection'. But what she was doing [was] she was going in a big sweep all night right around us and the next morning she'd be out there bang right in front of us again.

When the 2/21st Battalion arrived at Ambon on 17 December 1941, it had been joined by a number of ancillary units: a troop of the 18th Anti-Tank Battery of the Royal Australian Artillery; one section of the 2/11th Field Company of the Royal Australian Engineers; a detachment of the 23rd Infantry Brigade Signals; the 104th Light Aid Detachment of the Australian Army Ordnance Corps; a detachment of the 2/12th Field Ambulance; the 23rd Dental

Unit of the Australian Army Medical Corps; members of the Australian Army Service Corps and, finally, personnel from canteen and pay services, and the intelligence corps.[67]

In all, Gull Force numbered 1131, most of whom had come from Victoria, as this was the state from which the 2/21st Battalion had been drawn almost exclusively (see Appendix III for this and following data). The ancillary units, in contrast, came largely from New South Wales. Unsurprisingly, many of these volunteers were young, single men. Nearly 70 per cent of the force were aged 30 years or younger; 76 per cent were unmarried. As was the practice of the day, most identified themselves as having some religious adherence: nearly 44 per cent were listed on their attestation forms as Anglican; 19 per cent as Catholic, and 36 per cent as non-conformist. These percentages were not significantly different from those registered for Victoria in the 1933 census, the last census before the Second World War. The patterns of residence of the 2/21st were also similar to those of other Victorians at that time, with half living in the capital city at the time of enlistment. Only 10.8 per cent of Gull Force were born overseas.

The officers were drawn from a higher socio-economic bracket than the other ranks, nearly 89 per cent of them having held professional managerial or non-labour jobs in civilian life. The majority of the officers lived in the capital cities at the time they enlisted. They were disproportionately Protestant and distinguished from the ranks by their previous military service. There is nothing intrinsically surprising about this profile of the officer cohort. Men with more education, management skills and prewar military training were likely to be given preference for commissions as Australia raised its second volunteer AIF. Nonetheless, the social differentiation between the officers and the other ranks presumably added to the tensions between the ranks that became such a feature of Gull Force's captivity.

3

CRISIS OF COMMAND, 1941-42

Ambon, the island Gull Force was intended to defend, is a beautiful small island in the Moluccas group, in the east of today's Indonesia. Only 53 kilometres in length, it nestles just to the south-west of the larger island of Ceram and is centrally placed between New Guinea, Timor, Sulawesi (Celebes) and the Halmahera islands. Its strategic value has long rested on its deep-water harbour. This penetrates between two mountainous peninsulas for about 16 kilometres, providing an anchorage that is well protected and deep, in that ships can come right into the wharves. An enclosed bay at the head of the harbour, Binnen Bay, offers even greater protection for shipping and naval aviation. Yet, the very topography that makes the island so striking made it a nightmare to defend in 1941–42. This was soon realised by the Australians sent to help defend it, but their warning that it was a lost cause would go unheeded in Melbourne.

AMBON'S PREWAR HISTORY

For more than four hundred years Ambon played a role in international affairs out of all proportion to its size. The reasons for this were not only its harbour but its spices, nutmeg and cloves. Unlike pepper and ginger, which grew naturally in many areas of Asia, nutmeg and cloves were native only to the Moluccas islands. As the demand for spices grew in the late Middle Ages, with the yearning to flavour the salted and pickled meat that figured monotonously in the European winter diet, so the attraction of Ambon to outsiders increased. At first, trade was dominated by a few Muslim Malay sultans who organised the production of cloves and nutmeg and exported these spices to Europe via sea and land routes.

Then, in the early decades of the 16th century came the first of the European naval powers, the Portuguese. Rounding the Cape of Good Hope in 1487–88, they reached the Moluccas in 1512. Ambon and Timor soon became the last in a chain of strategic ports, stretching from the Indies to Portugal via Malacca (now Melaka), Ceylon (now Sri Lanka), Goa, the Persian Gulf, and the east and west coasts of Africa. The Portuguese control of their 'garrison empire' was comparatively tenuous, owing to the shortage of manpower in Portugal. Yet they attempted, with some success in the Moluccas particularly, to convert the local peoples to Christianity. The Spanish Jesuit Francis Xavier also visited Ambon, in 1542, converting many of its inhabitants to Catholicism.

The Portuguese hold on the 'spice islands' was soon challenged. In 1579, the British explorer and privateer Sir Francis Drake anchored off Ternate, an island of the Moluccas to the north of Ambon, on his voyage around the world. Then, in 1595, the Dutch, another naval power of northern Europe that was emerging to challenge the dominance of the Iberian powers, sent their first expedition to the region.

In 1602, they defeated a Portuguese naval force off Bantam (near Singapore) and three years later seized Ambon.

The British soon contested Dutch control of the Indies by establishing posts in many of the same islands. This rivalry culminated in 1623 in the so-called Amboyna massacre, in which nine Englishmen and some Japanese traders in the area were executed for supposedly plotting to overthrow the Dutch fortress on Ambon. The Dutch claimed that they had the jurisdiction to try the British on Ambon, but the incident became a *cause célèbre* in Britain at the time. Indeed, it still figured three hundred years later in the education of some of the men of Gull Force. Walter Hicks, a private with the 2/21st Battalion, knew little of 20th-century Ambon, but engrained upon his memory from his school days was the date, '1623, Amboyna massacre'. It was with a sense of premonition that he arrived in Ambon in late 1941 to see that a memorial to the victims of this massacre included his namesake, John Hicks.

In the aftermath of the Amboyna massacre, the British withdrew from the region, leaving the Dutch in control of Ambon and the neighbouring islands. With the exception of a short period during the Napoleonic Wars (1805–15), this situation prevailed until the Second World War. Dutch administration of the Moluccas was wanting, in many respects, in that the Dutch East Indies Company strove during the 17th century to maintain artificially high prices for cloves by restricting production, thereby driving the Ambonese growers into insurrection on several occasions. These disturbances, and the attempts by the local population to augment their income by smuggling spices to other foreign buyers, were suppressed, often with bloodshed and the destruction of clove trees. Nonetheless, the Ambonese, because of their Christianity, had a reputation by the 20th century for loyalty to the Dutch and sympathy with European values. To quote a Dutch historian writing paternalistically in 1936:

> The Amboynese is strongly built and rather dark of colour. Like most Easterlings, he is not over fond of labour, but he is intelligent and studious. As a Christian he feels himself in close contact with the European, and thus makes a most faithful subject of the Government. In the army he is a much desired element on account of his courage, adaptability and his love of order.[1]

A STRATEGIC NIGHTMARE

For all its intriguing past, in 1941 Ambon posed major challenges for those trying to defend it. The island is small, but its coastline is long and its terrain rugged. Steep, heavily vegetated mountains rise from the sea along every coast. In 1941 there were only two roads of any quality connecting the major settlements and fortifications. The airfield, at Laha, was on the opposite side of the bay to Ambon town and could be reached only by motor launch or a primitive track.

Clearly the island could be defended only by a large well-equipped force, but the local KNIL (*Koninklijk Nederlands Indisch Leger* or Royal Netherlands East Indies Army) troops numbered only about 2600.[2] They comprised several small and understrength companies of a mix of conscripts, from

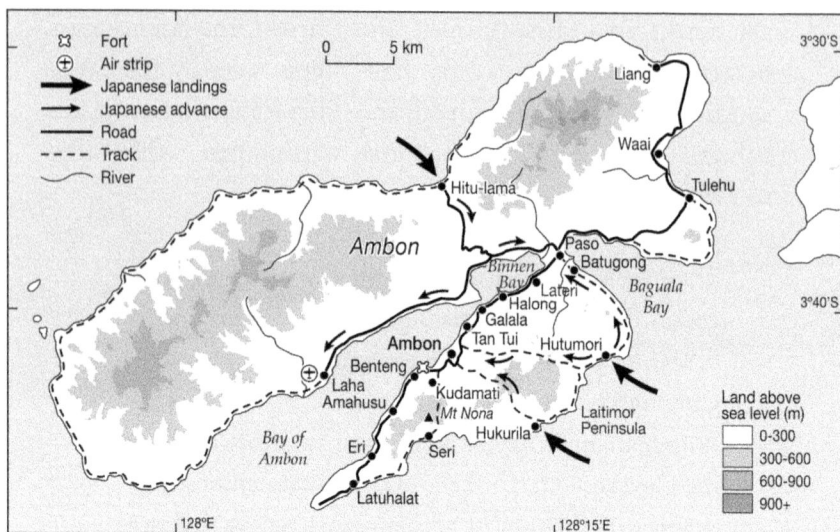

Map 3.1: Ambon, January–February 1942

Europe, Ambon, Java and other areas of the Netherlands East Indies.[3] Many of the units, which were mainly led by Dutch officers, were below strength and some of the troops had little, if any, training. According to one Dutch officer, the 'Home Guard' was issued with shoes, helmets and weapons only a few days after the war with Japan began. Prior to this, they had had no chance to use a rifle.[4] In addition to these troops, there was a detachment of Dutch engineers to operate searchlights and a company of coast and anti-aircraft artillery. The artillery, a mixture of fixed and mobile guns, was stationed at what the Dutch assumed to be strategic places on the island: Laha, Paso (at the narrow junction of the two peninsulas) and the environs of Ambon. The most impressive fortification, a fixed battery with underground communications, was at Benteng, just south of Ambon town. This commanded a view down the bay to its mouth and across the water to Laha.[5] The Dutch, however, had very few anti-aircraft guns and almost no air or naval support for their land forces. A number of Dutch naval aircraft were based at Binnen Bay, but they were withdrawn when the Japanese air raids intensified in mid-January 1942.[6] At Laha airfield, the Dutch had only two Brewster F2A Buffaloes, an aircraft that one authority has described as 'one of the few U.S. failures of the war'.[7]

Gull Force, too, was poorly equipped for the task assigned to it. Despite the recommendations of Lind and Roach after their 1941 reconnaissance trips, the force had no field artillery or anti-aircraft guns when it arrived in Ambon. Nor had the other reinforcements that Roach thought necessary – additional anti-tank guns, more 3-inch mortars, anti-aircraft guns, more automatic weapons and two additional infantry companies – arrived.[8] Gull Force did have limited Royal Australian Air Force (RAAF) support at first. One squadron of Hudson bombers (no. 13 squadron) arrived on 13 December 1941, and for a short time in January some American Catalinas joined the Dutch aircraft at Halong. These aircraft, however (or at least those that survived the Japanese air raids in January), were evacuated shortly before the invasion of Ambon began. No aircraft supported the Allied forces on the island when the Japanese attacked late on 30 January 1942.

The chances of successfully defending Ambon were compromised, too, by the short time Gull Force had on the island before the Japanese invasion. After their arrival in mid-December 1941, the officers were taken by the Dutch on tours of the prepared defences and positions, while the troops inspected those parts of the island that were accessible by road.[9] But there was no thorough reconnaissance of the remote areas of the island. The only Australians with detailed knowledge of Ambon were the personnel from the Australian Army Service Corps (AASC) who had been sent there in mid-1941 to prepare for Gull Force's arrival.

Meanwhile, Roach was obliged to coordinate his operational plans with the Dutch troops under the command of Lieutenant-Colonel JLR (Joseph) Kapitz, and to accept the Dutch assumption that the Japanese would attack either on the northern coast, at Hitu-lama, or at Paso, but not on the southern coast of the island, the Laitimor Peninsula. The terrain in this area was too rugged and steep, Kapitz argued, and the tracks between the south coast and the villages of Ambon and Paso too primitive to permit an attack from those directions. As it happened, the Japanese landed there, as well as at Hitu-lama. According to Dutch sources, Kapitz was also anticipating a Japanese landing at Waai or Tulehu to the north-east of Paso but he seems not to have told the Australians of this.[10]

Roach concluded that he had little option but to disperse his forces to the defensive positions already partly prepared by the Dutch. His original intention was to commit as few troops as possible to preliminary dispositions, holding the bulk in readiness to counterattack when the Japanese plan of attack was revealed. But the barracks prepared for Gull Force at Tan Tui about 3 kilometres to the north of Ambon town were found to be too vulnerable to attack from the air.[11] Consequently, Gull Force was divided into smaller groups, manning positions at Laha airfield, Eri and Latuhalat at the tip of the Laitimor Peninsula, and Amahusu and Mount Nona, the high (490 metres) plateau above Ambon, which commanded a view over the whole of the southern Laitimor Peninsula. The decision to allocate nearly two of Gull Force's companies to the defence of the airfield at Laha was justified, but the dispersal of the remaining units was a measure that Roach presumably accepted because of the shortage of time and the constraints of cooperation between allies. Originally, early in January, A Company of the 2/21st Battalion was stationed at Paso with the Dutch troops. This arrangement, however, was not a success, partly because of language difficulties and partly because of what one Dutch officer called 'different reactions of both nationalities to certain occurrences (raising of the alarm, confinement to barracks, occupation of positions, etc.)'. After 10 January it was agreed that A Company should be positioned at Eri.[12]

The gravity of Gull Force's situation was not immediately apparent to the other ranks in their first days on Ambon. Relieved to be deployed overseas at last, they were enchanted with the island. Ambon is, in many respects, the quintessential tropical paradise: dramatic cloud formations, blazing sunsets, coconut palms, tropical fruits and spices. The temperature averages 27°C with little variation throughout the year, although the humidity is stiflingly high, thanks to an average annual rainfall of 3454 millimetres on some parts of the island. The Australians also revelled in the warm welcome of the local inhabitants, and the idyllic scenes of fishermen returning at sunset, singing in harmony as they paddled their praus.[13] They took delight in breaking the conventions of Dutch colonial life, paying the exorbitant asking price for any commodity and fraternising with the Ambonese to the point of treating rickshaw drivers to rides in their own vehicles.

The barracks at Tan Tui, meanwhile, seemed a paradise in contrast to Winnellie. The long wooden huts, with atap roofs, stretched up a slope from the bay of Ambon to the splendid home of the local Chinese planter and merchant after whom the site had been named. The quarters, for officers and ranks alike, were light, airy and comparatively spacious. 'Quite luxurious', 'more like a holiday camp than an action station', is how some members of Gull Force described Tan Tui. Keith Mellor, then a 21-year-old lieutenant, later remembered: 'I had a room with a large four-poster bed, with mosquito net and pillows and sheets all provided, a dressing table, a marble wash-stand, an armchair and a little verandah with a glorious view over the bay. It was really quite delightful'.[14]

That said, the barracks at Tan Tui, like the accommodation at Laha airfield, were not finished when the Australians arrived. Water was not yet laid on to the kitchen and ablution areas, and there was no electric light.[15] As for the latrines: apart from a few septic tanks, there was a supposedly temporary wooden structure, built out over the bay, which served as a natural sewage system. This installation, known to the troops as the 'bridge of sighs', would become, during captivity, a vantage spot for fishing and an important meeting place for the prisoners, out of sight of the Japanese.

The troops might not have been fully aware of their vulnerability until the first Japanese air attacks on 2 January 1942, but not so Roach. Given that little had been done in response to his earlier reconnaissance trips, he had profound concerns even as he left Australia. On 13 December 1941, he wrote angrily to Scott, then serving as the staff officer at Army Headquarters (AHQ), Melbourne, which had operational responsibility for Gull Force. Stressing the urgent need for additional troops and equipment, Roach criticised the 'unpardonable stagnation' of the past seven months. This pointed to 'a policy of "wait and see" prevailing over reality and expediency'. He warned that '[i]f any of my excellent fellows do not arrive at their destination it will not be a case of "gallant sacrifice" but of murder due to sheer slackness and maladministration'.[16]

As soon as he reached Ambon, Roach wrote again to Melbourne, reiterating the deficiencies in Gull Force's equipment, and the 'imperative' need for guns and machine guns. Thanks to a clumsy system whereby Gull Force's lines of communication for maintenance matters went through 7th Military District in Darwin, some of Roach's messages were not read in AHQ Melbourne for days.[17] Increasingly restless, he advised by signal on 24 December that the combined army forces on Ambon were inadequate to hold vital localities for more than a day or two 'against determined attack from more than one direction simultaneously'. Even with the additional supplies requested, Gull Force's position would be 'precarious' if it lacked air and naval support.[18] The Dutch forces, Roach reported three days later, had only five days of ammunition supply and were proposing to vacate five forward posts in the event of simultaneous attacks from two or three directions: 'admittedly' he conceded, 'they have not very favourable alternatives with their present strength'.[19]

On 26 December, the Deputy Chief of the General Staff, Major-General Sydney Rowell, finally replied: while Bren carriers would arrive on Ambon in the first week of January 1942, the additional units Roach requested were 'not repeat not available'. The task of Gull Force then was, 'in cooperation with local Dutch forces … to put up the best defence possible with resources you have at your disposal'.[20] To this, Roach replied on 29 December that 'All [on Ambon were] most eager to administer salutary punishment [to the enemy]'. He felt 'confident enemy will waver before Australian fire and bayonets'.[21] But this was bluster. Roach's intelligence officer, (Captain) Rod Gabriel, later recalled that when Roach received Rowell's message, he placed his hand over his metal badge of rank on his shoulder and said, 'This metal means nothing to me, but the lives of over 1100 men do'.[22] On 1 January 1942, Roach wrote to Scott:

> I find it difficult to overcome a feeling of disgust, and more than a little concern at the way in which we have seemingly been 'dumped' at this outpost position, in the first place without any instructions whatever … and in the second place with (so far) a flat refusal to consider any increase in fire power and the number of tps., whilst the co-operation and assistance from the other two arms of the Service must be of very limited value indeed.

Repeating his prediction that Gull Force would be able to hold out for only two or three days against a large-scale attack from several directions, Roach asked:

> It is beyond my comprehension – and I am not alone in this – why this policy of dissipation of strength, which is not adequately supported, is allowed to continue.
> … I cannot be convinced that the throwing away of

a Force like this and that of Leggatt's [on Timor] for
the sake of anything up to a three days delay to the
enemy, is worth the sacrifice of so many valuable lives,
and valuable material … It is surely the policy, either to
hold this, and other smaller localities, to safeguard the
North of Australia, or not to hold them. If it is to be
the former, then adequate means should be place at the
disposal of the Comd. to carry out his role.[23]

Roach admitted that he was speaking 'very frankly, but I
would feel very guilty if I did not do so, and many valuable
lives were thus lost due to the fact that your HQ had not
been made fully aware of the situation'. He asked that his
letter be escalated to the minister (there is no evidence that
it was).

Japanese air attacks on Ambon intensified, with seven
flying boats dropping 33 bombs at three points on the
island on the night of 6–7 January 1942. Air raids occurred
almost daily thereafter. Roach signalled on 11 January
that 'prospects are gloomy'.[24] Then, two days later, he took
the radical step of recommending to Melbourne that Gull
Force should be evacuated. The support he had requested
could not be expected, and if Ambon were to be attacked by
combined enemy forces such as were then operating in the
Menado area in north Celebes (Sulawesi), the men of Gull
Force could not hold out for more than a day. It would be
a 'purposeless sacrifice of valuable man power and arms' to
leave them on Ambon.[25]

Roach's advice to Melbourne was emotionally charged.
By some accounts, he was in poor health at this time. His
letter to Scott of 13 December was written from hospital

in Darwin, and Macrae maintained in a later report that Roach suffered from a 'breakdown just before embarkation and his health ... deteriorated on Ambon'. By 10 January he was 'very exhausted'.[26] When Roach returned to Australia in mid-January, he underwent medical treatment for several months (though we do not know why).[27] Yet, his fellow officers of the battalion, when interviewed in the early 1980s, denied that Roach was unwell.

Whatever his state of health, Roach's assessment of the vulnerability of Gull Force was rational – and it was supported by his close colleagues on the ground. Macrae endorsed in writing Roach's letter of 1 January, as did (Captain) Edgar Tanner, an intelligence officer sent to Ambon by AHQ to liaise with Gull Force. He arrived on 10 January and within three days told Sturdee that Gull Force should be evacuated. Any delay in doing this would result only in 'disaster and [the] futile sacrifice of valuable men'.[28] Moreover, the senior RAAF officer on Ambon, (Wing Commander) ED Scott, sent a signal to Melbourne on 11 January noting that Japanese air bases were now established about 360 miles (580 kilometres) away, and urgently requesting immediate reinforcement with fighters and dive bombers. Without these, only 'token resistance [would be] possible with [the] present unsuitable aircraft', all of which would certainly be destroyed within a day's action by carrier-force enemy forces.[29]

ROACH'S RECALL

This intelligence from those on the ground failed to change opinion in Melbourne. On 13 January, Roach was told to cease his messages at once, given that 'your staunch defence will have important effect … in regard future Australian–Dutch cooperation'.[30] Then, on 14 January, Rowell ordered Roach to return to Melbourne:

> It is apparent from messages received at Army Headquarters since your arrival at Ambon and from letters written by you to Lt.-Col. W.J.R. Scott, that you have not the necessary confidence in your ability to conduct a resolute defence of Ambon in co-operation with the local Dutch forces … [you] have generally given the impression that you have accepted defeat as inevitable even before being attacked.[31]

Roach later claimed that he first learnt of his recall from Kapitz, a situation that was 'very embarrassing for both of us' and was not 'the right and decent way'.[32] Then he heard from Melbourne that the command of Gull Force would be taken by none other than Scott, who had been at the receiving end of Roach's messages and had volunteered on 11 January to go to Ambon to lead Gull Force in his place.

This was an extraordinary intervention: to replace a commander at a time when a major enemy attack was known to be imminent, with a man who had no familiarity with the battalion he was to lead or the terrain on which it would fight. The decision was taken in consultation with Sturdee, although it seems that the minister for the army, Frank Forde, was not informed until a day or two later.[33] No one in Melbourne was prepared to accept Roach's advice and evacuate Gull Force. Such an operation might well have been logistically impossible, given the shortage of shipping and the Japanese dominance in the air near Ambon. But no decision-maker even asked for an assessment of the feasibility of evacuation. Nor was any serious consideration given to how long Gull Force might last if left in Ambon. Scott said later in his 1946 report:

> [Gull Force] did in fact hold up a complete Japanese
> Division with its transports and adequate Naval
> and Air support for at least two weeks and inflicted
> heavy loss upon the enemy. ... had 'Gull Force' been
> withdrawn from AMBON before the Japanese attack,
> the Japanese Division with its Navy and Air Force
> support could have proceeded straight to Darwin.
> ... I am unable to say whether this force would have
> been destroyed on arrival at Darwin during January/
> February 1942, but there can be said to be at least
> considerable doubt on this point.[34]

However, this is a retrospective rationalisation and there is no evidence that at the time AHQ calculated the benefits and costs of a delaying action. Rather, as decision-makers faced with cognitive dissonance often do, they answered a substitute question: how could they silence the man who told them what they did not want to hear?

We do not have a record of what Sturdee said to his minister when seeking approval for Roach's recall. A draft memo prepared for this purpose was apparently not sent – a good thing given its tortured argument:

> The force provided, in co-operation with N.E.I.
> forces, is considered sufficient to retain the island

against attempted occupation on a light scale. To
provide sufficient forces to withstand a major attack is
entirely beyond our means. Great value should accrue,
however, if the enemy is denied the island except by
the employment of overwhelming force.[35]

However, Sturdee told the commander of KNIL, General
Hein ter Poorten, and the recently appointed supreme
commander of the American–British–Dutch–Australia
Command (ADBA), General Archibald Wavell, that Roach
was dismissed because he had made it clear since his arrival
at Ambon that he had 'no spirit to conduct a resolute
defence if attacked'. His latest messages indicated a 'probable
deterioration morale all troops Ambon [sic] which may be
beyond power of new Australian commander to improve
rapidly'.[36] Wavell responded by saying that the matter was
one for Australian authorities to determine but:

> So far as I can judge position at Ambon not critical
> and in any case I am opposed to handing out
> important objectives to enemy without making
> them fight for it. Quite appreciate feelings of lonely
> garrison but am sure Australians will put up stout
> fight whatever happens. No doubt it is wise to change
> commander.[37]

Some weeks later, when writing his official despatch on the
operations in South-East Asia, Wavell wrote:

> From the standpoint of higher strategy the situation
> [in early 1942] bore a distinct resemblance to that

when we went to the assistance of Greece a year earlier.
It might then have been more prudent to let Greece
go and concentrate on holding Crete and our gains
in Libya. It might possibly have been more prudent
here to let the N.E.I. go and to concentrate on making
Burma and Australia secure. But undue prudence
has never yet won battles or campaigns or wars, and
from the political point of view it would have been
as unthinkable to abandon our stout-hearted Dutch
allies without the utmost effort to help them as it
would have been a year earlier to leave the gallant
Greeks unsupported. Our assistance to Greece cost
us Crete and placed us in great difficulties in the
Mediterranean; our attempt to hold the N.E.I. has cost
us Burma and has placed India and Ceylon in danger;
but that in both instances we took the right, the only,
decision, I have no doubt. Just as I still believe that our
expedition to Greece was by no means the forlorn hope
it may have appeared, so the Allied attempt to defend
the N.E.I. might well have had a more fortunate issue.
The principle of engaging the enemy as closely and as
far forward as possible must be maintained at all costs
and will in the end bring victory.[38]

The Allied defeat in Greece in April 1941 was, by any
standard, a comparison that had nothing to commend it. But
it seems – to employ the insights of decision-making theorist
Daniel Kahneman – that Wavell responded to this new crisis
situation within an established pattern of associated ideas
from the past, ideas that determined how he interpreted the
present as well as his expectations of the future.[39] Hence, he

invoked the logic of one failed military campaign to justify another.

As for 'resolute defence', 'stout fight', lack of 'spirit', 'lonely garrison': these are best described as 'high diction', the elevated rhetoric that besets so much of the discussion of war and obscures its reality.[40] These distancing clichés obscured poor strategic decision-making by resorting to value judgments about the qualities Australians should display in war. As senior Allied commanders saw it, Allied soldiers had to put up the best fight possible with whatever resources could be spared. They were meant to manifest honour, courage, determination and a willingness to die. Was this not what their forebears had done at Gallipoli and on the Western Front? Wavell, for one, lost an eye and won the Military Cross in the Second Battle of Ypres in 1915. Sturdee had served as engineer in highly exposed sites such as Steele's, Quinn's and Courtney's posts on Gallipoli at a time when it was clear that the Allies were not going to prevail in this campaign. He had won the Distinguished Service Order for his work in 1915 and 1916. Thus, Sturdee read Roach's warnings as cowardly rather than rational. In 1955 he wrote to Gavin Long, the official historian of Australia in the war of 1939–45, commenting on the chapter on Ambon:

> I think that [your draft has] let Roach off lightly, he was a squealer from the moment he got to Darwin and I was concerned with his effect on the fighting moral [sic] of his battalion. From the time that he arrived at Ambon he never let up. His final message was demanding that ships be sent to Ambon to take the force out … As it turned out I should have left him

there to go into the bag and saved a good man like Scott for further useful service ... I might say I did not receive any similar squeals from Timor or Rabaul.[41]

THE MYSTERY OF SCOTT

Perhaps even more opaque than the thinking of senior commanders was Scott's motivation. His offer to take Roach's place was made when the Japanese had already occupied Kuala Lumpur and were only 320 kilometres from Singapore. As he later told official historian Lionel Wigmore, when commenting on a draft chapter on the Ambon campaign in 1954: 'You must remember that I was very well aware that I was taking on a job which held out no hope of survival, and without any of the physical training which such a job required.'[42] How do we explain this extraordinary decision?

Scott's career prior to 1942 was intriguing and complex.[43] A product of Sydney Grammar School and son of a bank manager in the New South Wales town of Bingara, Scott had a distinguished record of service in the Great War, serving in Gallipoli and France. Twice mentioned in dispatches, he was awarded the Distinguished Service Order for his work at Flers on 14 November 1916. But – almost certainly significantly for his later life – Scott also suffered considerable wartime injuries and ill-health: malaria at Gallipoli in 1915; shell shock at Pozières in 1916; concussion when he fell from a horse in France in 1917; and 'debility' in 1918.

In 1919, Scott was responsible for arranging the shipping for the repatriation of the AIF from Britain, a role that he seems to have performed with distinction. It was at this time that he met and began a friendship with Eric Campbell who, 12 years later, founded the paramilitary organisation, the New Guard. The impression Scott made on Campbell was vivid and enduring.

> As we were tossing out in Plymouth Sound [in the
> SS *Anchises*] Scott, in full uniform and heavy top
> boots, came out with the small pilot boat to collect the
> embarkation papers. In the choppy sea he had to climb
> a rope ladder from the boat to the saloon deck and at
> times he dangled precariously. The troops were making
> bets as to whether he would make it or fall in the sea.
> But he hung on tenaciously and made the ascent and
> descent safely.[44]

Whatever qualities Scott may be said to have lacked, personal bravery was not one of them.

On his return to civilian life in Australia, Scott became an insurance broker, but he was also a familiar figure in the anticommunist movements, which sprang up in response to the supposed threat of left-wing radicalism and industrial unrest after the Russian Revolution and general strike of 1917. In 1920, Scott became treasurer of the King and Empire Alliance, a conservative group set up to 'counteract disloyal doctrines' in the community. It seems that he was responsible for recruiting a secret army that would take over the state should the Labor government of John Storey (1920–21) attempt to introduce 'Bolshevik' measures. In the event, Labor (under Storey's successor, James Dooley) was defeated in March 1922 and Scott's army, of which little is known, was never mobilised. The whole incident, however, was immortalised in the novel *Kangaroo* by the British author DH Lawrence whom Scott met in mid-1922. According to Robert Darroch, Scott became the model for Jack Callcott in the novel Lawrence wrote almost immediately afterwards.[45]

Although the King and Empire Alliance was dissolved after 1922, Scott seems to have maintained his paramilitary activities throughout the 1920s. In 1925, according to Campbell, Scott was asked by Prime Minister Stanley Bruce to raise a force of 500 'stalwart ex-AIF men', who were supposedly to help the police in the event of there being civil disorder when two waterside workers' leaders, Thomas Walsh and Jacob Johnson, were deported. As in 1922, the political situation was defused, since the High Court ruled that the deportations were illegal, but Scott apparently encountered no difficulty in mobilising the required 500 men.[46] As this suggests, Scott maintained close links during this period with the world of ex-servicemen and the RSL. He was one of the founders of Legacy, a state councillor of the RSL in New South Wales and, after July 1922, commanding officer of the 55th militia battalion. When, in May 1920, 150 000 ex-servicemen sabotaged a Labor Party meeting in Moore Park, which was called to protest the deportation of certain aliens, Scott spoke on the rival platform set up by the RSL. A year later he was prominent in an ex-servicemen's mass demonstration in the Domain, inspired by the burning of the Australian flag by radical activists on May Day.[47]

When the Australian Labor Party (ALP) leader Jack Lang, was elected premier of New South Wales in 1930, Scott again emerged as a leader of the forces of conservative reaction. Together with a group of militia officers and

Sydney businessmen, he created what later became known as the Old Guard. His responsibilities seem to have included recruitment of paramilitary forces. According to Darroch, by early 1932, Scott had plans to oust Lang by force of arms, and at one point the troops under his control were apparently within days of mobilisation. The dismissal of Lang by the governor, Sir Philip Game, however, ensured that the Old Guard, like its rival the New Guard, 'went into recess, with the knowledge that it could still be called up … if needed'.[48] Whether at any time in all these shenanigans Scott met or had correspondence with Roach, up to his own clandestine activities in Victoria, we do not know.

To add to the complexity, in the 1930s Scott became an enthusiast for all things Japanese. He visited Japan in 1934, collaborated with Japanese consular officials, and wrote articles for the *Sydney Morning Herald* praising Japanese industry and defending that country's foreign policy. In the first of these articles, published on 17 October 1932, Scott justified the Japanese invasion of Manchuria. Many of his other articles in the following three years continued to be sympathetic towards Japanese expansionism and critical of the United States, China and the League of Nations.[49] Superficially these activities would seem to label Scott as a pro-Japanese appeaser, and it has even been suggested that he was a potential Australian Pétain (that is, a collaborator in the event of a Japanese occupation of Australia).[50] Such an interpretation, however, might be too simple. In Darroch's opinion, Scott might have been involved in some elaborate intelligence game, cultivating the Japanese under military orders. But, as Darroch himself admits, there is insufficient evidence to do more than speculate along these lines. As it was, Scott's membership of the Australia–Japan Society, an organisation suspected by the Commonwealth Investigation Branch of espionage activity, proved a complication when in April 1935 Scott joined military intelligence: he was refused access to secret files.

Throughout these years of clandestine political activity, Scott's private life was far from happy. His two marriages ended in divorce and, at least in the late 1930s, he seems to have been under considerable stress. His stepsons recall that on occasions he would come downstairs brandishing a revolver and threatening to go out into the garden and shoot himself.[51]

When the Second World War broke out, Scott was recalled to full-time military service, and was appointed in June 1940 to the General Staff in Melbourne. From February to May 1941, he commanded the guerrilla warfare training centre for independent companies at Wilsons Promontory. On his return to AHQ, he assumed the role of liaison officer for Gull and Sparrow Forces.

His offer to take over command from Roach was made in a personal and confidential note, written on 11 January 1942, to the Director of Military Operations and Plans (DMOP), and attached as something of a postscript to an analysis of the aircraft available in the area of Gull Force. Writing at 2315 hours – not the optimal hour for rational thinking – Scott pondered the possible repercussions should Gull Force be the first objective chosen by the enemy:

> A stubborn resistance & a good fight even against
> overwhelming odds now, must stiffen resistance
> everywhere and clinch our association with the N.E.I.

Not to mention the effect on the U.S.A. Withdrawal or a weak resistance will set the pace for future threats or worse ... It could affect the action of A.I.F. troops in Malaya. ... I am convinced that there is a political significance behind this which may well be worth consideration at least.

Hoping that his views would be taken 'as a very ernest [sic] opinion that much rests on this position in Ambon and not as an impertinence from a junior officer', he claimed that he would be 'proud indeed' to take over command of Gull Force immediately: 'I have no particular belief in my ability but I have a definite belief in my ability to inspire confidence in men and to lead them. I apologise for blowing my own trumpet in this way, but for the first time in my life I feel it perhaps justified'.[52]

Unlike Wavell and Sturdee's decision-making, Scott's carried a high personal risk, and we can only assume that he was persuaded of the political and strategic value of the Ambon operation. He made a note in the margins of an earlier message from Roach that predicted that Gull Force could not last for more than a day or two. 'Well worth it – what's the force there for?'[53] Scott seems to have read Roach's protests as the utterances of a man unfit to hold an important command position. He later described Roach's cable of 11 January as 'hysterical'.[54] In contrast, he had a record of being a man of action. Possibly he felt demeaned by sitting out the war in an office in Melbourne. Perhaps he thought this was his last opportunity – he was already 53 – to lead men in battle. His brother, Lieutenant-Colonel (Alan) Humphrey Scott, had died while acting in command of the 56th Battalion at Polygon Wood in 1917.[55] Charles Bean concluded in his official history of the AIF in 1917 (published in 1933 and presumably read by Scott) that had Humphrey survived, he would 'almost certainly have risen to brigade command'.[56] Did Scott hanker to emulate his lost brother's success in command? Possibly, too, given Scott's experience with independent companies, he thought that Gull Force might retreat in the face of the Japanese attack and hold out in the more remote parts of Ambon (as the remnants of Sparrow Force and the 2/2nd Independent Company did in Portuguese Timor).

Whatever his motivation, it seems clear that Scott fell victim to his own illusions. If he hoped for promotion – his critics in Gull Force claimed that he 'white-anted' Roach for this purpose – he was to be disappointed. The rank at which Scott transferred to the AIF, on the day before he left for Ambon, was the same (major acting lieutenant-colonel) that he had held previously in the Australian Intelligence Corps. Not until September 1942 was he confirmed in the rank of lieutenant-colonel – by which time he was in a POW camp on Ambon and knew nothing of his promotion.[57]

ROACH'S PENALTY

As for the hapless Roach, he flew back to Australia as soon as Scott landed in Ambon. No officer at AHQ met him to ask what intelligence he might have about the Japanese. He had only one very short interview with Rowell on 22 January.[58] After seeking legal advice, Roach submitted a complaint to AHQ in early February 1942, requesting that the operational order recalling him from Ambon on 14 January 1942 be cancelled and destroyed. The change in command of Gull Force should be recorded as being for administrative and operational purposes only and without any detriment to himself. His service with the AIF should be deemed 'satisfactory'.

> Events have proved [he wrote in a ten-page handwritten letter on 9 February 1942] that the 'men on the spot' have, on more than one occasion in this War, held a broad and sometimes a more accurate view of tactical requirements and probable results than have men at superior HQ. ... [Ambon] was not a case of 'good men for a rotten cause' but rather one of dissipation of force (admittedly a question of policy).

Given that he had 27 years of almost continuous service, including years in the interwar militia when many officers carried on only at some inconvenience and expense to themselves, Roach maintained that 'it is a bit "rough" to feel that one is, in effect, "turfed out" (as a man might be with a criminal record), relieved of his Command, and dismissed the Service, presumably as the price for candour'.[59]

However, the Military Board decided that Roach had been removed 'for good and sufficient reasons'. A few weeks later, on 9 March 1942 he was discharged from the 2nd AIF and placed on the reserve of officers. For some months, while Roach was unwell, he found it 'impossible to indulge in any normal activities'.[60] But in June 1942, he met with Minister Forde, who referred him to the Commander-in-Chief, Thomas Blamey – who refused to see him. Still smarting from a sense of 'grave injustice', Roach complained again in November 1942, this time to the Governor-General in Council. Once more he sought to have the operational order recalling him from Ambon on 14 January 1942 withdrawn, on the grounds that it was unjustifiable and cast an unwarranted reflection on his personal attributes and his methods of command.[61] The legal advice to Forde (and through him to the Governor-General) stated that:

> whether a senior officer is competent and suitable
> for use on the active list is essentially a matter for
> the determination of the Commander in Chief,
> acting of course on the advice of his senior officers.
> … If the Governor-General, acting of course on the
> advice of his executive council, considers that the
> C.-in-C. is not competent to select his immediate
> subordinate officers, it would be a question of
> removing the C.-in-C., but while he holds that
> position he surely must be responsible for the
> selection of his fighting officers.[62]

Hence, Roach's complaint was dismissed – though 'as an act of grace' he was deemed entitled to certain payments'.[63]

Roach could not let matters rest, raising his grievances again in November 1943. The Adjutant-General Major-General CEM Lloyd paid Roach the courtesy of meeting him in early December 1943, but soon wrote that Blamey considered it impossible to withdraw an order made by an authority that 'shortly afterwards ceased to exist' (presumably a reference to the dissolution of ABDA in February 1942). Nothing in the files, Roach was told, 'basically affects your military reputation'.[64] There the matter rested until the war ended, and the liberation of Gull Force revealed the terrible human cost of the deployment. Roach raised the matter of his treatment once more, citing *inter alia* the magnitude of Gull Force's casualty list.[65] But this petition, too, was dismissed.

The Army said it saw no further purpose in pursuing the correspondence.[66] Clearly, no one in authority was willing to concede that Roach had been right. He was to remain the fall guy for the ill-conceived deployment of Gull Force to Ambon.

4
BATTLE AND DEFEAT, FEBRUARY 1942

Roach's predictions of doom for Gull Force might have been seen as defeatist in Melbourne, but they were accurate. The change of commander, from Roach to Scott, was only a symbolic gesture. It did nothing to change the situation on the ground. Gull Force remained poorly resourced and without the air and naval support that might have given it some chance of success. When the Japanese attacked in massive force in late January 1942, the defence of Ambon would last only four days before Gull Force went into captivity.

PRELUDE TO BATTLE

The Japanese quickly established air superiority in the first weeks of 1942.[1] On 16 January, a large daylight raid killed four AIF personnel, destroyed some of the RAAF's Hudsons on the ground and demolished fuel dumps. The two Dutch Brewster Buffaloes – what (Wing Commander) Scott called 'the whole bloody [Dutch] air force' – were shot down while trying to intercept the Japanese fighters.[2] At Laha, the Dutch Bofors anti-aircraft guns proved ineffective, and the Australians resorted to trying to shoot down Japanese aircraft with Lewis and specially mounted Vickers guns. When the US air personnel were withdrawn on 20 January, the guns from their abandoned Catalinas were installed on special mountings and they too were also used as anti-aircraft guns. On the south side of the island, however, no anti-aircraft fire was put up, lest it reveal the Australian and Dutch defensive positions.[3]

As the air attacks increased, the morale of the Dutch troops began to waver. It had probably never been strong. Some of the NCOs were disgruntled at their failure to receive the promotions they had been promised, and communication between the officers and the local troops was poor. The impunity with which the Japanese bombed the island further eroded confidence. The commander of the Dutch Reserve Corps, Lieutenant BJ Huizing, wrote later:

> At air raids, false or not, and regardless of where
> the enemy aircraft were, the golden rule [of sub
> commanders] was: 'get into hiding.' The troops
> remained passive! There was no check on possible fears
> … This led to seeking cover unnecessarily, sometimes
> to panic, often out of proportion to the enemy threat;
> this was made worse by the example of officers and
> NCOs.[4]

The impact of the air raids, Huizing thought, was worsened when the Dutch officers, including Kapitz, continued to assert that the Japanese would not attack Ambon until they had defeated Java. In fact, the invasion of Ambon occurred more than a month before the attack on Java, and when it happened, some of the local troops abandoned their uniforms and melted into the anonymity of the Ambonese villages. Others, one Australian believed, collaborated with the Japanese, acting as guides to the Japanese forces.[5]

The morale of Gull Force seems to have weathered the air attacks better, although men became exhausted by having to move into slit trenches night after night. The situation had its humorous side. To quote Thomas Clark at Tan Tui, 'Some of the boys [sic] antics at getting out of bed were rather humerous [sic] including the capers of my friend … trying to untangle himself, from his mosquito net and at the same time climbing into his trousers'.[6] But at Laha, troops were forced to move from their poorly camouflaged barracks to temporary accommodation about an hour's march from the airfield. This site was less sheltered and the arrangements for boiling water broke down. With drinking water being drawn from the creeks, dysentery broke out. Malaria, too, spread as men had to leave their mosquito nets to shelter from the night air raids. The considerable wastage from illness weakened the men even before the Japanese attacked.[7] A (lucky) victim of malaria was the commander of C Company, the 25-year-old (Captain) DA (Donald) Sandy, who was evacuated on the last plane leaving for Australia and would survive the war. His place at Laha was taken by (Major) MWH (Horton) Newbury.[8]

The Australians on the southern side of the bay focused on preparing the positions they were to defend. The Eri and Amahusu lines were rugged defensive systems of trenches and dug-outs stretching up the steep hills from the bay of Ambon. The gradients on the shoulder falling from Nona to the sea were 1 in 6, or steeper. All the food, ammunition and water that the Australians might need had to be carried up these punishing slopes. A certain amount of Ambonese labour was employed, but much of the hard work fell to the Australian troops. Macrae suggested later that these two weeks of carrying supplies over rugged terrain in the hot weather might have 'been a factor in subsequent events'.[9]

The arrival of Scott unsettled the troops, although he later recalled that Newbury showed him some 'kindness' and 'sympathetic understanding of my unenviable position'. Newbury shared his tent with Scott on his first night when he could scarcely stay awake through exhaustion.[10] But the change of command had little effect on Gull Force's defensive preparations since Scott had no time to make any significant changes. When the Japanese attack finally came, the Australians occupied essentially the same positions that Roach and Kapitz had finally agreed on some three weeks earlier.

On 29 January, air reconnaissance reported the movement south from Menado of an armada of Japanese ships: five warships, 17 transports and five unidentified vessels some hours astern.[11] Instructions from higher command at Bandung triggered the destruction of all the major installations on Ambon. This included the oil reserves, bomb dumps, and most of the facilities and the runway at Laha. The last of the surviving RAAF Hudsons, with the exception of one that was badly damaged, had been evacuated that day. One over-enthusiastic Dutch mess sergeant even destroyed some food dumps at Laha, prompting his despairing commanding officer to record: 'The man is insane! So we do not have any food for the time being'.[12]

Everyone was now aware of the critical situation they faced. AT (Alan) Murnane wrote in his diary on 30 January:

'We felt a bit shit-house at this stage, it was evident the japs [sic] were really coming and we had no air or naval support whatsoever'.[13] Years later Ron Green recalled:

> we watched from our position as, down at the edge of Ambon town, near the wharves, our engineers blew up the fuel dump sky high to deny it to the Japanese. We watched in ... sombre silence this seeming symbol that we had burned our bridges behind us, that our fate had already been sealed.

The parting comments of some of the RAAF personnel were also discouraging. 'If you could see what was coming in that convoy,' they said, 'you'd find a canoe and start paddling for Australia'.[14]

THE JAPANESE ATTACK

The land attack on Ambon came on the night of 30 January (see map 3.1, p. 50). According to the Dutch official history of the campaign, 5300 of the Japanese troops who had captured Hong Kong were used for the assault.[15] Under the command of Major-General Takeo Ito, they included the 228th Infantry Regiment, one battery of mountain artillery, two batteries of anti-aircraft artillery, one company of engineers, and various support services. En route to Ambon, at Davao in the Philippines, they were supplemented by the 1st Kure Special Landing Division and two sections of the 1st Sasebo Special Landing Division.

Under cover of night, the Japanese marines landed

at Hitu-lama on the northern coast, and Hutumori and Hukurila on the southern coast of the Laitimor Peninsula. The latter was the area that the Dutch had thought to be impenetrable and was only lightly defended by a few detachments of local troops. These were quickly swept aside and within hours of landing the Japanese were making their way, with the aid of local guides, along the tracks to Paso and Ambon town.[16] The logic of the Australian and Dutch strategy was shattered. Their defensive positions on the Laitimor Peninsula almost all faced the Bay of Ambon, while those at Paso faced north and north-west. The Japanese were now threatening them from the rear, and advancing on positions that were weakly defended. Stationed at Ambon town and the nearby Kudamati were Gull Force's service units (pay, postal and medical personnel), local police forces and recruits who had only recently arrived from Australia or, in the Dutch case, from Ceram.

Learning of the Japanese attack, Scott and Kapitz made some changes to the disposition of their troops. Australian support personnel (mainly the AASC and the 2/12th Field Ambulance) who were stationed at Galala were ordered to Kudamati, while a Dutch company, then at Eri, was also brought up to help deny the enemy the approaches to Mount Nona and Amahusu. But this did little to slow the Japanese advance. By the afternoon of 31 January, the Japanese had reached the hospital that was less than a kilometre north of Kudamati. The town of Ambon fell into Japanese hands early the following morning. With this, the first Australians went into captivity. According to (Sergeant) Ron Leech, a member of the 2/12th Field Ambulance, known for his irrepressible humour:

I saw one of [our] captains … He was bailed up in the street with these strange-looking people talking to him. I thought they must have been the French Foreign Legion. They were funny-looking people with a rag hanging down from a hat. Never having seen a Jap before in battle dress, I thought, 'Hello, we have reinforcements'. When I went down, they thrust a machine-gun at me and gave it a wave, and I thought I'd better go and let the captain know we were in trouble. The Jap officer said, 'Okay'. So I went up and as I was going up I said, 'You wouldn't believe it, the first bloody Japs we've seen, and we're prisoners!' And some of the troops thought I said, 'The first Japs and *we've* prisoners'. So they all came running down to see our prisoners![17]

With the capture of Ambon town, the Australians on the Laitimor Peninsula were cut off from the Dutch. Kapitz had already abandoned his plans to meet the Japanese at key coastal positions and instead concentrated most of his troops in the vicinity of Paso. This left Hitulama defended by only a platoon of troops, who quickly abandoned their positions.[18] As the bridges on the road to Paso remained intact, it took the Japanese only hours to threaten Paso from the northwest and to reach the outskirts of Laha.

The Dutch defence of Paso soon collapsed. Its defensive works were incomplete, and thanks to Kapitz's last-minute change of plans, many troops were unfamiliar with the terrain. Some panicked and fled when they came under fire. Others remained but, according to the disdainful Huizing, were 'an indolent herd, over-tired and spiritless'.[19] The Japanese, therefore, had little difficulty in penetrating Paso's defences when they attacked from the north and south at noon on 31 January. Communications were broken with Kapitz, who only two hours earlier had decided to move his headquarters to Nontetu on Binnen Bay – without informing either Scott or some of his own officers. By evening, the greater part of Paso was in Japanese hands, and later that night, with the Dutch forces in disarray, Kapitz surrendered. Huizing, who had fallen into Japanese hands at Paso and was then forced to direct them to Kapitz, later described the scene at Dutch headquarters:

> When I arrived … I went into the battery. It was almost full moon and I could see fairly well. When I came to a group of sleeping people, I said to no-one in particular, 'Is Lt-Col. Kapitz here?' A man raised himself up and said, 'Yes, that's me, what's the matter?' 'I said, 'There's a Japanese officer who wants to talk to you, sir.' Lt-Col. Kapitz answered, 'Well, let him come over here'.[20]

As historian Roger Maynard later quipped, the Dutch rule on Ambon came to an end 'not so much with bang as a whimper, or in this case, a yawn'.[21] The Dutch resistance had lasted less than 24 hours.

TRAPPED: KUDAMATI AND ERI

The position of the Australians in the south of the Laitimor Peninsula was now untenable. The Japanese directed their attacks first against Kudamati. The transport personnel there, under the command of (Lieutenant) DW (Denis) Smith, drove back the attack, but the Japanese then tried to outflank Kudamati by driving a wedge between it and the battery at Benteng. They almost succeeded, given that most of the Dutch personnel and some of the Australian troops in the vicinity had vanished. But through the efforts of those men who remained, the Japanese manoeuvre was contained. This success, however, was rapidly nullified by the fact that at about 0900 hours on 1 February the guns of the Benteng battery were destroyed by the Dutch commander, who concluded that it was irresponsible to leave the battery intact with the Japanese close by in such strength.

The entire firepower of the Japanese could now be concentrated on the Australian positions. The troops at Kudamati, together with much of the battalion's ammunition, stores and transport, were surrounded on three sides. Their telephone communications with Scott's headquarters, which he had relocated from Amahusu to Eri late the previous day, were cut. Moreover, with the guns at Benteng silenced, the Japanese destroyers, which had previously been confined to patrolling across the mouth of the bay of Ambon, could enter the harbour and shell the Australian positions. One Japanese minesweeper was sunk by the mines the Dutch had laid (for which the Australians at Laha would pay a terrible penalty later) but the Japanese were willing to risk such losses.

The Japanese now threatened the Australian positions in the Amahusu line. Throughout 1 February, the Australians at the end of the line at sea level managed to repel repeated attacks with machine-gun fire and the use of mortars further up the hill. But on the far end of the line, high on Mount Nona, events developed in a way that meant the whole of the Amahusu position was abandoned by the end of the day. At noon, about 300 Japanese troops were observed making their way up Mount Nona from the north-east. By mid-afternoon they had reached the plateau. The Australian 5th Platoon waiting for them, under the command of (Lieutenant) WT (Bill) Jinkins, repulsed several fierce attacks by the Japanese during the afternoon and evening. Jinkins later wrote:

> [The Japanese] managed to get to within 30 yards
> [of the Australians] before being challenged. When
> challenged they replied 'Ambonese' and we opened
> fire, whereupon the JAPS cried out and withdrew to
> dead ground. The JAPS immediately reformed and
> uttering what was apparently a war cry rushed our
> positions. The rush was stopped by Tommy Gun fire
> and Grenades … Rifle grenades then drove them
> back a further 100 yards. Attempts to attack our
> positions from either flank were also broken up
> by rifle grenades.[22]

None of this was known to Scott. Communications between Nona and battalion headquarters were broken, and when another platoon, sent up as reinforcements from further down the Amahusu line, reached the plateau at 2000 hours, it failed to make contact with Jinkins. Its commanding officer, (Lieutenant) Sam Anderson, was wounded in the legs by a Japanese hand grenade and instructed his men to leave him and retreat rapidly down the mountain. The news they took with them was so alarming that Scott and other senior battalion officers concluded that Mount Nona was under Japanese control.

In fact, it was not. The Japanese on the plateau withdrew at about 2300 hours because, it seemed, their troops were suffering casualties from their own mortar fire. With the pressure removed, Jinkins and two others rescued Anderson, weak from loss of blood, and during the night led the platoon westwards (though they could not rejoin the rest of battalion trapped to the south). Ultimately the platoon took up a holding position above the road near Amahusu.[23]

Late on the night of 1 February, Scott concluded that the Amahusu line was untenable and ordered all Australian troops to retreat to Eri. The evacuation took place under the most difficult conditions. The darkness, enemy fire and rugged terrain were compounded by the presence of more than a hundred panic-stricken local troops. Hungry and thirsty, they had been coming from further up the Laitimor Peninsula since early in the afternoon. In the words of Ron Green:

> The Dutch troops appeared to be out of control and
> were cluttering up our line of withdrawal. To continue
> to try and move down the trench line was hopeless, so
> we climbed out of there, and finding our way through
> the barbed wire entanglements protecting the trench
> system, eventually reached the road at the bottom.
> We then walked about a mile, past a blown bridge,
> to a rendezvous where we boarded our 15 cwt trucks
> which, with the lights extinguished, sped us back to
> Eri … along the narrow road.

The Japanese pressure on the Amahusu line continued throughout the night, but the mortar platoon of D Company held off the attack, firing their weapons with such rapidity that they glowed red and hot. When the withdrawal was finally completed, the last covering Australian troops under (Captain) JF (James) Major scrambled down the cliffs to the beach and made their way on foot along the water's edge to Eri.

Scott supposedly intended to concentrate his troops at Eri and hold out until air and naval support arrived from Australia. He had requested this support from Melbourne in the last message he sent from the telegraph at Laha before the airfield was cut off by the Japanese attack. But Scott knew better than anyone, given his recent tenure at AHQ, that no supporting forces were going to materialise. By the morning of 2 February, large numbers of Australian and Dutch troops were holed up in the tip of the Laitimor Peninsula. Food was in short supply, the men were exhausted by lack of sleep, supply dumps had been raided by the fleeing local troops and the prized waterhole near the beach was being shelled by Japanese destroyers in the bay. Little was known of what was happening at Laha, but the mortar and gun fire heard over the past two days suggested that fighting there had been fierce. One of the Australians trapped at Eri, Thomas Clark, recorded in his diary: 'Most of the fellows have borrowed my New Testament, as things up to date are pretty tight as far as our chances are concerned. I suppose we all know the real meaning of fear now, and no wonder, for it is no picnic'.[24]

The Japanese made no attempt to storm Eri by land but relied instead on their air and naval forces to bring the resistance to an end. Japanese planes machine-gunned the roads, attacking anything that moved and directing the fire of the destroyers in the bay. Shelling continued throughout the afternoon of 2 February. Australian casualties were not great, since, in Macrae's words, the Japanese seemed to 'hold their hand', but scrub fires broke out in the upper sections of the Eri line. To quote Thomas Clark:

> Eventually the shells ignite the growth on our hill-top, and as none of us wish to be roasted, we are ordered to get out of our trench and into the jungle. We made for a ravine, which prior to this, we decided was too steep. It's marvelous how these Zeros make us change our minds. Fortunately, none are hit, on our run across the hundred yards clear space.[25]

The morale of some Australians crumbled. Macrae met several cases of men leaving their lines without authorisation, or individuals declaring that 'they might as well toss it in'. Scott was confronted on the afternoon of 2 February by a soldier who insisted 'these men have had a gutful and won't fight'.[26] Opinions differ as to how widespread this disaffection was. Scott maintained that the morale of the entire battalion was low; but Macrae insisted that the unrest was limited to one rifle section and a few other individuals. In his opinion, the majority of the battalion was still willing to fight and felt that there had been 'too much sitting down and taking it'. He gave the men 'a fighting talk about being better dead than a Jap. prisoner'.[27] Green, then commanding 17 Platoon, later confirmed the more positive assessment. When he offered his men the opportunity on 2 February to take part in a last, almost certainly suicidal, raid on Ambon, they agreed to do this without exception. These, incidentally, were the same

men who in Scott's unofficial report were condemned for
slack discipline in Darwin.[28]

By the end of 2 February, it was all over. An ambulance
trying to carry some wounded Australians to the hospital at
Ambon on 1 February was sent back by the Japanese with
a message telling Scott of the Dutch surrender and advising
him to do the same.[29] Certain officers resisted the notion,
since the battalion had suffered only minor casualties and the
units originally based at Eri had not even joined battle with
the Japanese. Nonetheless, on 3 February, Scott decided to
surrender. By then, parties of Australian troops had begun
moving along the road to Ambon town carrying white flags,
and the Japanese flag had been seen flying over the airfield
at Laha.

On Scott's instructions, the medical officer Bill Aitken
made his way by ambulance to the Japanese lines at Amahusu
to obtain their terms of surrender. Meanwhile, in a bizarre
happenstance, a note from Kapitz to Scott, and a message
from the Japanese, urging the Australians to capitulate,
fell into the hands of Jinkins, still in hiding at Amahusu.
Intent on getting the message to Scott, Jinkins made his way
on bicycle to a Japanese roadblock and thence to Benteng
barracks and the residency where the commander of the
Japanese regiment forces, Ito, was based. After meeting with
Kapitz, who provided a second letter for Scott, Jinkins was
accompanied by the Japanese back to the Amahusu line, and
given a captured AIF motorcycle to make his way to Scott
at Eri.[30]

The troops at Eri prepared to march into captivity. They
did their best to destroy their weapons and trucks, bury
their ammunition and render their grenades useless. '[W]e

mutilate our machine guns and throw away the parts', Thomas Clark wrote. 'Gosh! We hate to do this, because we are proud of our gun, and the way we kept it.'[31] Then, they fell into their units and marched to Amahusu. James Armstrong later wrote:

> [T]here we met the Japs. There were quite a few had not seen the Japs till now. And I myself didn't like the look of them. … everything seemed so quiet, no guns booming or planes going overhead. We made a meal of what we happened to have … We were allowed to go down to the sea to wash. It was real good. We then lay down on the ground and went to sleep. No worry about anything tonight, the first good night's sleep for days. We were now P.O.Ws.[32]

The Australians who had been trapped at Kudamati, unable to join the withdrawal to Eri, surrendered at noon the same day, their stocks of food and ammunition exhausted.

CATASTROPHE AT LAHA

On the opposite side of the bay at Laha, the rest of Gull Force faced an even worse situation. A Japanese advance party reached the village of Lelua within 15 hours of having landed. A major assault on the airfield did not begin, however, until more than 24 hours later, by which time the Japanese had been reinforced, possibly by some of the troops that had captured Paso.

According to Japanese and Australian sources, the men defending Laha fought fiercely.[33] One of the few survivors who escaped to Australia, Lieutenant IH (Ian) McBride, recalled:

> heavy machine gun and mortar fire was directed at
> our positions on the eastern side of the aerodrome
> and small parties of the enemy infiltrated between the
> platoons holding that area ... there was hand to hand
> fighting. The enemy were located, because of their
> habit of talking and calling out in a high pitched tone
> to each other. ... The fighting took place in an area
> covered by tall grass ... The enemy failed to make use
> of the natural cover afforded them and seemed to be
> poorly trained in night fighting. Had it not been for
> their habit of talking to each other it would have been
> difficult to locate them.[34]

However, the strength of the Japanese air and naval support meant that only nine hours after the assault began, the battle for the airfield was over.

Late on Monday 2 February, the Australians at Laha began negotiations for surrender.[35] According to a Japanese account, Newbury and at least ten of his men approached the Japanese under a white flag. They were escorted to Japanese headquarters at the village of Suakodo and detained overnight in the village school. The next day some representatives of the Japanese approached the Australian and Dutch positions at Laha. A Japanese soldier, Takada Haruo, later stated:

finding that the Australian troops had vacated the
airstrip defensive positions we proceeded towards
the jetty where we saw signs of enemy movement.
At the building near the jetty we were met by a party
of Australian officers and one Dutchman … After a
discussion they agreed to surrender their troops who
amounted to about 150 Australians, 2 or 3 Dutchmen,
and 2 or 3 natives. The troops were lined up on the
airstrip and after a roll call had been made they were
billeted in the neighboring barracks under Japanese
guard.[36]

What then happened to these and the other men who
surrendered at Laha is not entirely certain. None of the
prisoners survived, but the later evidence of Japanese
personnel and local Ambonese, and the excavation of four
mass graves discovered by the Australian War Graves Unit in
November and December 1945, tell a terrible story.[37] Some
of the Australians and Dutch taken prisoner were seriously
wounded or ill and died shortly after surrender.[38] But on
6 February, a group with Newbury in the lead was taken
out. According to the later testimony of a Japanese warrant
officer:

The prisoners had their hands tied behind their back,
but they were not blindfolded. Whilst they knelt on
the ground, Japanese executioners cut their necks with
Japanese swords. Many heads fell off the bodies but
there were also some partly cut off. However, death
was almost instantaneous. As soon as one execution
was over, another followed … About ten [Japanese]

carried out the executions so that each of them
beheaded at least from two to three prisoners. The
rest of the party was engaged as guards escorting, one
by one, the prisoners from the Native School to the
execution ground.[39]

The bodies of these men were thrown into a shallow grave
and possibly burned.

That evening a group of air force personnel, who had
not escaped the island, were also killed. In the following
two weeks, all remaining prisoners at Laha were executed.
To judge by the remains in mass graves found after the war,
many had violent deaths: shattered jaws, broken skulls and
one with a hole in the skull that suggested a bayonet might
have been thrust in and rotated. Perhaps some men suffered
head injuries inflicted by a large wooden club that was found
in one grave.[40]

Several reasons have been given for these executions.
One was the practical difficulty of holding so many
prisoners when Japanese troops were needed for other duties.
Another was the difficulty the Japanese had controlling the
Australians; supposedly they were uncooperative and inclined
to try to escape (as indeed some of them did). The Japanese
commander Hatakeyama Kunito said after the war that the
prisoners of war 'harboured resistive [sic] malice against us
… the general situation at the time … necessitated inevitably
the execution of the POWs … for the purpose of avoiding
our forces being destroyed by the enemy'.[41] Revenge also
seems to have played a role. The troops who slaughtered the
Australians probably included the crew of the minesweeper
that had been sunk in the Bay of Ambon.[42] Possibly, too, the

executioners included members of a Japanese platoon whose commander had been killed in the battle for Laha.[43]

Motives such as these have led soldiers throughout the history of warfare to kill rather than spare their prisoners of war. But the massacre of 229 Australians at Laha occurred little more than a decade after the third Geneva Convention protecting the rights of prisoners of war had been signed by nearly 50 governments of the world. Japan had been one of these signatories, but it had never formally ratified the convention. The tragedy at Laha was the first sign of how little the principles of international law and humanity would shape the Japanese treatment of Gull Force in captivity.

GULL FORCE'S PERFORMANCE

It is difficult to judge how well Gull Force performed in battle, especially as at least a quarter of the men had no direct contact with the enemy. Scott's postwar reports implied that the Australians' defeat was accelerated by the 2/21st Battalion's being poorly trained and undisciplined. However, when the Australians engaged the enemy in close combat, it seems that they often performed as well as the Japanese dominance in numbers and firepower allowed. On Mount Nona, 5 Platoon inflicted a heavy toll on the Japanese before it was forced to withdraw. At Laha, too, the Japanese appear to have suffered extensive casualties while overcoming the Australian and Dutch resistance. A court of Inquiry convened in May 1942 concluded that, on the basis of the evidence provided by men who had escaped Ambon in the aftermath of battle:

each of the scattered elements of the [2/21st Battalion] offered resolute and effective resistance for several days, and surrendered only when further defence was not reasonably possible. The troops exhibited a high morale and inflicted on the enemy considerable losses, while our losses were light.[44]

Most famously, on 1 February, in a memorable display of skill and bravery, Driver Bill Doolan covered the withdrawal of an advance patrol that had met the Japanese on the outskirts of Ambon town. Perched in a tree, Doolan used the weapons at his disposal to inflict such severe losses on three truckloads of Japanese infantry that he became a folk hero among the Ambonese population. His grave would become something of a shrine, marked by a wooden cross and adorned with flowers during the war. His exploits were also immortalised in a ballad:

> From his tree the Australian Doolan killed many
> men of Japan.
> He did not run away or move back.
> Until at last he was killed by the men of Japan.
> The Australian soldier Doolan died by the side
> of the road.
> His grave is under the gandara tree ...[45]

This poem would also enter Australian national memory of Ambon. In 2024 Doolan's exploits hold a prominent place in the section of the Australian War Memorial's exhibition on prisoners of war that deals with Ambon. Presumably its heading, 'He did not run away', taken from the poem, is not intended to imply that others did. As we have seen, some cracks in Australian morale did occur at Eri and these might arguably have accelerated Gull Force's surrender.

However, it was only a matter of time before Gull Force was defeated. Its surrender was attributable not to failings of its own but to the overwhelming might of the Japanese forces and the failure of the Australian Army to provide the resources needed for the force to survive.

SCARS OF DEFEAT

The men of Gull Force knew that they had been abandoned, and they were angry – both at the time and for decades after. On their return to Australia at war's end, some families and federal politicians demanded an inquiry into whether 'valuable Australian lives were recklessly and fruitlessly thrown away' on Ambon, Timor and Rabaul.[46] But nothing came of this. The political and military elites closed ranks, and Forde told parliament that Gull Force had been 'adequately supplied' and that 'its gallant stand [was] one of the epics of the war [that] enabled the Allies to reinforce and ultimately to turn the tide'.[47]

However, the veterans themselves, when asked in the 1980s why Gull Force had been defeated, replied: 'We had nothing'; 'We had no show at all'; 'We were there only to say there was people there'; 'Virtually we were there to be taken'.[48] Sam Hillian, a corporal in the AASC, remembered: 'Resentment was the keynote of my feeling all the way through, great resentment against the people who got me there and the people who were responsible for me being there'.

Of course, in February 1942 these emotions could not be vented on those people who were 'responsible', namely the senior commanders safe in AHQ Melbourne. Hence, in a classic instance of misdirected aggression, many men in Gull Force blamed their officers. Alan Murnane wrote, 'Every section of the Battalion is disgusted with the way the officers handled the little bit of action we saw. There was no co-operation whatsoever and no one seemed to know what the other fellow was doing.'[49] More specifically, many men blamed Scott. He was the local embodiment of the command in Melbourne, and the man who had orchestrated the recall of the popular Roach. Macrae wrote later: 'a lot of the men directed their resentment towards Scott ... it was quite ridiculous as Scott wasn't responsible for the strategic situation. They all blamed him for it ... I think that even some of the junior officers did that, but they were always looking for someone to blame.' Macrae himself remained the personification of loyalty to Scott, who would write in 1946 that Macrae's loyalty 'from start to finish has been one of the best and finest things which I have met in a long life'.[50]

The other ranks in Gull Force, it should be said, were not unique in holding their officers to account. Tensions between ranks in the aftermath of defeat seem to have been common. At Changi POW camp, for instance, in the first days of the Australian 8th Division's captivity, one officer wrote, '[t]he troops, and most officers thought they had been "sold a pup" in Singapore, and there was a feeling of bitterness and frustration. Many troops tried to take out some of their bitterness against the officers, and the reaction of the latter soon showed up the good officers from the rest'.[51] However, the toxic memory of Scott's presumed role in Gull Force's downfall lasted beyond the days of its defeat. It continued to pervade relations between the commanding officer and his men for the next three-and-a half years – although, as we shall see, Scott soon gave the ranks considerably more cause to hate him.

Another legacy of the defeat on Ambon was the disdain that many in Gull Force felt for the Dutch. The seeming reluctance of the Dutch officers to fight, and the decision to destroy the guns of the Benteng battery, were condemned as the weaknesses of men corrupted by years of colonial life in the tropics. To quote the later opinions of two officers of the 2/21st Battalion: first, Keith Mellor:

> [The Dutch officers] had been living there on the
> fat of the land for far too long, strings of servants ...
> I can recall the first time that I went out [to the steep
> Amahusu line] with a Dutch officer and native carriers
> and so on. When we got the trucks pulled up at the
> bottom of the road, [the Dutch] said, 'You go up there
> and we'll wait for you here. We'll be here when you
> get back'.

And Rod Gabriel:

> We went out to the lines on the Bay ... it was steep
> climbing ... and the C.O. said, 'Let's go up.' And the
> Dutch said, '11 o'clock, time for a beer'. So by the
> time you drive back and have a beer it is then time for
> afternoon siesta, because they just shut down in the
> afternoon ... The mere fact that there was a war on
> was just incidental.

Scott, in particular, despised the Dutch. His first impressions of Kapitz had been positive but this gave way to contempt. His postwar report stated:

> It has not been possible to ignore the Dutch troops
> or their Commanding Officer. It is unfortunate that
> there is nothing to be said which could be regarded
> as bringing credit either to the one or the other. My
> unhappy experience with these people both at Ambon
> and Hainan leave [sic] me convinced that there is no
> one characteristic which an Australian or a Dutchman
> could find in common.[52]

Like so much of what Scott wrote, this is jaundiced and unjust. The disdain for the Dutch among the other prisoners also owed much to the hot-house atmosphere of defeat and captivity. Australians of that time were not known for their multicultural tolerance. But this negativity served to accentuate Gull Force's isolation and inward focus. Scott, for his part, had no rapport with other senior Allied officers with whom he might have shared the stresses of leadership. With the exception of a small coterie of friends, he became remote and withdrawn, and his isolation almost certainly affected his ability to handle the delicate and desperate problems of command in captivity.

PART III
ESCAPE, 1942

5
ESCAPE FROM AMBON, 1942

Surrender meant years of privation and, for many of Gull Force, a slow death from hunger and overwork. A few Australians, however, were able to escape from Ambon and make their way back to Australia. To judge by the popular literature of the Second World War, escape was the quintessential activity of prisoners of war. They supposedly did nothing but tunnel, forge documents and plot with the intention of eluding their captors. Such experiences, however, were typical only of prisoners of war in certain parts of the world, particularly Western Europe. Even then, escape was an option largely for officers who felt a duty to escape and had the time to plan, given that they were not required, under the third Geneva Convention of 1929, to do manual labour. In contrast, escape for prisoners of the Japanese was often impossible. The distance between their place of capture and their homes was immense, the terrain beyond their camps was often impenetrable, and the local populations were so physically and linguistically distinct as to make disguise for an escapee impossible. In addition, the Japanese made it brutally clear that they viewed any attempt to escape as a capital offence. The 52 escapes of Gull Force are thus remarkable achievements, made possible by a mix of personal courage, the help of local people and a lot of good luck. Most men escaped in the early months of 1942 before the Japanese had established tight control over Ambon and the surrounding islands in the Arafura Sea. The exception to this was a party of six Australians who escaped from the POW camp on Hainan Island in April 1945 (see chapter 11).

ESCAPE FROM SOUTHERN AMBON

The first men to escape from Ambon took advantage of the confusion immediately after Gull Force's defeat. One group came from a fighting patrol that had set off from Eri late in the night of 2–3 February, under the command of Macrae, to investigate rumours that the Japanese had landed at Latuhalat on the south-western tip of the Laitimor Peninsula. Another cohort, consisting of mostly walking wounded from the battle for Laha, escaped from the Regimental Aid Post near the airfield just before it was overrun by the Japanese.

The first group learnt that Gull Force was about to surrender when they were above Latuhalat on the morning of 3 February. A few hours earlier, Macrae had fallen violently ill after eating some nuts from a tree, and when stretcher-bearers summoned from Eri arrived, they brought news of Scott's decision to capitulate. Macrae and another officer with the party, 22-year-old former student (Lieutenant) WAM (Wilf) Chapman, decided that any members of the patrol who wished to escape should be allowed to do so. In a sliding-door moment for himself, Macrae judged that he was in too much agony to join them. He was taken back to Eri while the rest of the patrol set off, under Chapman's leadership, to find some way of getting off the island.[1]

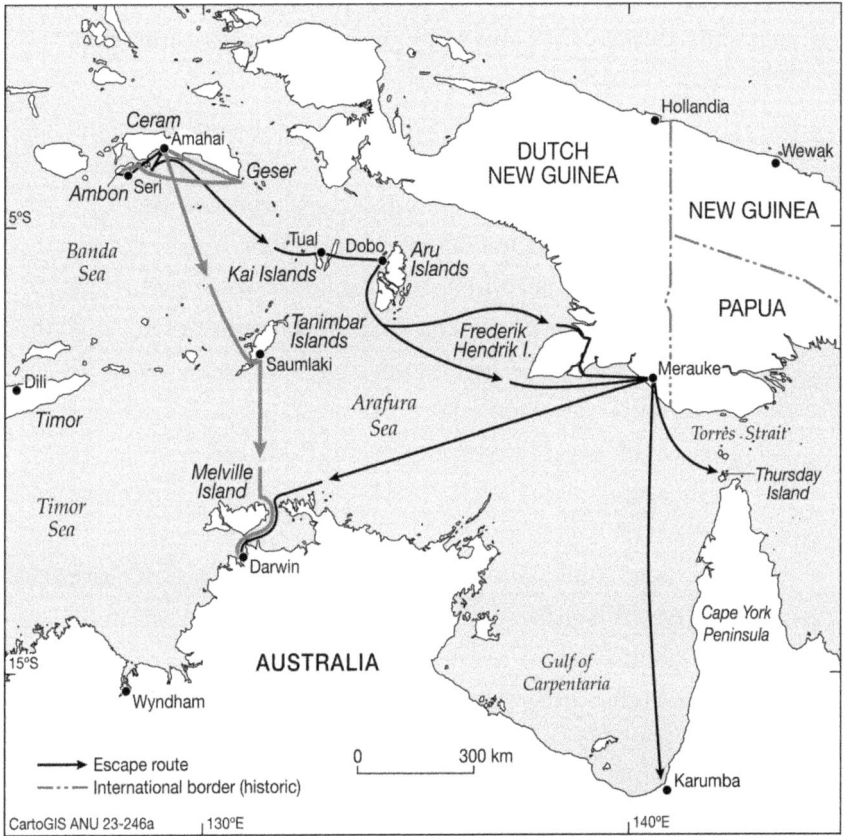

Map 5.1: Escape routes from Ambon, 1942

Just before dark, they managed to find the small village of Seri on the southern coast of Ambon at the foot of formidably steep mountains and gullies. The local owners were willing to let them use one of their boats. It was scarcely seaworthy, leaking like the proverbial sieve, and with very poor sails and rigging. Only some of the Australians had any sailing experience, but, galvanised by the fear of falling into Japanese hands, they loaded some water and coconuts and set sail. Two local people were persuaded to go with them. As (Bert) Grady's diary records:

> Then the fun started three or four new [sic] quite a bit about sailing the rest nothing. If those who new [sic] had done the lot themselves or issued plain instructions we might have been some use, but to shouts of unfurl the sail, pull on the jib and hoist the boom it was a fine old mix up. So much so that our two natives went overboard and swam ashore. However, just as it seemed we would go on the rocks the wind freshened and we were away.

As the boat took off, two Japanese naval vessels were patrolling the southern coast of Ambon. The Australians had no choice but to sail between them, trusting that the Japanese would think they were Ambonese engaged in inter-island trade. The gamble paid off, and although a violent storm that night broke the boat's rudder and ripped one of its sails to pieces, the party managed to limp into Titawaai on the small island of Nusa Laut, to the east of Ambon, on 5 February.

There, they were welcomed by the local population with pots of lukewarm tea, pineapples and other fruit. The Dutch controller on the neighbouring island of Saparua also offered assistance, once Chapman had made contact with him with the help of the local rajah and a borrowed prau. Almost everything the Dutch gave Chapman, however, was lost when the prau sank on the return journey to Titawaai. On 8 February the group finally sailed for Ceram.

The putting to sea ... was a terrific job [Grady wrote], the tide was against us but after much pushing and shoving we got started ... and started rowing ... After about an hour and a half we were about 200 yards off shore and just holding our own from being washed back again. In the meantime the bread [the native women had been preparing in the afternoon] had cooked and a canoe brought it out, but owing to the rough seas it was almost impossible for the canoe to come alongside. In the process of trying it capsized and there went our bread. Two of the six water-sodden loaves were rescued and were not much the worse for their ducking. We were by this time about all in with the rowing ... just then a offshore breeze sprang up, the sail filled and we were away. It was dark by this time and we settled down to sleep. This was soon rudely disturbed by a grating grinding noise and a cry of 'We're on a reef' from the helmsman.

Fortunately, the boat was not badly damaged and could be lifted off the reef. But then the winds proved fickle, and it was not until the afternoon of 10 February that the Australians reached Amahai on Ceram.

Again, they were delayed by problems with their boat, and by Chapman suffering an infected elbow, but the time at Amahai passed almost pleasantly. The exhausted men relaxed in the village hospital and hunted game in the jungle. They had very little money and food on the island was becoming scarce, but the local population shared what they had. The Dutch controller and missionary were hospitable, the latter even putting on a sumptuous meal for three of the

Australians – rice, chicken, vegetables and wine, all served from sparkling china and a snow-white tablecloth.

By 14 February, the repairs to *Belching Bertha,* as the Australians had named the boat, were completed and the party set off for Geser, at the eastern tip of Ceram, with three villagers as navigators. Some way along the coast they learnt from locals paddling out from a village that the Japanese were present further along the island. So they split into two groups: one led by Chapman remained with the boat, while the other made its way along the coast by land.

The group in the boat reached Geser in four days, even though more storms blew up, ripping out the leaking boat's jib again. Once more, they received a warm welcome from a swarm of local praus and the controller. Replenished with supplies of food and a new crew, they set off on 21 February for Tual in the Kai islands. As always, they were playthings of the weather – at times becalmed, at times battered by storms – but four days later they anchored off Tual. Then, in an extraordinary coincidence, they heard Australian voices calling to them in the darkness. It was the rest of their party from whom they had separated some days before.

This group had managed to make its way along the coast of Ceram, alternately walking or being carried in villagers' canoes. They had met no Japanese and their most serious problems had been lack of food and the many rivers, which they had to cross by wading out into the ocean to find a sandbar. They had reached Geser on 22 February, only one day after Chapman and the others had left.

At Tual the Australians radioed the Dutch headquarters at Bandung, asking for instructions and transport home. Two days later Bandung replied, telling them to make their way to Dobo, in the Aru Islands, where a boat would arrive to take them to Darwin. The Australians soon found a launch, which seemed 'a queen after our old tub' and reached the Aru Islands on 1 March.[2]

At Dobo, however, the promised boat did not appear and as the days passed, nerves became frayed, food supplies dwindled, and fears of capture by the Japanese grew. A Japanese air raid on 12 March finally convinced the Australians that they could wait no longer. The next day they took to the seas again in two Dutch boats, one an auxiliary ketch with an engine, *Arcadia* (under Chapman); the other a sailing vessel, *Gloria* (under Warrant Officer LC [Leo] Warren). By this time their numbers had been swollen by some Dutch civilians, including the owner of *Arcadia*, and a small group of Australians who had escaped from the prison camp at Ambon early in March.

At first the two boats stayed together, the arrangement being that the motorboat would tow the sailing boat when the winds were light. But on the night of 15–16 March, the two craft became separated. According to the Australians on *Arcadia*, this happened because of rough weather. *Gloria* was far faster in fresh winds and had to be cast off when it had kept coming up to the stern of the other boat. However, the men on *Gloria* claimed that they were left becalmed – and without adequate rations – by *Arcadia*. A court of inquiry, held after both groups reached Australia, investigated the circumstances of the escape, and Chapman was cleared of any implication that he had neglected his duties.[3] But the men who were on the sailing boat maintained, when interviewed in the 1980s, that they were desperately short of food in the last part of their journey.

According to their accounts, once *Gloria* had lost contact with *Arcadia*, it headed for Merauke on the coast of Netherlands New Guinea (now South Papua, Indonesia). This was the previously agreed rendezvous, since news had been received that Thursday Island had been bombed. For several days, *Gloria* was out of sight of land, and rations became short. The Dutch missionary on board became panicky, insisting that they were lost and should turn back. He changed his mind when offered the option of being thrown overboard. Several of the Australians had malaria, and by 20 March there was only one tin of bully beef and peas, and two tins of preserved fruit per day for the 23 people on board. The situation improved a little when a fish obligingly jumped into the boat, to be smothered instantly by at least ten Australians, but by the time the party reached land, the men were reduced to eating fried flour and water.

Land was at last sighted, after a week at sea, and on 28 March *Gloria* reached Merauke. Since there was no sign of the *Arcadia* party, it was decided they would set out independently for home. As AS (Alec) Hawkins told the story years later, the Dutch controller would not allow them to take his diesel-powered patrol boat, so they impounded him in his home, and set off heading due south. It took them only three days to reach Karumba on the Gulf of Carpentaria. The local population, having satisfied themselves that this was not the vanguard of a Japanese invasion, gave the very hungry arrivals 'a great feed of bread and cheese'.[4] Soon a Sunderland flying boat, on its regular ferry trip from Brisbane to Darwin, happened to arrive, and took the escape party to Townsville, and ultimately Brisbane. There they were 'made to look like soldiers again', before they finally set off by train to Sydney – and then, at last, a reunion with their families in Melbourne.[5]

Meanwhile the other group, on *Arcadia*, were making slower progress, even though their boat had an engine. They chose a different route to Merauke, via the Princess Marianne Strait, which separates Frederik Hendrik Island from the mainland. Navigating the strait, they became grounded on a sandbank. For a maddening two weeks, besieged by mosquitoes, they tried to refloat the boat. Fortunately, food was not a problem, given the proximity of land and helpful villagers, but eventually the waiting was too much for five Australians. They set off for Merauke on foot, judging (as it turned out, accurately) that they would get there before *Arcadia* did. When the boat was finally refloated and reached Merauke, it made contact with Australia. Within two days, an RAN vessel arrived to tow the Australians and 22 Dutch civilians back to Thursday Island.

ESCAPE FROM LAHA

Most of the other Australians who escaped from Ambon took a similar route, island hopping from Ambon to Ceram and thence to the Kai islands, the Aru islands, Merauke and, finally, the north coast of Australia. The men who escaped from the Laha side of Ambon were mainly casualties from the fighting.[6] Their medical officer, (Captain) S White, gave them permission to leave when it was clear that the airfield, which was a short distance from the Regimental Aid Post, had fallen to the Japanese. Some of the men were seriously ill. The only Australian officer in the party, (Lieutenant) Ian

McBride, was weak with the loss of blood from an injury to his arm, which had been operated on only the night before.[7] Stan Shaw made the whole journey to Australia with a piece of shrapnel lodged in his neck. It kept 'weeping and draining for about three weeks' but then closed up.[8]

This group spent three days and nights making their way by local tracks across the precipitous mountains behind Laha to the coast of Ambon opposite Ceram. There they met several others who had escaped from Laha, making their number about 20. For more than a week they remained on Ambon, sheltered from the Japanese by villagers. But it was clear that they were putting the Ambonese at great risk and eventually, when McBride was able to travel, they decided to leave the island for Ceram.

For practical reasons, they decided to travel in small groups. As they made their way along the island chain and through Merauke, however, they met each other at various points. Some of them joined forces with two Dutch officers also escaping from Ambon, while others met some American airmen who had suffered burns when their Catalinas had been shot down. After the usual frustrations of shipping, weather and navigational confusion, these various groups made their way safely to Australia – in McBride's case, landing at Karumba.[9] Here, so one source would have it, they were fired upon by Australian troops.[10] The story is probably apocryphal but remains in circulation to this day.

ESCAPES FROM TAN TUI

Back on Ambon, it became much more difficult to escape once Gull Force was under Japanese guard at Tan Tui. Nonetheless, 13 of Gull Force managed to do this. The first two were R (Ronald) Macpherson and Ben Amor. In the first weeks of their captivity, they slipped out of the camp at night under the fence, which was then only a few strands of wire, and accumulated a stockpile of supplies.[11] One night early in March they made their break. Two brothers, Don and Vic Findlay, were meant to join them but missed the rendezvous in the dark. (They were later sent to Hainan, and both survived the war.) Macpherson and Amor set off along the usual route from Ambon without mishap. They again had the help of villagers on various islands, one of whom informed the authorities that the Australians had gone in a different direction from that which they had taken. Eventually, in late April, at Saumlaki in the Tanimbar Islands, they joined a party led by Jinkins, which, as shall see, left Tan Tui some two weeks after them. They sailed with them to Darwin. 'Everyone was very excited', Ben Amor later wrote, 'sharing news and scrounging cigarettes from the Soldiers ... One chance in a thousand and we made it.'[12]

Four more Australians, (Corporal) FA (Frank) Redhead, RB (Rupert) Goodall, WC (William) Dahlberg and D (Donald) Johnson, left the POW camp on 9 March 1942. Unlike Macpherson and Amor, their escape had the approval of Scott and Macrae. By all accounts their trip to the Kai islands was uneventful. At Dobo, as mentioned, they joined forces with some of the Australians escaping from Eri, and sailed to Merauke, and then, with the help of an RAN vessel, to Thursday Island.[13]

The last escape from Ambon was led by Jinkins, who planned it with great thoroughness from the moment he became a prisoner.[14] For six weeks in February and March 1942, he made 13 reconnaissance trips outside the wire at night and established contacts with friendly Ambonese. His selection of the escape party was equally meticulous. Two of the seven were trusted friends. One of these, (Lieutenant) AG (Gordon) Jack, was asked to choose a fourth member of the party. The other three were chosen by Jinkins because of their skills. Holding instructional classes within Tan Tui, supposedly for the edification of the prisoners, Jinkins identified those in the camp who were trained in astral navigation and the maintenance of diesel engines. He selected as the final members of his party a diesel mechanic, Harry Coe, who in civilian life had maintained a diesel-driven milking machine on his own farm; and (Lieutenant) ROD (Roland) Rudder and (Corporal) C (Cliff) Warn, both of whom had considerable sailing experience.

Scott and Macrae were aware of Jinkins' plans and contemplated joining the escape. Ultimately, however, they remained on Ambon. Their reasons for doing so have been debated. According to Scott's later account, he felt torn between two conflicting duties: to escape to Australia with the tactical and strategic information he had acquired during the fighting on Ambon; or to stay with the men under his command. After consulting two officers, he finally decided that the latter was his primary responsibility. He hoped that the considerable knowledge of the Japanese he acquired in the interwar years equipped him to handle relations with the enemy. As for Macrae, Scott maintained that he was urged by fellow officers to stay on Ambon since Scott himself was 'a stranger to the battalion and did not know any of the officers or men, their qualities or their weaknesses'.[15]

This version of events was later challenged by Jinkins. In his recollection, Scott insisted on being included in the escape party on the very day before it planned to leave Tan Tui. He was dissuaded only when Jinkins enlisted the support of the medical officer (Captain) Bill Aitken, who told Scott, in a tense confrontation, that the haemorrhoids from which he had been suffering for some time prevented his walking even the shortest distance unaided and made him unfit to join any escape.

Jinkins' party left Tan Tui on 17 March 1942. Since three of the group were officers, whose absence from the camp would be more difficult to hide from the Japanese, their places in the officers' lines were filled by three of the other ranks. Sergeant S (Stanley) Piggin assumed the identity of Jack; GA (Geoffrey) Waring substituted for Rudder, and Sergeant CM (Clifton) Wilson for Jinkins. The Japanese never discovered this subterfuge, and when Wilson and Waring died later in their captivity, they were buried under their assumed names. After the war, their graves were renamed, and their real identities made known to the Imperial (later Commonwealth) War Graves Commission (IWGC). The survivor, Piggin, was awarded a British Empire Medal in 1947 on the grounds that if he had been discovered as assuming an escaped officer's identity, he would have been executed.[16]

The first part of Jinkins' escape went only partly to plan. The praus and paddlers that he had arranged in advance were waiting on the southern coast of Ambon with food and supplies. But a tropical storm struck early on 18 March, drenching everything. It forced the escapers to put to shore at Hutumori, the site of one of the Japanese landings in January. Afraid of being betrayed by local spies, the party set off as soon as the rain stopped, even though they were now forced to sail past Paso in daylight. Fortunately, they saw no Japanese and were able to reach the island of Haruku safely by mid-morning. From there, they made their way in a hired (and very expensive) prau to Amahai on Ceram. The difficulties of finding a motorboat kept them in Amahai for three days, and when they finally set off, they had to contend with not only variable weather but also with persistent engine troubles. They reached Geser on 24 March.

By this time Geser, which had been the port of call for the past six weeks for up to 70 Australians, Dutch and Americans escaping south, was running short of food. The island also had little oil, since stocks had been destroyed earlier to prevent them from falling into Japanese hands. Jinkins and his party, therefore, had to wait some days for oil from the Bula oilfield on the north coast of Ceram. When this arrived, they found themselves unable to start their boat's engines, and had no choice but to accept the Dutch controller's offer of two native praus. In these they set off painfully slowly in the light winds. Arthur Young, the log keeper and diarist of the party, sought relief from the tension by writing:

> Much disappointment evident with us, especially one skipper Jinkins who dother say mighty little which is a sure sign that he is not pleased. He being one to speak

at great length when there is speaking to be done ...
One Lieut Rudder, who is a fine sailor, and has salt
in his veins, do sit dejected-looking near the tiller,
betimes swinging the rudder for pastime. Alec do busy
himself making cocoa, so taking advantage of our
being becalmed. And so to some reckoning, when we
do find that it is one fortnight but one day since we did
escape, and not much progress made, we being now
but three kilometres [sic] off Ceram.

The next day, however, the winds freshened and by 1 April
the party had reached Tual. There they decided to go not
to Dobo, as Australians escaping from Ambon before them
had done, but to head for the Tanimbar islands. This was
the more direct route to Australia, but it involved a voyage,
unbroken by islands, across the Arafura Sea.

To complete this stage of their journey, Jinkins bought a
prau and hired a new crew, but the latter investment was far
from a success. To quote Young again:

At Toeal [Tual] we acquired the services of three
natives, a skipper with an asinine laugh, and of
Papuan descent, and possibly of a long line of
missionary munchers, whose apparent good humour
kept us amused while our sense of humour lasted,
but after two or three days of bumping about, the
cackle of the skipper and his habit of not giving direct
answers to our questions ... made us ready to throw
the crew overboard ... Once we showed the old man
a map of the Banda Sea, correctly oriented, feeling
that he was not quite acquainted with our position

at that moment. 'Twas then that we realised that he could neither read nor write, and he explained that he had never used a map, which probably accounted for our arrival at Poeloe Moloe, about 25 miles west of our course, after three days from Toeal. We were then obliged to sail SE into the wind to reach Ridol, on the island of Larat ... [At Ridol] we dismissed our very unpopular crew, choosing to sail the Java ourselves with only a native crew.

It took the Australians several days of difficult battling with the winds and prau to reach Saumlaki on the southern end of Jandena, where the Dutch controller and his wife managed to cope with their gargantuan appetites. Finding a boat that was suitable to take them to Darwin proved more difficult. After five days the controller agreed to let them take a 40-ton government schooner, but this the Australians managed to ground on a reef as they left Jandena in a strong southerly gale. Since the boat could not be refloated off the reef, the Australians had no option but to return to Saumlaki in lifeboats.

Several days of waiting followed, during which they were joined by Amor's group, and a motor launch from Tual carrying 18 Dutch civilians, including women and children. This was the boat in which Jinkins' party finally made its way to Australia – although gaining possession of it was far from easy. The Dutch civilians disliked the arrangement the Australians proposed: namely, that they and the single Dutchmen should take the boat, leaving the Dutch families to be rescued later by a plane, which the others would send back from Australia. Jinkins refused to leave two Australian officers on Jandena as a guarantee of his good faith. Then, it was the turn of the crew of the motorboat to refuse to sail the craft to Australia. Finally, after hours of fruitless negotiation, they were 'persuaded' to do so by the Australians marching them on board in a not especially friendly manner.

Eleven Australians and six single Dutchmen finally left Saumlaki on the evening of 1 May. By 3 May, they had sighted Melville Island, but since they had incomplete maps, they were not certain of their position. At 1000 hours the next day, they saw a familiar sign of Australian civilisation: a beer bottle floating in the water. 'Must be near Darwin', Young noted in the log, and at 1730 on 4 May they finally arrived in Darwin harbour. Their journey from Tan Tui had taken 48 days, only 20 of which had been spent travelling.[17] When finally back in Melbourne, Jinkins met with Sturdee who said, 'Lad, we never expected to see any of you again.'[18]

It was some time before the escape of Jinkins' party was noticed by the Japanese on Ambon. The ruse of substituting other ranks for the missing officers worked, and the escape of the other men was covered by a classic POW stratagem. During roll call, Scott talked to the Japanese who were counting the prisoners, while Macrae moved men, who had already been counted, up the lines to be counted again. The Japanese, however, finally learnt of the escapes, and retaliated by moving the officers from their quarters to the huts occupied by the men. They decreased the area of the camp and built a new double-barbed-wire fence 3.7 metres tall. Machine-gun posts were installed at all angles. Roll call was held every evening at about 1830 hours and surprise roll calls at any time. Worse, the Japanese declared that if any prisoner were found to be missing, the officer in charge of his hut would be executed. If the prisoner himself were recaptured, he, too, would be executed; and if he remained at large, an Australian of comparable rank would be killed in his place.

These regulations contravened the Geneva Convention, but given the Japanese threats, Scott decided to ban further escapes. One already planned to take place under the leadership of (Captain) J (James) Major was cancelled, and in the next three and half years no other Australians escaped from Ambon.[19] On Hainan, even though Scott refused to sign any declarations that bound him and his men to promises not to escape, no one broke out of the camp until April 1945.

A RESCUE PLAN

Jinkins planned to arrange the rescue of Gull Force when he reached Melbourne. At first it seemed that he might succeed. At the highest levels of the Australian Government there was now a deep, if belated, concern about the Australians lost in the Netherlands East Indies and Rabaul. On 19 May, Forde, with the backing of Prime Minister John Curtin, asked Sturdee to explore the possibilities of rescuing prisoners of war. The director of naval plans, Commander HC Wright, was delegated to draw up plans for potential raids on Ambon.[20]

The plan proposed by Wright, and supported by Jinkins, envisaged a commando raid on Ambon of up to 40 men supported by two destroyers. The ships would make their way up the Bay of Ambon under the cover of darkness and then approach Tan Tui. (The waters were navigable to the edge of the coral reef adjoining the camp.) The commandos would storm the camp, supported where practicable by the prisoners themselves. Meanwhile, other prisoners would swim or use dinghies to reach the nets hanging from the sides of the destroyers.[21]

The plan was a bold one, particularly in its assumption that the destroyers would be able to make their way, loaded with prisoners, back down the Bay of Ambon. On the basis of Jinkins' intelligence, however, it was assumed that the Japanese naval defences were comparatively light and that the bay had been cleared of mines. The RAAF, it was believed, would be able to provide some fighter protection and intercept the Japanese by bombing Laha and Halong. The prisoners, moreover, were reportedly ready, in the event of an Allied attack, to cut the communications and lighting circuits of Tan Tui camp.[22] Despite the risks of the operation, it was thought that about 80 per cent of those interned on the island could be rescued.

Several senior officers in the Australian and Dutch navies gave the plan their approval, although in the case of the Dutch, who would be required to provide a cruiser to support the operation, this was given reluctantly.[23] Then, the planning came to an abrupt halt when the US commander of the South-West Pacific Forces, Vice-Admiral HF Leary, vetoed the proposal. In his view it was 'entirely impracticable', given the narrowness of the Bay of Ambon, the likelihood of the Japanese air and naval forces attacking in such a confined space, and the probability that the force would be detected before it reached its objective. He wrote on 3 June:

I think we would lose two of our fighting ships and in addition not add to our prestige by an attempt of this nature. If the camp were on an open coast where a direct approach were possible it might be a different matter. In addition ... the attack on these vessels by air while loaded with prisoners would be disastrous.[24]

Leary may have been acting under political instructions, as Jinkins was told informally by a senior source after the war.[25] More likely, it was the manifest risks of the rescue operation that doomed it, especially as it was thought, on the basis of Jinkins' information, that the prisoners were being treated well by the Japanese. Plans to rescue Gull Force were therefore shelved in mid-1942. Less ambitious schemes to establish an escape route out of Ambon were attempted later, but the Dutch agents infiltrating the island were captured by the Japanese.[26]

AFTER ESCAPE

Perhaps the most remarkable thing about these escape narratives is that all the Australians who left Ambon in early 1942 managed to reach Australia. They made – to use European POW parlance – 'a home run'. Their success was due to the relative proximity of Ambon to northern Australia, the scattering of islands in the Arafura Sea that provided useful stopping points, the generous assistance given by the local inhabitants and the Dutch controllers, and finally, their sheer luck in staying one step ahead of the Japanese.

Of the escapers, Jinkins would go on to have a notable war career. He was not inclined to rest after his eventful journey across the Arafura Sea and the battle on Mount Nona. Instead, he joined the Special Operations Directorate (also known as Special Operations Australia), a unit that conducted covert operations behind Japanese lines in South-East Asia. In July 1942, only weeks after his escape, Jinkins was back in action, leading an unsuccessful attempt to occupy the Aroes and the neighbouring Tanimbar Islands. Over the next three years, he would engage in a series of dramatic operations in North Borneo and the surrounding region. The stories of Operations Python, Politician and Semut 4 have been told elsewhere. Suffice to say here that all these operations, which aimed at collecting intelligence about Japanese movements, shipping and installations, and laying the groundwork for future sabotage and underground resistance, involved great risk.[27] Operatives went hungry, suffered malaria and black water fever and, if captured by the Japanese (as many were), faced torture and execution. Beyond this, the US submarines that delivered the operatives to Borneo were vulnerable to Japanese attack and even 'friendly' collisions. But Jinkins – to judge by his record of regular volunteering – seems to have loved the work and to have had a talent for it. Awarded an MBE for his efforts in organising the escape from Ambon, Jinkins was mentioned in dispatches in early 1945.[28] He was also recognised by the US Navy with the Submarine Combat Insignia for four successful patrols in US submarines – a unique distinction for an Australian.

The other men of Gull Force who returned to Australia did not have such drama-filled careers, but almost all of them served out the war. Of the 45 who can be traced from the surviving records, eight were discharged from the Army in 1942–44 on medical grounds (malaria being a possible contributing cause in some cases). One died of burns when an oven exploded in 1944.[29] Only one, Frank Redhead, was killed on active service, in Balikpapan, Borneo, on 1 July 1945. The rest of the men who escaped Ambon lived. The call they made, in the chaos of early 1942, was the right one.

PART IV
PRISONERS ON AMBON, 1942-45

6
FIRST MONTHS, TO OCTOBER 1942

All soldiers contemplate the possibility of being killed or wounded in action, but rarely do they anticipate becoming prisoners of war.[1] The transition to captivity is profoundly disorienting. In combat, soldiers have been purposeful, part of a highly structured and goal-oriented organisation. As prisoners of war, they are 'dependent, helpless, lacking identity and self-esteem'.[2] Furthermore, their previous authority figures, the officers of their unit, have limited power to protect their interests from their captors, who may impose a regime that is alien and seemingly arbitrary. In these circumstances, prisoners of war have been observed to react with stunned disbelief, numbness, a sense of humiliation, fear of the future, and anger against their officers and high command, such as we have already seen in the case of Gull Force. In time, these feelings diminish, as prisoners adjust to their new situation. They create, as far as is possible, a new life and home in the prison camp. If the captivity is prolonged, however, a deep sense of futility develops, manifesting as increasing irritability, diminished enterprise and initiative and, often, deep tensions between the prisoners of war. If the captivity continues for several years, and the conditions of internment deteriorate, the prisoners may suffer psychological damage, which impairs their ability to establish personal relations, both within the camp and in later civilian life.[3] As AL Cochrane, himself a prisoner of the Axis powers in Europe, said after discussing the matter with many prisoners of war, 'in general one could say that the first year was spent in adaptation, the second was the best year, the third began to be a strain, and the fourth and following years left no one unscathed'.[4]

ADAPTATION

The trajectory of Gull Force in captivity conformed in many ways to this pattern. Survivors recalled in the 1980s that they felt numb, disgusted and disgraced – emotions intensified by the racial divide from the Japanese.[5] To quote Don Findlay, 'It wasn't very nice when you saw these little blokes smaller than we were.' Ron Green, for his part, maintained, 'I, and I am sure the others, were proud of the AIF and of our own unit, and I felt that somehow we had let the AIF down even though I knew that we had not been given a chance, and that in our circumstances defeat was inevitable.' Every member of Gull Force had a deep fear for the future, both for themselves and for their families who, for all Gull Force knew, might be facing Japanese attacks on Australia.[6] The uncertainty about how long their captivity might last and how the war might end was also deeply demoralising.

Yet, if this anxiety was typical, the first days for those Australians captured on the Laitimor Peninsula were not as dire as they might have been. Prisoners in other theatres of war had to endure, soon after capture, primitive transit camps, death marches, train journeys in cattle trucks, exposure to the elements and even starvation. When American and Filipino troops, captured on the Bataan Peninsula in the Philippines, were forced in April 1942 to march some 160 kilometres to their internment camp without any reliable issue of food or medical attention, thousands died.[7] Gull Force, in contrast, had to march perhaps 20 kilometres from where they surrendered to their already established base at Tan Tui.

Here, the Australians were assigned one compound; the 300 or so Dutchmen, another area. The barracks had been ransacked during the recent battle, but conditions were generally reasonable.[8] The camp still had no electricity, but did have kitchens, a hospital of sorts and latrines (unorthodox but hygienic). Although water had to be carried from where a pipeline from a spring ended, some 15 metres below the camp, the only times that water was scarce were when Japanese ships came to the port of Ambon and filled up their water tanks over two to three days.[9] The prisoners' accommodation was timber huts, 30 metres by 6 metres, roofed with atap (palm leaves) and fitted with concrete floors.[10] Up to 70 men could sleep in each hut.[11] Initially, there was no problem with overcrowding. Bedding was in short supply, since the Japanese soon confiscated some of the Australian supplies, but the prisoners were able to find adequate substitutes.

Importantly, in contrast to Laha, the Japanese captors on the Laitimor Peninsula side of the island were initially quite benign. Those prisoners who escaped in March 1942 remembered their guards as being friendly, handing out cigarettes and 'treating us with every courtesy and consideration'. Dahlberg, in his evidence to an Australian court of inquiry about events on Ambon in July 1942, said, 'our captors acted like gentlemen and treated us like gentlemen'.[12] Jinkins, too, reported that the Japanese treatment was 'as fair as it could have been'.[13] Although prisoners' watches and personal possessions were commandeered by Japanese soldiers, on at least two occasions these were returned when complaints were made to senior Japanese officers. The private responsible for one theft was physically punished in front of a group of prisoners.[14] At this time even the Japanese interpreter at Tan Tui, Ikeuchi Masakiyo, who would later become the embodiment of capricious sadism, seemed to be reasonable.

The Japanese control of the prisoners' movements was also lax in these early days. While guards were stationed at regular points around the camp, armed with automatic weapons, they did not patrol between the posts and the area was not illuminated after dark.[15] Hence the prisoners were able to slip out of the camp at night to scrounge extra food and, as we have seen, plan their escapes to Australia. According to one estimate, as many as 50 or 60 Australians were outside the camp on any one night at this time.[16] All this, of course, began to change in April 1942, when the Japanese discovered the escape of Jinkins' party and tightened the security of the camp. But even then, conditions inside Tan Tui were far from harsh.

PRIORITY ONE: FOOD

Nothing matters more to the survival of a prisoner of war than food. For the first 20 months of Gull Force's internment, the Japanese supplied about 480 grams of rice per man per day. This was occasionally supplemented by small amounts of fish and vegetables.[17] The prisoners supplemented these meagre rations from a variety of sources. The first was their own army supplies, which had been stockpiled in Tan Tui and elsewhere on the island during the preparations for the Japanese invasion. The depots had been raided by the local population during the fighting, but the Australians were allowed to go out under escort, and retrieve as much food as they could find. An officer of the AASC, (Captain) Sam Rose, remembered:

> we went into a hut and a native woman was on a bed
> up there about that high. One fellow said, 'Mama very
> very sick.' We could see underneath what was there.
> We got Mama off … lifted the mattress and there
> were all the bags of sugar and everything else, flour
> and so forth.

In this way 'a quite decent supply' of flour, sugar and tinned food, including the ubiquitous bully beef, was added to the Japanese rations for at least the first three or four months after Gull Force's surrender.[18] The various cooks throughout the camp – messing was managed by individual huts at this stage – were able to make the monotonous rice slightly more palatable. They were also able to cook bread, using three times the usual quantity of stale yeast. They even created cucumber sandwiches.[19]

The second source of additional food was trade with the local population. The main road on the island went through the camp and one day each week the Japanese allowed the Ambonese to hold a market. Working through a nominated agent from each hut, prisoners purchased sugar, sago, fruit, eggs, peanuts and other goods, including tobacco.[20] The financial resources of individual prisoners varied, and the Australians were less well off than the Dutch internees, some of whom had come into the camp directly from their own homes and had the cash to pay higher prices for food.[21] Nonetheless, the market was an important source of food for the prisoners, until the Japanese stopped it in 1943 – supposedly because the Ambonese were by then too short of food to have anything to sell.[22]

A third source of extra food was stealing from the Japanese. Any moral inhibitions the Australians may have had about 'scrounging' disappeared. Stealing became such a way of life – and Australian ways of thieving so inventive – that some of Gull Force later doubted whether they could ever be trusted to walk through a supermarket again on their return to Australia. But however skilled they were at theft, they risked a beating if caught.

Finally, the Australians produced their own food. Within the perimeter of the Tan Tui camp, gardens sprang up everywhere. Cassava, the local staple, was the most popular crop, but peanuts, chillies and tomatoes grown from the seeds of tinned tomatoes were also coaxed into life with the aid of Ambon's benign climate and heavy rainfall.[23] Some prisoners set up fish traps in the bay.[24] Others fished from the comfort of their seats in the 'bridge of sighs'. Yet others kept chickens. Those who could not bother with these chores slipped out of the camp at night to collect coconuts or whatever else could be found.[25]

In their efforts to find food, the prisoners formed small groups of two to eight men. These 'syndicates', which pooled resources, were sometimes based on existing friendships but could be simply pragmatic: what Eddie Gilbert called 'marriages of convenience'.[26] Each prisoner had different skills and different opportunities to scrounge for food. Those working on the wharves, for instance, had an obvious advantage. The understanding was that if one man shared his spoils, then the others in the syndicate would reciprocate when he was confined to camp or assigned to a less profitable working party.[27] This mutual support system might be read as a testament to the legendary Australian capacity for mateship, but similar arrangements of convenience emerged elsewhere: for example, among American prisoners in the Philippines and between internees of various nationalities in Sumatra, where the syndicates were called *congsies* after the Chinese word for a small group or organisation.[28]

PRIORITY TWO: WORK

Beyond food, the other major issue shaping life in captivity was work. This impacted largely on the other ranks, since the Japanese did not regularly require the officers on Ambon to do manual work.[29] In this, at least, they respected the 1929 Geneva Convention. Later the officers were forced to work on Japanese vegetable gardens, but this happened infrequently. Generally, the officers were left free to administer the camp and to act as supervisors of working parties (although the Japanese stopped them from going out with the men in 1944).

The other ranks, in contrast, were required to perform manual labour. At first, this was either camp chores, such as digging holes and burying rubbish, or light work such as cutting grass. Only about 50 of the prisoners were employed in this way in the first weeks.[30] Gradually, however, the Japanese demanded larger working parties and assigned them to heavier tasks. These included unloading ships, handling bombs and ammunition, repairing roads, making a rifle range and, as the Allied air forces began to appear from May 1942, digging air-raid shelters.[31] The Geneva Convention prescribed that the work of prisoners should have no direct connection with the operations of the war; prisoners should not be employed in the 'manufacture or transport of arms or munitions of any kind, or on the transport of material destined for combat units'. But when Scott complained to the Japanese commandant in July 1942, he was told:

> Don't be puffed up,
> Don't be grow impudent,
> Don't be grow vain,
> Don't be intrusive,
> Don't be too forward,
> to say such a haughty protest for our orders to work by you Australian. And you must attempt nothing beyond your strength as Prisoners of War. Shut your mouth better.[32]

At no stage did the Japanese pay officers or men on Ambon for their work, although they did so on Hainan and in many other camps in the Asia-Pacific.[33] They promised payment – at the rate of 25 cents per day for officers, 15 cents for NCOs, and 10 cents for private soldiers – and demanded that the Australian officers keep records of the work, but, as

(Lieutenant) John van Nooten later wrote, after two months they 'just wiped it and never paid anything'.[34]

Despite all this, most of Gull Force welcomed the working parties when they first began. Outside the camp, men could scrounge food and contact Ambonese villagers who were often willing to slip the prisoners food and cigarettes. Finally, work offered some change from the tedium of life in the camp.

PRIORITY 3: MENTAL HEALTH

The challenge of staying emotionally and mentally healthy was intense. To mitigate against the boredom, and the sense of their lives being wasted, the prisoners established a camp 'university'. The expertise of one man was shared with the others. Mathematics, languages, science, soil erosion, accountancy, shorthand, law, motor mechanics, English literature, bridge and vocational guidance for the younger members of the battalion: these were some of the classes offered almost daily in early 1942. In addition, there were reading circles, debates, a library made up of books collected from throughout the camp, and lectures on travel and subjects of general interest. An Agricultural Society was formed. Sport, too, was a feature of life in the weeks before working parties. The day began with 15 minutes compulsory physical exercise, followed later by more exercise (for those who wanted it) in the 'gymnasium' constructed by the prisoners. Boxing, wrestling, volleyball, cricket and deck tennis were also arranged.[35] A fierce basketball competition culminated in a final between the officers and men of the transport unit.

The prize was a tin of tobacco, a valuable commodity since on Ambon, as in many other POW camps, cigarettes became the currency of the camp economy.[36]

During these early days, Gull Force also enjoyed regular concerts by the 2/21st Battalion band, whose instruments had somehow survived the looting undamaged. Even the Japanese enjoyed the regular concerts. Gull Force found it also had considerable amateur theatrical talent. One prisoner could remember and perform the 'Albert and the Lion' monologues by Stanley Holloway, then popular in Australia. Another man wrote a type of 'Dad and Dave' serial, complete with female impersonators. Costumes were produced with endless ingenuity from clothing within the camp. Dutch women interned in a nearby camp provided female clothing, and split coconuts resolved the problem of reproducing the female anatomy. Even a curtain was made for the 'stage', meticulously decorated with replicas of the badges of all the units that made up Gull Force.[37]

ESCALATING VIOLENCE

At first all these activities were tolerated by the Japanese; but after about six months, restrictions were progressively introduced. The number of concerts was limited, sporting fixtures were cut, and lectures were censored before they were allowed to be given. All the books of the library were registered and many of them confiscated for the duration of the war.[38]

These changes reflected a wider change in Japanese attitudes, which began about June 1942. What caused this is unclear. Perhaps it was a reaction to the first signs of Japanese strategic setbacks, at the major naval battles of the Coral Sea and Midway in May–June 1942; however, many of Gull Force attributed it to a change in the personnel administering Tan Tui. For a short period in early 1942, the camp had been under the control of the Imperial Japanese Army, but soon it was transferred to the Japanese Navy. The force responsible for guarding the prisoners was a detached platoon of the 20th Garrison Unit (Marines), consisting of about 40 NCOs and men under the command of a warrant officer. The commander of this platoon was automatically camp commandant and responsible for discipline and security within the camp. He, in turn, reported to the successive commanders of the 20th Garrison.[39]

For the first half of 1942 this commander was an innocuous figure, but in June he was replaced by Captain Ando Noburo. Nicknamed 'Handlebars' by the Australians because of his sweeping moustache, Ando took a keen and spiteful interest in the prisoners under his command. He issued a new set of orders, restricting not only entertainment and instructional classes, but also conversation with the local population. All potential weapons – shovels, knives, axes and tools – had to be handed in to the Japanese. They were issued thereafter only at working parties. The keeping of diaries was forbidden, and nightly inspections of the camps introduced. All ranks were ordered to stand to attention as the commandant made his rounds. Ando also instituted surprise searches, in which the Japanese descended on the camp without warning and searched everyone's belongings. Additional irritations were a prohibition on eating between meals and the issuing of orders in Japanese only. Ando also insisted that all prisoners, bar Scott, should salute the Japanese sentries, whatever their rank.[40]

Under Ando the level of physical violence also escalated. Making frequent inspections of the camp, he punished any individual who irritated him. On one occasion he struck (Major) George de V Westley with his sword in front of several other prisoners; on another, he rushed into the isolation ward of the hospital and, without reason, attacked a very ill man.[41] In a third incident he broke into the room the Australian officers were using as a mess and, in the words of (Captain) JM (John) Turner,

> immediately shouted out a torrent of Japanese, nothing
> of which could be understood by those present … As
> no one understood what was being said Capt Ando
> became enraged and using a cane about 3 feet in
> length he slashed myself three or four times across the
> face, severly [sic] bruising the cheek bone then half a
> dozen times across the chest which was bare leaving
> bruises and weals which took some days to heal.
> He treated Lieut Chaplin in like fashion, and made
> two attempts to strike Captain Major. He then left,
> striking the cook, Pte Williamson several times before
> departing.[42]

In July 1942, this violence exploded in a profoundly disturbing incident. About 30 of the Dutch male prisoners interned in Tan Tui were caught by the Japanese trying to communicate with their wives who were detained in a nearby camp. Apparently, they had permission to send letters via the interpreter Ikeuchi, but when it seemed that these were not getting through, the Dutch men entrusted notes secretly to the Ambonese at the market. Some of these were personal letters, nothing but intimate remarks; but when they were intercepted, Ando ordered that the Dutchmen should be punished.

The beating took place on a hill in front of the Japanese guard headquarters, only 25 to 35 metres from the Australian compound and visible to everyone in Gull Force. According to one of the young Australian officers, John van Nooten:

> Ando addressed the guards (who would be about 40 to 50 in number) and on his direction they rushed about collecting weapons. They collected pick handles, iron bars, star pickets, wire cable, in fact anything that they could lay their hands on … The beating was the most terrifying and bestial performance imaginable. It must have lasted some 2 hours or so and the result was that there were 18 stretcher cases, 3 men died and quite a few suffered from fractured bones, concussion and internal injuries as well as the terrific contusions and wounds that the majority suffered.[43]

More graphically than any other change in their circumstances, this 'Dutch garden party', as the Australians called it, signalled that the relative calm of the first months of their captivity was over. Even though the Japanese, with an inconsistency that often confounded their prisoners, sent cakes and wine to Kapitz with a message of regret, attended the funerals of the Dutch they had killed, laid wreaths on their coffins and made gifts to their relatives, the image of that merciless beating on the hill haunted everyone.[44] Among the

Japanese involved in the violence was Ikeuchi. Although only a civilian attached to the navy, he was gradually assuming the role of camp manager, the intermediary through which the Australian officers had to channel all their requests to Ando. His involvement in this beating was a sinister sign of what Gull Force could expect from him in the future.

In the months that followed, the level of violence experienced on working parties increased. Japanese guards began to beat the prisoners without provocation and to punish them for offences such as receiving food from the Ambonese. In one incident in August 1942, described by (Lance Sergeant) WD (William) Harries:

> several Ambonese threw pineapples, tobacco and soap
> on the ground near us. I told the men not to pick
> them up, knowing the consequences. At lunch time,
> the Japanese guard motioned me to take them and I
> distributed the goods amongst the men. He then lined
> us up, kicked everyone severely in the shins and body
> and punched several heavily in the face. There was
> nothing wrong with the work.[45]

A regular source of friction was the obligation to salute the Japanese guards, even when passing a sentry house between the sleeping huts and the 'bridge of sighs'. One evening Turner failed to give an appropriate salute on this well-trodden path. He was given 12 strokes with a heavy stick and made to stand in the rain for an hour clad only in his pajamas. Other prisoners were beaten severely for the same offence.[46]

LEADERSHIP ISSUES

As the Japanese treatment of the prisoners worsened, so too did relationships within the prison camp. Notably, the leadership provided by the officers of Gull Force came under strain. As was their practice throughout the Asia-Pacific, the Japanese did not segregate the officers from the other ranks in separate camps. They interned all ranks together and allowed the Australian military hierarchy to remain in place. Thus, Gull Force's officers had daily responsibility for internal camp administration. It was they who chose the men for working parties, administered the distribution of rations and maintained discipline within the camp. The distancing of the Japanese from these matters was almost certainly an advantage, in that the officers could form a buffer between the ranks and their captors; but it meant that the officers performing these inherently contentious roles faced the challenge of maintaining the legitimacy of their command.

Their difficulties were compounded by the fact that captivity changed the sources of the officers' authority. Within the traditional military setting, officers were able to draw on a mix of formal and informal authority: formal (or as it is sometimes called, legitimate) authority being the position that they held by virtue of their commissioned rank and the system of military law that sanctioned non-compliance with orders; informal authority being the officers' competence – military expertise and fighting skills – and personal qualities such as bravery, charisma and concern for the men they led.[47] Despite the issues with Gull Force's discipline in Darwin already discussed, it seems that the men of Gull Force did not seriously contest this authority during the period of training and preparation for battle. The army was, after all, an institution, whose purposes they supported when they volunteered for military service in 1940. Authority, it has been said, is 'a bilateral process in which those exercising command and those giving compliance share common goals and norms': norms that are shared and reinforced by the larger group or community to which both the leaders and the led belong.[48]

The defeat of Gull Force, as we have seen, threatened all this. Not only was the authority of the army as an institution shattered, but the qualities that might have made an officer effective in earlier days did not necessarily command respect in the POW camp. Leadership is inherently situational. The traits required to exercise it vary with changing circumstances. In 1942 there was no template as to how officers trained to command in battle should lead in captivity. Moreover, the sanctions by which command and discipline were normally enforced were now largely ineffectual. It meant nothing to deny a man his leave when he could not take it. His pay could not be docked, given that he was not receiving any (docking pay that was accumulating in Australia was too remote a sanction to have much effect). Nor was there much point in reducing a man's rank. Of course, a man who needed disciplining could be confined to 'barracks' in Tan Tui, but this denied him the opportunity to scrounge food outside the camp on working parties. Extra fatigues inside the camp and the reduction of rations were also morally questionable sanctions when the prisoners were already overworked and hungry. This left three other options: corporal punishment, detention within some form of Australian-managed 'jail', and handing men over to the Japanese for discipline. But in early 1942, none of these methods were acceptable to either the officers or men of Gull Force.

The exception was Scott. At some time early in their captivity, so Scott claimed in his postwar account, some 'bad elements' appeared. Officers were being openly heckled, and NCOs who tried to get men to work were laughed at. 'Discipline was disappearing rapidly and the bitterness of prison life was beginning to be felt. It was apparent that the whole organisation of the camp would suffer.' Scott thus decided to call a parade of all the Australians in the camp, and 'to tell them just where they got off'. To the mass of silent prisoners assembled before him, he announced that 'he had been a soldier too long to allow any man under his command to dictate to him'. His orders issued through his officers must be strictly obeyed and the strictest discipline maintained. Everyone's life, he said, might depend upon this. Should large numbers of prisoners refuse to work or to obey orders, then he would go to the Japanese and inform them that he had no control over his men. He would insist that he and his officers be removed to another camp. Should individuals be guilty of a disciplinary offence, such as stealing from their mates, refusing to obey orders or being insolent to their officers, then they would be taken to the Japanese commandant for punishment. He said he was 'determined, for the sake of everyone, that law and order would be maintained, and would not have the welfare, and perhaps lives, of all placed at the mercy of the minority'. Scott further said that he would recommend that miscreants would lose pay when they returned to Australia. Any NCO who 'did not do his job' would revert to the ranks.[49]

This speech was no idle threat. Shortly after it was

given, according to (Captain) Rod Gabriel, one prisoner who refused to obey an officer's orders on a working party was handed over to the Japanese for punishment. Fortunately, since this was the period of Japanese restraint, he was simply detained for a while in the guard house.[50]

Scott's threat to hand Australians over to the Japanese for punishment was resented bitterly within Gull Force. His approach violated a core principle of leadership: namely, that the leader's role is to protect the interests of the men he leads against external threats. Although Scott claimed to have the interests of the collective at heart, he was willing to abandon individuals to their enemy. Even if the Japanese had been inclined to treat these men humanely, Scott's resort to a form of 'coercive authority' – obtaining compliance from subordinates by threats of force – was almost certainly unacceptable to Australian soldiers. As we have seen, the Anzac legend accorded a central place to mateship and a more informal style of command and sanctions. Thus, a private in the 2/21st, Reg Brassey, said, 'If you can't punish men yourself, you shouldn't be where you are. If you're supposed to know how to lead, but have to hand men over, then you shouldn't be in the job.'

We can only speculate as to Scott's motives. Perhaps, having taken command of Gull Force voluntarily, and then been denied the victory or the noble death that he imagined, he directed his anger against the men whom he thought responsible for his humiliating status as a prisoner of war. Another contributing factor might have been Scott's age. When he took command of Gull Force in January 1942, he was 53, the oldest battalion commander in the 2nd AIF. Perhaps he had simply lost the tolerance needed for leadership, and the ability and willingness to understand the problems of men often 30 years his junior. Perhaps, as he grew older, the authoritarianism that his earlier political activities suggest was a part of his personality became more pronounced.

Whatever the explanation of Scott's behaviour, it confirmed the principle that leadership requires different skills in different situations. The assertive, influential leader of the interwar paramilitary organisations became the withdrawn, alienated commander when confronted with the unprecedented and unique strains of a POW camp. The enduring impression conveyed by survivors of Gull Force when interviewed in the 1980s was of a man who never fraternised with the ranks, who stayed aloof and closeted in his hut, unaware of and unconcerned with the problems of his men. As (Lieutenant) Colin McCutcheon, who knew him well on Hainan, commented later, the ranks 'never felt they had a friend in their CO'.

TO HAINAN

For many men in Gull Force, the question of Scott's leadership ceased to matter late in 1942. On 15 October, Ikeuchi announced that the prisoners on Ambon were to be divided. Most would remain on Ambon but almost a third, together with almost all the Dutch prisoners, were to leave for an unknown destination. The new camp, Ikeuchi assured them, would be 'in the nature of a convalescent camp', with medicines and proper treatment available.[51] As a result, many of the other ranks included in the draft were selected from the prisoners who were ill. At the insistence of the Japanese, almost all the Australian Army Medical Corps personnel were also included, leaving only one Australian dentist, (Captain) PM (Peter) Davidson, a Dutch doctor, (Captain) JHQ Ehlhart, and a few medical orderlies with the majority of the Australians on Ambon.

Scott, Macrae and 12 other officers were assigned to go with the contingent of 267 Australians and 233 Dutch prisoners. Remaining on Ambon were 528 Australians, including 24 officers, 14 Americans (interned in the camp from late 1942 after escaping from the Philippines), and six Dutch (the Dutch were staying to clear the tank mines).[52] They were left under the command of Westley, the only remaining major, who remained in this role until the end of the war.[53] The Roman Catholic padre, VE (Vincent) Cochrane, went with the group leaving Ambon; the Anglican padre, CH (Charles) Patmore, remained behind. Such possessions as Gull Force held communally were carefully divided before the contingent left for Hainan. Every man remaining on Ambon was left with at least one blanket and a greatcoat or service dress. All food was left on the island since 'those remaining would require every scrap they could get'. The departing prisoners were limited to only one parcel of baggage each; two, if they were officers. The Dutch who disregarded this regulation were caught out in a surprise practice pack and parade, and summarily punished by Ando. One man was hit over the head with a generator, the Dutch padre was slapped about the head with his Bible, and all the sick men were made to march, and then run, a certain distance with their gear in Ambon's stifling heat.[54]

The departure date was 25 October 1942. Before the prisoners boarded the small freighter, *Taiko Maru*, Ando addressed them through an interpreter. Australians, he said, had good discipline, 'nearly as good as the Japanese, and if it continued they would have a good trip. If not, they would be punished severely. The Japanese were quick-tempered and must be obeyed.' As if to prove his point, he ordered the last Australian to board the freighter, the adjutant Turner, to salute him – and then struck him with a stick.[55]

In the event, the members of Gull Force who left Ambon were the more fortunate; they suffered a much lower death rate than those who remained behind. But it did not seem so in October 1942. Ambon, after all, had the advantage of being familiar, and travelling by sea was a hazardous undertaking in a time of unrestricted submarine warfare. Most importantly, Ambon was comparatively close to Australia, and it seemed likely that it would be liberated early in the war. It would not be so.

7
SURVIVING, 1943-44

The situation of the Australians on Ambon deteriorated markedly after the departure of Scott and others for Hainan. The tightening of regulations under Ando, and the brutality of the 'Dutch garden party', proved not to be isolated incidents. Rather, they marked the beginning of a regime that would become progressively more severe in 1943–44. The more the wider strategic context for the Japanese deteriorated, the greater seemed to be their frustration with the enemy they had captured. Furthermore, as the Allies started to counterattack, the prisoners were exposed to a new and, at times, more devastating risk: the bombing of their camp by so-called 'friendly' forces.

NOVEMBER 1942 EXECUTIONS

A dreadful incident in late 1942 signalled these changes. Aware of prisoners going out of the camp at night in search of food, the Japanese laid a trap. Sometime in the first two weeks of November, four Australians were apprehended. Like the Dutch in July, they were taken to the Japanese headquarters where they were beaten and tortured throughout the night within the hearing of the prisoners in the camp.

The following day, the Japanese announced that all the prisoners would be punished if other individuals who had been going out at night failed to confess. If the offenders admitted their 'crime', they would be given only light punishment. Since it seemed that the four already captured might implicate others under torture, some men gave themselves up over the next 24 hours. But the Japanese wanted more. They set up an identification parade in which local people walked along the lines of the assembled prisoners pointing out anyone they had seen being illicitly outside the camp.[1] Decades later, the terror of that parade still haunted survivors. What if an Ambonese selected someone by mistake? 'After all they all look the same to us, so we might look the same to them.' Possibly the Ambonese, who had been beaten themselves, might nominate anyone, guilty or not, in order to save their own lives.[2] As it happened, one of the men identified in the parade had not been in the habit of going 'under the wire'.

Eventually, the Japanese collected about 25 Australians to join the four already at their headquarters. These men were then tortured over several days. In the worst cases, the Japanese suspended the men from a branch of a tree, with their wrists tied with cable above their heads. Hanging there, with their toes barely touching the ground, the men were beaten with pick handles, pieces of timber, star pickets, iron rods – anything the Japanese could lay their hands on. Many prisoners were also burnt with cigarette stubs, on their noses, necks and other parts of the body. Their genitals were kicked and their stomachs jumped on. At times the victims were given the food that the other prisoners were able to provide once a day. During the night, they were tied in a circle around a tree, forbidden to lean back against the trunk at any time. The next day the beatings resumed. As van Nooten recalled later:

> the original beatings lasted an hour and half. They gave them a spell and beat them again for probably another hour and then the beatings were just at odd intervals whenever any particular guard felt like giving more punishment to anybody who seemed to have taken it fairly well or anybody who was moaning.[3]

When the Australian who had never gone outside the camp at night protested his innocence and volunteered to swear to his truthfulness on the Bible, the Japanese replied that they had no use for 'that Devil's book'.[4]

The injuries of the Australians were severe. At least one suffered internal injuries around the kidneys, and all had contused buttocks, in some cases swollen to twice their normal size. Since the Japanese tended to inflict most blows between the small of the back and the knees, one prisoner lost use of his legs for three to four months.[5] After two or three days, some of the Australians were sent back to the camp. Others were kept for varying periods until only 11 men remained in Japanese hands. Some weeks later Ikeuchi came to the camp and said, 'You can take these beds away – they have been executed.'[6] Indeed, these men had been removed by truck on 22 November 1942, decapitated and buried in a mass grave.[7] The news of this ghastly event had a profoundly sobering effect as it spread through Tan Tui. As Eddie Gilbert said, 'After that we had learnt what the Japanese meant by "light punishment".'

THE BOMBING OF TAN TUI

The next disaster, three months later in February 1943, was the bombing of Tan Tui by American aircraft. From September 1942 on, the Japanese had commandeered some of the huts inside the camp for their own use. At first, they stored only foodstuffs, small arms ammunition, furniture and refrigerators; but by early 1943, they had accumulated at least 91 000 kilograms of high explosives inside what originally had been Gull Force's transport sheds. These were only 4.6 metres away from the Australian officers' quarters, 60 metres from the camp hospital and within 23 metres of the compound where 200 Dutch women and children were interned. These civilians had been moved to Tan Tui after the Dutch military personnel in the camp had left for Hainan in October 1942.[8] The Japanese claimed that there was no other storage facility on Ambon suitably protected from the weather.[9] But in making the camp a munitions dump, the Japanese were again ignoring the Geneva Convention of 1929, which specified that prisoners could not be used as a means of rendering areas immune from bombardment.

The Australians knew how vulnerable the camp was to aerial attack, but their attempts to have Tan Tui marked as a POW camp and the hospital roof painted with a red cross were rejected emphatically.[10] When the adjutant (Captain) John Hooke challenged Ikeuchi, he was threatened with execution and told that he should remember his status as a prisoner of war: 'You have no rights, do not be puffed up, international law & Red Cross Convention is dead.' Ikeuchi said that he did not like the bombs being near him any more than the prisoners did. The Japanese also claimed that ten of their own hospital ships, marked with red crosses, had recently been sunk in the vicinity of Ambon.[11]

On 15 February 1943 the worst happened. Late that morning day US B-24 Liberators bombed Tan Tui. In the words of Keith Mellor:

It was a bright day, bright sunshine, just on lunchtime. An engineer officer was up on the roof fixing the atap on the officers' hut which was the one closest to the bomb dump. Alongside it was a refrigeration unit … and George Russell, another officer, and I both walked out there. As we did, we spotted some Liberators coming in over the sea plane base and we saw this plane which appeared to waggle its wings. I said, 'Oh, he's been hit.' (It was the first time I'd seen a plane unload a load of bombs.) Well, he wasn't hit, he was unloading on us! The first salvo of bombs fell across the Dutch women's and children's camp and into the bomb dump – and set it on fire. One fell into the refrigeration unit and it blasted both of us over and it blew George Russell over the top of my head … he hit me with his knees as he went over and I thought I'd been wounded. I kept looking for blood but there wasn't any. Anyway, when we both got up, we saw that the bomb dump was alight … so George raced off to warn the Dutch women and children to get down and I came back to try to get the troops, hospital people and all the people in the huts there into the long concrete gutters that lined the road through the centre of the camp.

The camp hospital at that time contained 40 to 50 patients, many of whom could not walk without assistance and some of whom were stretcher cases. Officers and men from across the camp converged to evacuate them before the bomb dump exploded. For nearly two frantic minutes the rescue work continued. Then, when the evacuation was almost completed, part of the dump went up in a massive explosion.[12] To continue with Mellor's account:

> I was standing on the other side of the road yelling
> for people to get down, just by the basketball court,
> when – I didn't hear the explosion – I was just lifted
> off my feet and carried through the air and deposited
> about 6 or 7 feet down near the basketball court. I can
> remember looking back over my shoulder and seeing
> up in the air huge timber beams from the huts about
> twenty feet long, just lazily circling a hundred feet up
> in the air or more. Everything was utter chaos.

Another prisoner, Leo Manning, found himself 'running up in the air. My feet were going but I wasn't moving'.

Tan Tui camp was almost totally destroyed. Walter Hicks later wrote: 'nothing bigger than four or five feet existed, and vast sections had vanished completely. The devastation was utter.'[13] The former bomb dump was now a crater measuring 36 metres by 18 metres by 9 metres. Only three huts remained and these were badly battered and damaged by fire.

For many weeks thereafter, Gull Force rebuilt their camp with minimal assistance from the Japanese. According to Westley, the Japanese 'treated it as a bit of a joke and blamed the Americans'.[14] A small quantity of atap was provided for roofing, but essentially the huts had to be largely reconstructed from the debris left over from the blast.[15] Prisoners extracted nails from pieces of timber and rethatched the roofs with palm leaves.[16] New cooking utensils were made from scraps of galvanised iron and aluminium. Ultimately, 18 huts were rebuilt. One was soon commandeered by the Japanese to serve as a store hut, and the rest housed up to 52 prisoners each.[17]

The Dutch nationals, meanwhile, were transferred to the township of Ambon where the women and children were crowded into 'a disgusting and inadequate' church. Their injured were admitted to a hospital on the outskirts of the town. Some months later, the Australians subsequently learnt, they were transferred by ship to Macassar.[18]

Perhaps more important than the physical destruction from the bomb blast was the psychological damage. It was a cataclysm that remained etched on the memories of the survivors decades later. The explosion, the deafening noise and the fires left them terrified. 'For days after we were too frightened to look up into the sky,' Arthur Deakin said. Moreover, the destruction of the barracks destroyed the world that the prisoners had managed to create during their first year of captivity. Those small but cherished possessions, which linked the prisoners to their past, had been lost.

Even worse, the bomb blast decapitated the camp's leadership. The short interval between the dropping of the bombs and the explosion of the dump was long enough to attract many officers to the epicentre of the disaster. The Anglican padre, Charles Patmore, was one of those killed. 'Chewing Gum Charlie', as he was affectionately known after the 2/21st's march from Trawool to Bonegilla when he had cycled up and down the lines of troops handing out gum, was mortally wounded while attending to the wounded and dying near the bomb dump.[19] So, too, was the remaining Australian medical officer, Peter Davidson, killed as he tended two men wounded in the initial fall of bombs. Hooke, too died, together with three other officers and four other ranks, including Wilson, who had been the stand-in for Bill Jinkins after his escape. About 20 other Australians were seriously wounded, some of whom died from their injuries later. In addition, there were about 70 minor casualties.[20]

The padre, the doctor and the adjutant were all respected for their professional competence and their personal qualities. Davidson, like doctors across the POW camps in the Far East – (Sir) Edward 'Weary' Dunlop and Albert Coates being the most famous – commanded authority because he had skills that were vital to the health of the group.[21] He was also, as Hicks later commented, 'the finest man I have ever met'.[22] After Davidson's death, the Australians had to rely for medical care on Gull Force's dentist, Marshall, and the Dutch doctor, Ehlhart. Both of these were tireless in their efforts to counter the effects on the prisoners of malnutrition and overwork. But the loss of Davidson was incalculable.

The death of Hooke was a comparable tragedy. Although only 25 years old when he died, he had emerged as almost the leader of the camp. Westley, in charge after the Hainan departure, had been catapulted into this leadership role on Ambon and it was one that he neither wanted, nor found congenial.[23] He preferred to delegate the daily administration of the camp to Hooke. It was Hooke who liaised with the Japanese, received their demands for labourers, argued with them about the fitness of men to go on working parties, battled with them about the pettiness of their regulations, and promulgated their orders within the confines of the camp. It was a thankless task that, by all accounts, Hooke managed well. Arthur Deakin said, 'He was so good even the Japanese respected him. When he was killed, the Japanese saluted him. He would stand no nonsense from the Japanese. No other officer commanded the Japanese respect.' J (Joseph) Julian likewise remembered Hooke as 'a man that stood up to the Japs … He was only a young fellow too, he was a beauty.' In the words of Manning:

> He was very honest for a start, a very upright man.
> He had that knack of looking someone in the eye
> when talking to him … He was a gentleman … He
> wasn't aggressive. He was a very straightforward sort
> of man and it would come out, even when he was
> playing basketball. He would join in, you could
> iron him out and he'd still get up.

Hooke, then, was very much the officer of the AIF tradition: approachable, accessible and visibly willing to defend the interests of his men. Some survivors believed that had Hooke lived, the fate of the prisoners on Ambon might have been different.

Some final damage from the bomb blast was the relationship between the Australian and Dutch prisoners, which was already fragile after the defeat in February 1942. The bomb blast killed some 27 Dutch women and children; and accounts of what followed are conflicting. According to several oral accounts in the 1980s, few, if any, of the

Dutch men in the vicinity helped the injured women and children or joined in the fight against the fires in the camp.[24] However, when this allegation appeared in the first edition of this book, Dutch informants claimed that some Australians returned to the Dutch camp after the blast to steal jewellery, gold and money. They also purloined the clothing of Dutch women for use in their concerts – to the utter fury of one Dutch husband interned in Tan Tui: 'It took six of us to hold him down,' Sergeant C Varkevisser recalled.[25]

Like the derogatory comments about the Dutch role in Ambon's defence, these opinions should be read with caution.[26] Between some Australian and Dutch prisoners, relationships were more respectful and deep personal friendships developed and lasted after the war.[27] The Dutch Sergeant Major FH Waaldyk, for example, was helped to migrate to Australia in the 1950s by (Sergeant) Percy Elsum, one of the Australians wounded in the bombing attack.[28] Nonetheless, something in the attitudes and mores of the Australians and Dutch complicated their memories of captivity. This was the case not only in Tan Tui and Hainan, but in other camps across the Asia-Pacific, where a similar mistrust was evident.[29] Fortunately, for those on Ambon, the Dutch doctor, Ehlhart, was a notable exception to Australian negativity. In the memory of survivors, he did a 'marvellous job'.[30]

All this damage, tragically, had been the work of the very aircraft that the prisoners had welcomed as a sign of Allied resurgence when they first appeared over Ambon in May 1942.[31] Did the United States Army Air Force (USAAF) know the prisoners of war were there when they bombed Tan Tui on 15 February 1943? Probably – although it is hard to be certain.[32] We know that senior Australian and United States officials knew of the existence of the prison camp in mid-1942, thanks to the briefing Jinkins gave them after his escape from Ambon. He provided a sketch map of Tan Tui, dated 17 March 1942, with a shed marked 'Arms store' on it.[33] Generally, intelligence of this kind, gathered by AHQ Melbourne, would have been passed to senior Allied commanders in the field and from there fed down to operational squadrons. But it is impossible to establish, from the surviving documentary record, whether the presence of Australians on Ambon was conveyed to the personnel who set the targets for US aircraft conducting bombing sorties from bases near Darwin and to the pilots of the Liberators that bombed Ambon.

The squadron which bombed Tan Tui on 15 February 1943, the 319th Bombardment Squadron of the USAAF, claimed in its later history that prior to February 1943, 'the Allies had had only very meager intelligence' on Japanese holdings in the region. The history of the 90th Bomber Group (of which the 319th was part) likewise stated that this stage of the war:

the only requisites for a bombing mission were an airplane that had a good chance of getting off the ground with sufficient gasoline and a load of bombs with which to strike the target. Briefing consisted of handing the pilot and navigator a map (which was often inaccurate itself) and wishing them luck. Information about the possible target was non-existent … Weather data could be found only one way, by going up and trying to get through it.[34]

The 319th Squadron history makes no mention of the POW camp at Ambon. It notes simply that the most consistently bombed target around that time was Ambon, where 'shipping and stores areas were destroyed'.[35] The operational records of the squadron for 15 February 1943, held in the Australian War Memorial, meanwhile, list the targets for that day as being shipping in Ambon and Binnen bays, and 'land installations at Ambon'. However, these same records show that on 13 February and the actual day of the bombing, Allied aircraft took aerial photographs over Ambon.[36] These show clearly the huts of Tan Tui camp, although unmarked by any signs such as 'POW'.

A charitable interpretation is that the crews of the Liberators operating on 15 February did not know that what they saw below was a POW camp. They might have thought it to be a Japanese garrison. But they certainly knew they had done substantial damage. One post-operational report recorded that the photos taken of the attack on Ambon showed 'a salvo on TENTOEY [sic] 2 miles NE of Ambon Town, which started fires'.[37] Another noted that: 'Numerous fires were started in the town area. An explosion and a huge column of smoke over 100 feet high and visible for 50 miles probably from a fuel or ammunition dump was seen in the bombshell area.'[38] This was no doubt the ammunition dump at Tan Tui, but it is not stated as such. Other archival records are silent about the raid and its effects.[39]

Whether the character of Tan Tui was known on 15 February or not, it is certain that it was soon confirmed. Some months later, the operational reports of other USAAF squadrons referred explicitly to the POW camp. In October 1943, the camp was cited as a point of orientation for aircraft attacking other targets at Ambon.[40] On 20 September 1943, some aircraft of the 380th Bombardment Group were 'assigned to bomb' Tan Tui. Fortunately for those on the ground, the malfunction of one aircraft prevented the release of the bombs. Another missed the camp; its nine 500-pound bombs and incendiaries 'fell in woods west of target with unobserved results'. Four fires were observed in the vicinity of the camp.[41]

But if this raid missed its target, so far as Allied targeting was concerned, there was no exemption for Tan Tui. It would be bombed again, with similarly devastating effects, in August 1944.

A TIGHTENING REGIME

The bombing of February 1943 was a defining moment for survivors of their time on Ambon. It seemed to mark the end of Gull Force's early period of captivity that, while harsh, was still tolerable. In the first year, the men were 'reasonably fit, [and] there was no great hardship'. The following 18 months, however, became 'harder and harder', and the final year, from August 1944 to the end of the war was 'by far the worst period', defined by terrible hunger, disease and death.[42]

In November 1943, the Japanese command of the 20th Garrison Unit changed, with Ando being replaced by a naval captain, Shirozu Wadami.[43] No one lamented Ando's departure, but his replacement, who would remain in command until September 1945, took little interest in the prisoners, visiting the camp only twice between the time he took over and the end of the war.[44] This allowed Ikeuchi to become the 'all-powerful force' in all matters relating to the prisoners of war. It seems that he rarely passed on to higher authorities the complaints made by Australian officers. Nor was he called to account by any of his superiors. Even visiting Japanese dignitaries did not inspect the camp, as they had done quite frequently in the earlier months of Gull Force's captivity.[45]

The Japanese control of the camp continued to tighten with a raft of ever more intrusive regulations. Japanese officers and sentries had to be saluted; so did cars carrying Japanese officers, and Japanese ships of war in the vicinity of Tan Tui as they raised and lowered their colours every morning and evening.[46] All prisoners had to 'be polite and careful in their speech', especially in the hearing of Ikeuchi. Bad language or 'slang' in his presence could expect 'severe bodily punishment'.[47] At nightly inspections of the huts, all prisoners were required (as of March 1944) to 'lie to attention' on their beds, not moving, talking or playing cards. Only the senior Australian in each hut was allowed to move, simply to salute the Japanese guard (whatever his rank) and then escort the patrol through his area.[48] In Ken Widmer's words:

They would normally march straight through, the sergeant major being armed. Providing the Japanese had had a reasonably good day nothing eventuated. They just marched through. But if something had gone wrong and the commander was in a bad mood he would start from one end of the hut and slap each person on the face with a resounding smack ... From another hut ... it sounded like a rally in a Davis Cup tennis match.

On one occasion a guard slapped almost every member of a hut because a single piece of paper was discovered on the floor. Another time, one of the Australians coughed as the Japanese patrol went through – the sergeant major in charge of the hut was beaten.[49]

After nightly inspections, prisoners were confined to their huts from 1930 hours until morning, the only acceptable excuses for venturing out being visits to the latrines or the hospital. Cooks could move to the kitchens at 0430 hours. Singing was permitted only between 1700 and 1800 hours, unless prisoners went to the latrines or the pigsty where they could sing between 1800 and 1900 hours. More seriously, prisoners could not leave the camp without Japanese permission. The penalty for doing this, even if not attempting to escape, was death. Contact with the local population was banned (from at least November 1943) and anyone entering a Japanese store without permission would incur 'severe punishment'.[50]

HARD LABOUR

From 1943 on, the demands of the Japanese for labour also intensified. Unloading ships, as in 1942, was a common task, but the pace of this work increased as Allied aerial attacks also intensified. Shifts continued day and night and might last up to 12 hours. Men might get only one shift off before they returned to another round.[51] The work on the wharves was exhausting and dangerous. One Australian was permanently incapacitated when something fell on him from the deck above. Bags of cement, bombs, ammunition and all manner of commodities were loaded onto the men's bare backs and carried to the warehouses. The cement bags often burst, coating the men with a film that they struggled to remove from their bodies and clothes.[52] Coal, another filthy cargo, was shovelled, seemingly without end, into the ships' holds.[53] Years later John Devenish could still remember the agony of working on Ambon's wharves.

> The bags of rice were pretty heavy, they weighed 250 pounds.[54] We weren't well at the time, but we had to carry these things. One man, one bag. You'd stand up and they'd put this bag of rice on your back, or your mates would, and then you'd walk 100 yards maybe, dump it on the track, and go back for another one. You did this all day. If you went down under a bag, and a lot of us did collapse, you got belted by a Jap guard until you stood up under it. That wasn't humanly possible. So a couple of your mates who were coming back empty handed from the loading trucks, would get each side, lift the bag so you could stand up under it, and you'd stagger off again.[55]

For all this, working on the wharves was welcomed because the cargo might include food, cigarettes or soap, all of which could be pilfered and traded.

Few of the other working parties offered such prospects. Some involved carrying rocks from creeks to construction sites across the island; others, the building of roads, air-raid shelters and pill boxes, the laying of foundations for oil tanks, the digging of slit trenches, the chopping of wood, and working on gun emplacements and gardens for the

Japanese.[56] In one high-risk operation, prisoners were ordered to dig storage tunnels or underground systems for radio stations, deep into the steep hills above Ambon town. They worked, in primitive conditions, by candlelight with small picks.[57] The Japanese supervising the work used explosives with an alarming abandon. Harry Williams tried to delay entering a recently dynamited tunnel to check that all the explosive had discharged, but the Japanese in command of the working party insisted on going ahead. Williams had no choice but to follow: 'It was wet and the fuse was out but the Japanese pulled it out. My heart was in my mouth because it might have gone off anyhow. But he would have gone up too!' Other workers were not as lucky. One staff sergeant, JF (James) Duncan, was injured when a falling coconut tree crushed his leg on 7 May 1943. He did not survive the amputation that the serious contusions required. Another Australian, JN (John) Tullett, drowned on 8 December 1943 when he and several other prisoners were ordered to swim about 230 metres, pushing timber that they were unloading from small wooden craft lying just offshore.[58]

A particularly dangerous assignment ordered by the Japanese was the extraction of the picric acid explosive compound from 225-kilogram high-explosive bombs. This 'blacksmithing work', as it was euphemistically called, involved cracking open the bombs and then extracting the compound by means of metal spikes and hammers. The prisoners protested at the dangers of this work, but to no effect. Eventually, on 25 November 1944, one of the bombs exploded.[59] In the words of one of the Australians present, Robert Bryans:

We were crushing the picric acid (which was in lumps)
by tapping the lumps with a metal hammer on a sheet
of canvas on the ground ... A Japanese supervisor was
extracting the picric acid compound from a bomb in
the same shed. He was loosening this compound from
a bomb of approx 500 lbs by driving a steel pike into
the bomb with a steel hammer ... At about 1345 hrs
I saw a flash from the bomb followed by a terrific
explosion. I was knocked over and burned on the legs,
arms and chest. I was dazed, struggled to my feet and
with the assistance of Ptes [Walter] Tuddenham and
[Athol] Grimison, dragged Pte [TR (Thomas)] Noble
from the shed.[60]

One Australian was killed immediately. He was terribly
burned and suffered almost instantaneous death from his
injuries.[61] Three others were shockingly injured and died
within weeks. Noble, who had his foot amputated by a
Japanese doctor immediately after the explosion – it was
almost completely severed – also died later.[62] The Japanese
supervisor, too, was badly injured. He lost a leg and an arm
and suffered other injuries.[63]

Beyond the risks inherent in much of their work, the
prisoners were exposed to Japanese violence. Men too sick
to work were beaten in an effort to make them move. Any
men working in 'slow motion' – one of the many offences
under Japanese regulations – were punished.[64] The language
barrier impeded communication. Many times, however, the
violence seemed to have no logic. The Japanese guards were
subject to a harsh disciplinary system themselves within
the Imperial Japanese Army, and they had no hesitation in

venting their own anger on those even lower than they in the military hierarchy.[65] Many examples of gratuitous violence could be cited, but four examples, described by Australians as evidence of war crimes after the war, suffice:

> [In 1943] I injured my right foot very badly and it got badly infected and I was in hospital for four months and when I came out of hospital I had no feeling in my foot … [it] was so swollen approx. three times its normal size, I was unable to wear a boot on it, but I was made to go out on QM work parties, and every time I slipped and fell over, which was quite often … I was always kicked and bashed until I got on my feet again.[66]

> It was a regular thing for someone to be beaten every morning, or jumped on or kicked. We were beaten for not being able to get about quickly or for being a bit late in coming out of our huts; it was generally for very paltry things.[67]

> I remember seeing two men … brought back to the camp after having been out on a work party … they were made to do the 'Lockheed Torture', which consisted of making them stand on one leg with the other leg held out behind and their two arms outstretched. They were kept standing like this for a half an hour or more. Previously they had been badly beaten at the work party.[68]

The 'White Lady' hit [MA Bolding] over the face with the flat of a shovel and [he] fell to the ground crying. The 'White Lady' then kicked him while he was on the ground and Bolding was unable to work for the rest of the day.[69]

Commonly, the Japanese would hit prisoners over the buttocks with sticks or pick handles. According to van Nooten, who became Gull Force's adjutant soon after Hooke's death, the Japanese wielded a pick handle 'like a baseball club – a full swing and a blow that [threw] a man forward on his face'.[70] At other times, prisoners had to stand to attention on a slab of concrete, bare-headed and looking towards the sun, for anything up to six hours. They were forced to hold heavy rocks above their heads for long periods. Or they had to maintain a body press position until they collapsed; or kneel on a log while holding another piece of wood between their thigh and calf.[71]

With grim humour, the prisoners gave the Japanese perpetrators various nicknames: The Black Bastard, The Mad Carpenter, The Blob, The Doll, The White Lady, Frill Neck, Creeping Jesus, Frog Voice, Giggling Gertie, Gold Tooth, Muttering Mick, Horseface, the Grey Mare and Pram Pruen (a corruption of the Malay word for girl or woman).[72] Not all the Japanese, it must be stressed, behaved badly. Several allowed the sick members of a working party to rest or return to camp. They turned a blind eye to the pilfering of food, or even gave the Australians food or other gifts when they were ill.[73] To quote Arthur Deakin:

On one of the work parties this Japanese – he was a happy sort of a bloke – was showing off in front of the natives and he was making our people throw punches at him so that he could throw them with jujitsu. Well, I had learnt jujitsu off a chap called Ron Leech ... and even if you gave me a thousand dollars now I couldn't tell you why I did it, but this particular day – whether I was fed up with him making fools of our people or not, I don't know – but I threw *him*. And he went off in to the bush. I thought, 'Gawd, I'm gone now, he's gone for a stick.' ... Everyone said, 'You've had it, Darkie' – and he came back with bananas and cigarettes and gave them to me! ... And every time he saw me after that I'd get cigarettes off him.

Some Japanese, being younger and smaller than the prisoners in their charge, seemed almost in awe of them. If a Japanese were Christian, too, that seemed to incline him to be more sympathetic towards the prisoners.[74] Other Japanese guards vacillated between violence and kindness, in a manner that never ceased to mystify the Australians. As Ted Winnell put it in later interview:

This little fellow wanted to arm wrestle with me, and I beat him ... So he gave me a packet of cigarettes ... I didn't smoke at all so I just gave the cigarettes away. Next thing, I look around and everyone's puffing cigarettes! So he asked me where my cigarettes were and I told him I gave them away. And he went crook with me ... gave me a hit over the ear – and another packet of cigarettes!

Leo Manning also recalled:

> [A guard] gave me a hiding [for stealing food] and
> my tail was red raw. [The next day] I got allocated to
> my job and it was the same guard, and the boys said,
> 'Change! Change!' … He glared at me and I thought,
> 'Oh no'. I wasn't looking forward to getting to my
> destination … but actually he called me over, then he
> sat me down, gave me half his dinner and gave me his
> cigarettes because he reckoned I didn't squeal or carry
> on. I'd done my punishment.

Even Ikeuchi was mercurial. Occasionally he apologised to
van Nooten for his failure to provide the supplies the prisoners needed.[75] SM (Stuart) Swanton meanwhile recorded in
the diary that he kept in shorthand for more than a year in
1943–44:

> Mister Eka burst in [to the hospital] on Monday
> morning and of his own accord discharged 6 patients
> whom he considered could go back to their huts. He
> told one chap that if he did not get up and exercise he
> would go to heaven. One of the boys had an accident
> on a work party today and was hit on the bottom by a
> truck. Had eight stitches in the wound and is now in
> hospital … Eka came down and told him he was sorry
> and gave him a packet of cigarettes.[76]

HUNGER

The most acute problem in these middle years of captivity was the decline in the rations supplied by the Japanese. Initially, they provided a fairly wide range of foodstuffs, including rice, meats, fish, vegetables and fruit (see Table 7.1). But from July 1943 onwards, the rations of rice and virtually every other commodity were progressively reduced. Almost the only rations that increased in the last two years were bananas, banana flowers and the nutritionally dubious 'greens' (that is, the tops of sweet potato and cassava plants).

The prisoners became progressively ever more reliant on alternative supplies of food. Gardens continued to consume a great deal of the men's energy.[77] So, too, did the keeping of chickens. Swanton, for example, bred chickens and had a regular supply of eggs, roast chicken on several occasions in 1943, and meals of rooster, cassava, onions, pumpkin, potato leaves and radishes. He wrote in his diary late in July 1943:

> I will remember one supper we had recently all the days of my life. This fowl which had been sitting and had become sick was almost dead and was lying on it's [sic] back with it's [sic] feet kicking in the air. We decided that we would kill it before it died of its own accord, and eat it. I think the axe beat it by about five minutes. One of the boys showed us how to pluck it dry i.e. while it was still hot ... [Murray] stuck it in a long meat tin and put it on the fire to boil. After it had been boiling for a while we decided to make some soup as well. I grated some cassava, cut up a couple of green tomatoes and Murray procured some onion tops

… We cooked it for about an hour, by then it was time to put the fire out according to regulations. I left it in the tin until the Commandant went through then got to work. The night was pitch black … I had to get the bird out of the tin and put it on a plate, then pour the soup out into three dishes. It was a picnic indeed. We had the soup first which was a bit burnt but very good and then as we could not see the bird, we just pulled her asunder by hand and ate whatever we got, a wing, a leg, the pope's nose or even a bit of breast. It was pretty tough but beautiful to the taste. After every bone had been cleaned down we put them in a dish and … left them out in the rain for the night. In the morning there was no sign of bones or even gravy on the dishes.

Raising chickens provided not only nutrition but some distraction from the dreariness of camp life. As Swanton admitted, he was 'very excited about getting nine chickens out from twelve eggs. They are such sweet little things, and have been quite restful to my mind watching them. Dozens of the boys have been up to see them.'[78]

As food production within Tan Tui reached substantial proportions (see Table 7.2), a flourishing barter trade grew up among the prisoners.[79] Prices were determined by market forces of supply and demand, with an enterprising corporal emerging as a middleman. Eggs were bartered for sugar, sugar for cigarettes and cigarettes for food. Many non-smokers believed that those who exchanged their rations for tobacco died more quickly. To quote Swanton again, writing on 26 April 1944: 'Every day one sees heavy smokers sacrificing their much needed meals for smokes.' Another

Table 7.1: Rations received from Japanese Naval Headquarters, Ambon, 1 January 1943 to 15 August 1945

Item[a]	1943	1944	1945
	(Quantities in kilograms, unless otherwise stated)		
Rice	98 750	68 281	15 915
Sago	–	20	1765
Maize	–	880	10
Flour	1496	3618	–
Sugar	2837	2488	522
Salt	3818	2207	637
Tea	421	195	92
Margarine	14	–	–
Yeast	1109	–	–
Biscuits	581	166	–
Matches	350	180	–
Milk	12 tins	–	–
Tinned meat & fish	8118 tins	234	–
Soup	79 tins	–	–
Fish (fresh & dried)	16871	9601	–
Meat (fresh & salt)	5056	820	–
Green vegetables[b]	8760	11 388	5385
Carrot & pumpkin	11 775	50	–
Cucumbers	12 140	4725	–
Potatoes[c]	41 670	26 111	19041
Melon & paw paw	5623	3785	–
Tomatoes	180	–	29
Egg fruit	960	1550	–
Bananas	–	4931	6496
Banana flowers	–	2170	6183
Coconuts	–	–	512
Matches	350	180	–

NOTES TO TABLE 7.1

ᵃ These are the major rations. Items like spices are not included.

ᵇ These consisted mainly of cassava and sweet-potato tops. Other vegetables in smaller quantities were bamboo shoots, bean shoots, cabbage (fresh and dried) and string beans.

ᶜ Mainly sweet potatoes and cassava.

SOURCE Official Japanese record, counter-signed by Major G Westley and Warrant Officer M Ryan, included in evidence at Ambon war crimes trial, NAA CRS A471 81709. On some occasions Ryan was forced to sign for more than he received.

Table 7.2: Garden produce harvested from Tan Tui POW camp, 1 January to 31 December 1944 (kg)

Cassava	2695
Sweet potatoes	2579
Greens (sweet potato and cassava tops, Chinese celery cabbage, pig weed, kankhon)	5008
Egg plant	783
Radish	1069
Beans	216
Pumpkin	169
Melon	65
Tomatoes	108
Cucumbers	120
Onions	35
Carrots	14
Papaya	365
Bananas (stems)	30

NOTES This report includes the annotation that in December 1944, garden produce gave each man 3 ounces (85 grams) per day.

All weights in kilograms except bananas, by stem.

SOURCE NAA A471 81709, pt 1.

valued commodity was salt, given the energy expended on work in the humid climate of Ambon. Some industrious Australians, as well as a few Americans, spent many hours painstakingly boiling down seawater.[80]

All these activities, however, became more challenging with the passage of time. In a vicious cycle, the lack of food reduced men's energy and resources for gardening and keeping chickens.[81] Furthermore, as prisoners became acutely hungry, stealing increased. The gardens were private initiatives, not communal, and the beneficiaries were individuals, not the collective. If the produce was shared, it was with an inner circle of friends, the syndicate. Mateship, then, had its limits. 'Bandicooting', that is, digging under a vegetable, removing its root and leaving the leaves undisturbed above the surface to wither a few hours later, became a highly developed art. As soon as a chicken started to grow plump, or a vegetable approached ripeness, it disappeared.[82] 'You had virtually to sleep with your garden', was how Ted Winnell recalled it later. Walter Hicks also remembered the desperation of losing his pumpkin.

> My pumpkin started to grow beautifully and I
> thought, 'I've had them before and they've vanished
> in the night … I'll fix them this time'. I got a cap off
> a mine detonator, a sort of steel cage, and there were
> some big steel spikes that went with it. I got this cage
> and put it over my pumpkin and I spiked it into the
> ground with these three-foot spikes, so that when I
> came to harvest it I would have to dig out these spikes
> because they were driven in at an angle. Honest to
> goodness, I went up there one morning and someone

came and said to me, 'Your pumpkin's gone'. I said, 'How could it go! They'd never get it out', (cause it nearly filled the cage). And I went up there – and they had cut it up with a knife into thin bits and pulled it out of the cage!

The gardens maintained by the officers for their own mess seemed especially vulnerable to theft. The other ranks approved of the bandicooting of the officers' gardens while condemning theft among themselves, which says much about relations between the ranks.[83]

Seeking to contain the individualism in food production, Westley ordered late in 1943 that all Australians should work on a communal garden. His logic was to increase food supplies by ensuring that all prisoners contributed to growing produce. But all that happened was that the men who were already motivated to maintain gardens split their time between private and communal gardening, becoming generally less productive; while those who had opted not to garden in the past simply continued not to do so. Westley had few sanctions at his disposal. As an inquiry set up to examine the Australian administration of Tan Tui after the war (see Appendix III) commented:

The 'bludgers' would not co-operate and even if coerced into spending the requisite time on the garden, did no useful or productive work ... [owing to] the general lack of co-operation and the completely individualistic attitude displayed by the men, the company garden was a failure. .. a long range policy should have been instituted in the early days of the

camp whereby all gardening was placed
on a communal basis and produce pooled.[84]

The real blow to private food production came in March 1944
when the Japanese ordered that any food produced in the
prisoners' gardens should be handed over to the central camp
kitchen. Gardens must be 'under company arrangements'.[85]
Finally, the Japanese banned private cooking.[86]

Making matters worse was the Japanese ban on contact
between the prisoners and the local Ambonese population
and the closure of the local market.[87] Sympathetic Ambonese
continued to secretly drop food or small packets of clothing
in the vicinity of working parties. But this carried high risks.
The Japanese were no gentler with the local population than
with the Australians.[88] The prisoners witnessed Ambonese
being punched, beaten and kicked by Japanese as they
used the road crossing the camp, bowing deferentially as
required. Ambonese were robbed of their merchandise
en route to the market and bashed if they refused to sell
goods to the Japanese. In late 1942, van Nooten watched as
a sentry knocked a pregnant Ambonese woman, who had
apparently committed no offence, to the ground. To the
applause of other guards, he kicked her in the stomach until
she lost consciousness. At other times, the Ambonese were
burned with cigarettes, prodded with bayonets, and strung
up by the thumbs, for no reason, van Nooten concluded,
other than to amuse the Japanese.[89] A local man earned
their wrath by stealing from the army store in March 1944,
and was bashed with a board for about ten minutes. Then,
according to Swanton, he was 'tied to a post and left in
the sun all day. What a sight it was to see the poor fellow

standing there practically unconscious and Japanese soldiers standing round reading a notice pinned on him. It reminded me a little of the picture of our Lord on the cross with the Jews all around.'[90]

With so many avenues for acquiring food denied, the prisoners invested huge efforts in 'scrounging' from the Japanese. Trading with the guards without Ikeuchi's permission was officially prohibited, although it seems to have flourished for a time.[91] Several prisoners unravelled their jumpers and balaclavas – far too hot for Ambon's climate – and, using knitting needles adapted from bicycle wheel spokes or wire, made socks, which they could trade with the Japanese for food or cigarettes.[92] A number of men also used the shorts made by the camp tailor for the same purpose, until Eric Kelly decided that he had had enough of making clothes for the Japanese. He brought a halt to this trade by issuing shorts, newly made, with holes neatly cut in them![93]

Failing trade, there was theft. A common ploy was for a prisoner on a working party to seek permission to go to the 'benjo' (toilet) and to slip away once the back of the guard was turned. In a few moments of freedom, bags of rice in the Japanese stores could be pierced with bamboo spikes and tins grabbed. Coconuts could be furtively stolen from trees.[94] The Japanese banned prisoners climbing trees or even collecting nuts already on the ground.[95] Coconuts, Ikeuchi said, belonged to the Emperor.[96]

Speed and ingenuity were the essence of theft. Keith Mellor, who supervised working parties on the wharves, recalled how he 'stood and watched, knowing that they were going to take those things. It's incredible. They used to disappear and I never saw anyone do it. Yet I knew they had them.' One Japanese guard left a working party briefly and returned to find a case of meat reduced to nothing but splinters. Bottles that were too large to be hidden in the prisoners' clothes were 'accidentally' dropped and their contents cleaned up.[97] Bravado worked when other tactics failed. (Lieutenant) R (Ralph) Godfrey remembered one man simply walking past a guard, with a jar of peanut butter in his hand, and placing it in his dixie. Other men stole from guards the very scarves and socks that they had previously sold them – only to sell them back again at some later date.[98]

Wherever possible, food was eaten at the site where it was stolen; or it was hidden in the jungle to be retrieved on a later working party. Both tactics involved risk, as an anecdote by Charles Crouch indicates:

We'd say to the Japs we wanted to go to the toilet … and as soon as we got behind the bushes, we'd run like the very dickens to the Jap rice store … One of you would stand at the front door while you got in and got the bag of rice out, and this day … Tommy Watson must have gone to sleep because the next thing there's this great roar and about three Japs and about twenty Muslims [appeared] … we went out of that hut like a rocket and round the back of the hut. I often feel sorry for the fox now, I know what it's like when the hounds are after you … Luckily their short legs couldn't go as fast as ours and [when we came] to a cross path … we went there and they went that way. I was running so fast and we came to a hill. I reckon I went like Donald Duck straight out into the air! … But we got back to the work party.

For the most part, however, the prisoners tried to smuggle their stolen goods back into the camp. Ingenious schemes were created: water bottles with false bottoms, stools with hollow seats and lap-laps with a double layer of fabric between the legs. The Japanese soon prohibited the use, on working parties, of seats or any other containers in which 'loot' might be concealed.[99] They took to bashing the men between the legs to see if a metallic ring gave away the presence of a stolen tin. If it did, the prisoner was punished. If it did not, he suffered the agonising consequences. When, despite everything, the prisoners got the stolen food home, they cooked it in the camp kitchen or on smokeless charcoal fires hidden under beds.[100] Somehow, the Japanese never noticed these, despite the overpowering smell of cooking in the huts during some inspections.

KEEPING CLOTHED

The battle to keep the prisoners clothed was not as difficult as finding food. Many Australians had become prisoners with only the clothes they were wearing in battle, given the looting of Tan Tui after their defeat. Some of what remained was lost in the bomb blast of February 1943. Despite this, the men remained reasonably clothed.[101] The Japanese issued about one lap-lap per man, some neck or sweat bands and about three bolts of khaki shirting. The camp tailor, Eric Kelly, managed to make the cloth into shorts. His sewing machine was kept working by an ingenious engineer who, on an improvised lathe, turned darning needles into grooved machine needles.[102] As it was, clothes did not matter all that much, since the heat and humidity for much of the year on Ambon meant that men were often more comfortable in lap-laps or G-strings.

A more intractable problem was footwear. The Japanese drew on captured Australian stocks to supply their own forces. When, on three or four occasions, they issued boots to the Australians, they supplied only the larger sizes for which they had no use. Eventually only about one-third of the prisoners had army boots.[103] Prisoners thus resorted to wooden clogs with a strap across the foot, or 'boots' made out of rubber tyres or canvas. A minority preferred to go barefoot, rather than make the effort to improvise shoes – a choice that had serious health implications in that it spread infection within the camp and contributed to the dreaded tropical ulcers.[104]

KEEPING SANE

The longer their internment, the greater the challenge for Gull Force of maintaining their mental health. Here, inclusive mateship played a positive role. Swanton recorded many instances of life in Tan Tui being brightened by individual acts of sacrifice and unselfishness: special meals for someone on his birthday; kindness, concern and, above all, food being lavished on the sick.[105] More widely, the prisoners managed to maintain some forms of entertainment, at least during 1943 and into 1944. These included the occasional talk by Westley and regular concerts. The Japanese offered the Australians some broken musical instruments, which had been owned by the Dutch, and with these and their own creations, some prisoners formed a kind of band to replace the one that had gone to Hainan Island. Homemade ukuleles, guitars and a bass (made out of an old meat case and a piece of copper signal wire) kept men distracted from the miseries of daily life – as well as providing them with one of the more exciting incidents of daily life.[106] According to George Williamson:

> Kelly and I were playing this night (in a cubicle in our hut) and I'm sitting on the bed with my feet on the ground, playing the guitar (he's playing the mouth organ) – and there's a storm going on, and at the corner of the hut was this great coconut tree ... touching the hut. We're playing away and next minute a great fireball comes straight out of the sky, hits the road and bounces and hits the tree and comes down into the hut. The strings on the guitar went red hot, burnt all me fingers. It run along the wire that was in the hut. The towels just burnt through and dropped to the ground. Anything that was on the wire just dropped on the ground. Kelly didn't get it as bad ... [because] he had his feet up on the bed. Some of the others were knocked out.

The importance of music to camp morale is manifest in Swanton's diary and would inspire his nephew, Lloyd, more than six decades later, to compose a mixed-media concert suite, *Ambon*, which included many musical references to the improvisation of camp life (see Appendix VI).

Other prisoners whiled away their free time with chess, cards (using homemade packs), riddles, puzzles of various kinds and reading what was left of the camp library. Sporting competitions were occasionally held, but by mid-1943 the men were too tired to view them with much enthusiasm.[107] Less strenuous was talk: conversations about home, family, girls, tomorrow's working party – and always, food. Like prisoners all over Asia, the men on Ambon spoke endlessly of their favourite meals, meticulously collected recipes, and planned a future in which they would farm, keep chickens or do anything associated with food.[108]

Such activities did something to maintain the Australians' morale as their physical conditions deteriorated. But the two things they needed most to keep hope alive, news of home and news of the war, were denied them. In the first 22 months of their captivity, no mail was received from Australia. Then on 26 December 1943, about 800 letters arrived at Japanese headquarters. Some were for Australians in Rabaul and Timor, but about 400 were for the prisoners on Ambon. Ikeuchi, however, only allowed some of the Australians to sort the mail, and then withheld almost all of it. Like some modern-day Tantalus, he released only the occasional letter, usually to a man who was dying or occasionally to an officer or an NCO.[109] Only when the war was almost at an end did Ikeuchi release the bulk of the mail, by which time the letters were almost three years old and most of the men to whom they were addressed were dead. At no stage during their captivity were the Australians allowed to send mail of any kind to their relatives. Even though Westley complained to Ikeuchi on this score, they were given not even the standard, and uncommunicative, postcards used by prisoners of war internationally.[110]

The Australians' deep sense of isolation was further accentuated by the fact that very few of them had any reliable information about the war. Walter Hicks, a former dux of his form at Melbourne High School, managed to learn Japanese with the help of one of the American prisoners, Michael Maslak. Working as a houseboy at the Japanese headquarters, he was then able to glean quite a bit of 'news' from the radio and newspapers he saw there. However, he did not circulate this information widely within the camp. He came to realise that his own security could be jeopardised by the ease with which others spread the news he had divulged to them secretly. The intelligence he collected, therefore, was shared only with a select circle of confidants. The rest of the Australians depended on far less reliable sources of information about the war: the size and frequency of the Allied air raids over Ambon, and the inevitable rumours, or furphies. According to these, which cynical prisoners numbered after the hole at the latrines from which they originated, the Allies took Singapore on two occasions in 1943 as well as Burma, Siam and Mindanao.[111]

BOMBED AGAIN

Allied air raids, of course, were very much a mixed blessing. While they indicated the growing Allied dominance in the region, they disrupted the prisoners' precious sleep, threatened their safety on working parties and inspired the Japanese to retaliation.[112] Then, on 28 August 1944, Tan Tui suffered a repeat of the catastrophe of February 1943.

In the aftermath of the earlier bombing, the Japanese had placed a red cross on the roof of the camp hospital and taken aerial photographs of the devastation. But this gesture seemed to be for propaganda purposes, and it lasted only a short time.[113] Westley and van Nooten complained strongly to the Japanese commandant about the failure to maintain this marking. But van Nooten was told that if he made any efforts to mark the camp, or continued to ask for this to be done, the commandant would personally execute him 'as an example in front of the remainder of the camp'. To make his point, the Japanese drew his sword and made a swing at van Nooten.[114] The prisoners more generally had been told that 'any sign of pleasure of excitement shown ... during an Air Raid will be taken as a HOSTILE ACT and the offender will be shot without further warning'.[115]

As it was, it did not matter if the camp was marked. At this time, the Allied air forces were pummelling the whole island of Ambon, even though US intelligence believed that 'the enemy has all but written the Ambon-Ceram area off as a major operational base'.[116] Tan Tui itself was not recorded as a target on 28 August; this raid was described as being aimed at 'the Ambon barracks areas and other targets'.[117] But Tan Tui's immunity was compromised by the Japanese Army's construction of a radio transmitting, receiving and direction-finding station within a few hundred metres of the camp. Anti-aircraft guns, placed just outside the compound, were also in the habit of firing on low-lying aircraft. Gun emplacements were situated at several places within the camp and just outside.[118]

The raid of 28 August was conducted by 62 Liberator bombers dropping 175 tons of 1000-pound bombs. The US prisoner, Ed Weiss, hiding in his air raid shelter, later wrote:

The B-24s had returned! In trail, these magnificent flying machines passed before my eyes, one behind the other, until I had counted 75, stretching from Amboina to Halong. I thought they were going to bomb Laha airfield but to my horror, they turned sharply left … and headed toward our side of Ambon island. I saw the bombs leave the aircraft and I knew we were in trouble … Lying prone on the dirt floor of the shelter, I felt myself being lifted about six inches into the air and then slammed down into the soft dirt of the floor, leaving me breathless. The concussions were severe and thick, black, acrid smoke filled the shelter trench. … When the black smoke cleared … I stood up, and in my exhilaration of bring alive, I extended my arm and clenched fist skyward, shouted, 'You bastards, I have survived, I have survived'.

Then the formation turned and came back for a second attack. 'The bombs followed the same track as the first, but now they were anti-personnel bombs [that] exploded horizontally, spreading thousands of deadly metal pellets from the ground to about waist high for a radius of 50 yards. They shred everything that is upright.'[119]

The effects on Tan Tui and the nearby Ambon town area were devastating. To quote the post-raid report: 'Many explosions resulted in the [Ambon] barracks; other buildings were demolished and the entire area was covered with flames and smoke rising to 10,000 feet.'[120] In Tan Tui itself, two Australians were killed by bomb splinters, a third died later and 15 were wounded. Many of the books remaining in the camp library were destroyed. In addition, the accommodation huts, which had been painstakingly reconstructed after the bomb blast of February 1943, were demolished. Given the weak condition of the prisoners and the refusal of the Japanese authorities to offer any help in reconstruction, only eight huts were eventually rebuilt. Five were used as sleeping quarters, one as a hospital hut and two for storage.[121]

Of this destructive August raid, the Australian official historian of the air war against Japan, George Odgers, wrote in 1957: 'Ambon which was heavily attacked by Liberators in August was practically destroyed. All the airfield facilities and buildings were flattened and the runways put out of order for a month. Almost daily attacks continued in September.'[122] The POW camp also failed to get any mention in Odgers' papers, now held at the Australian War Memorial. In this, and all other official sources, nothing was said about the devastation of Tan Tui.

The 2/21st Battalion marching though Albury, New South Wales, en route to Bonegilla. Those identified are Stanley Robert Hawksworth (second from front, left file) and Edward John Thomas Hinch (marching immediately behind him). Hinch was executed on 20 February 1942; Hawksworth died of illness on Ambon on 24 June 1945. *Australian War Memorial P10805.002*

The train that carried the 2/21st Battalion and other units of the 23rd Brigade to Darwin. The train was reportedly so slow that troops could play football alongside the track and keep pace with it. *Courtesy of Gordon Kent*

Officers of the 2/21st Battalion prior to their departure to Ambon. Left to right (sitting under tree only): Lieutenant Rod Gabriel, Intelligence Officer; Captain Charles Patmore, Chaplain, killed in Ambon during 15 February 1943 air raid; Horton Newbury, executed in the massacre at Laha, Ambon; Lieutenant John Davis, also executed at Laha; Lieutenant Noel Thomas; Lieutenant William (Bill) Aitken, Regimental Medical Officer; and Lieutenant Colonel Len Roach, Commanding Officer. *Australian War Memorial P03156.003*

Lieutenant-Colonel Len Roach, photographed at Darwin, 1941.
His calls for Gull Force to be evacuated from Ambon in January 1942
resulted in his dismissal and recall. *Courtesy of the family of John van Nooten*

Major Ian Macrae, second-in-command of the 2/21st Battalion, at
Darwin 1941. Captured with Gull Force in February 1942, he led
a successful escape from the prisoner-of-war camp on Hainan Island
in April 1945. *Courtesy of the family of John van Nooten*

Tan Tui camp, Ambon. This photo was taken after the war, after the camp had twice been devastated by Allied bombing. Four-fifths of the prisoners of Gull Force died in this camp. *Australian War Memorial 118253*

The primitive regimental aid post at Tan Tui. *Australian War Memorial 118259*

Ikeuchi Masakiyo, the Japanese interpreter who became de facto camp manager at Tan Tui, and the agent of much of the prisoners' suffering. For his role in maltreating the prisoners of war, he was executed in 1947. *Australian War Memorial 019312*

F O'Donoghue of Hawthorn, Victoria, standing beside the grave of the 11 Australians executed in November 1942 for breaking out of Tan Tui camp in search of food. O'Donoghue went to Ambon with the first relief party in 1945 to greet his brother, only to find that he had been executed by the Japanese. Later, the bodies in this grave were moved to the Ambon War Cemetery, established on the site of the Tan Tui camp. *Australian War Memorial 019313*

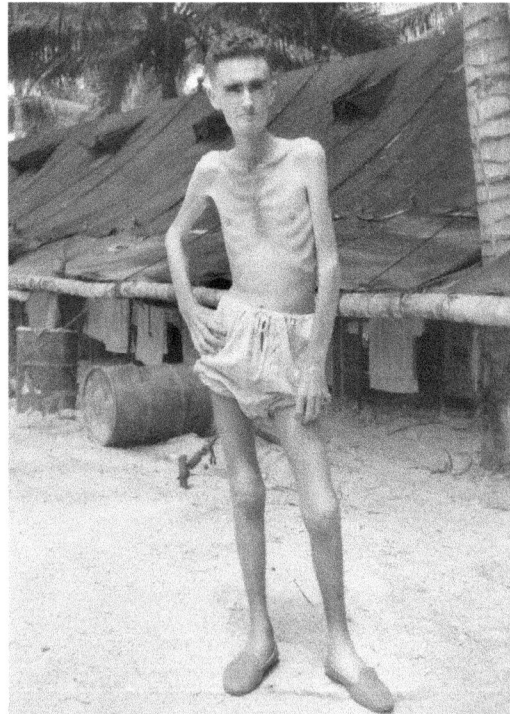

Private Leo Ayres, 12 September 1945. Like so many of the 2/21st Battalion, he was a victim of years of starvation and overwork. *Australian War Memorial 116271*

Top left Stuart Swanton, whose diary is one of the few surviving contemporary accounts of life as a prisoner at Tan Tui. He died on 14 August 1945, one day before the Japanese surrender. His nephew Lloyd was inspired nearly half a century later to compose a mixed-media suite, *Ambon*, in his honour. *Australian War Memorial P10827.003*

Top right The face of a family's loss. Thomas Hutchins, 2/21st Battalion, died on 4 September 1945 at Ambon, aged 32. Four of his brothers served overseas and one in Australia; all five survived the war. Four of his cousins died as prisoners of the Japanese, one at Rabaul and three at Ambon. *Australian War Memorial P07442.003*

Left Lieutenant John van Nooten photographed before he left Australia. From early 1943, at the aged of 25, he carried the burden of being adjutant on Ambon, responsible for mediating between the prisoners of the Japanese. *Courtesy of the family of John van Nooten*

A church service at Tan Tui led by Chaplain Charles Patmore, who was later killed while assisting the wounded during the bombing raid on 15 February 1943. *Australian War Memorial 136290*

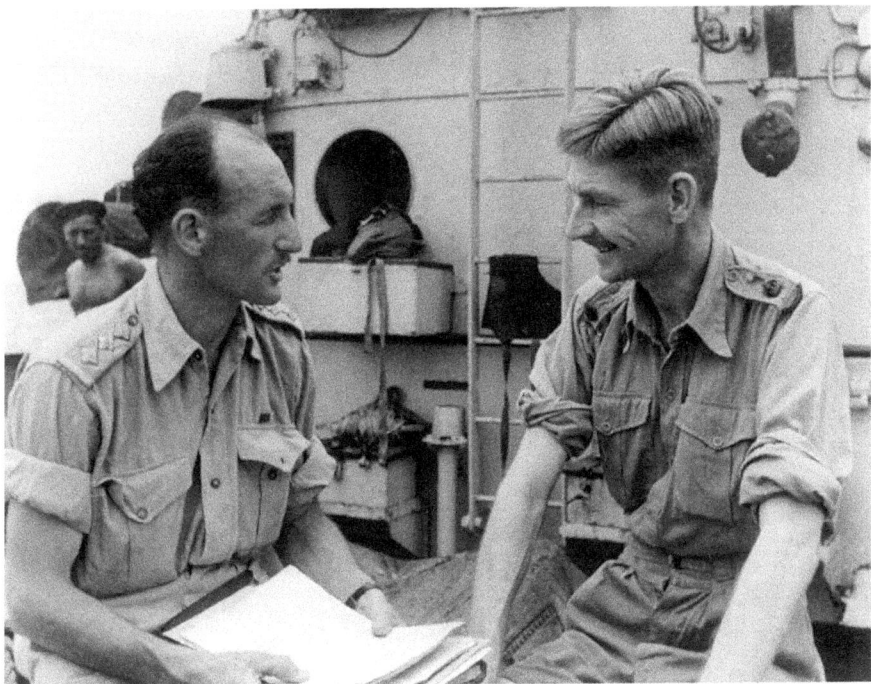

Major George de V Westley (right), in discussion with an officer of the force liberating Ambon, September 1945. The most senior commander at Tan Tui after Scott's departure for Hainan in October 1942, Westley struggled to provide leadership, and became deeply unpopular as conditions in the prisoner-of-war camp deteriorated. *Courtesy of Leo Manning; original photo Commonwealth Department of Information*

The view of Tan Tui from
the air moments before
the 319th Squadron of the
United States Army Air
Force bombed it, triggering
a massive explosion of an
ammunition dump, on
15 February 1943. The
prisoners' presence was
known to senior Allied
military officials, but
whether the aircrew knew
this was a prisoner-of-
war camp is not known.
Courtesy of Ian Elsum

Prisoners waiting on the wharves of Ambon for liberation, 10 September 1945. Identified left to right: FP Dihood; JR Culton (behind); Lance Sergeant CH Nye (with walking stick); Jack Panotie; Harry Braeter; Lieutenant GR Pullin; 'Darky' Lee; T Kellet; J Wilson; Staff Sgt Eric Kelly; Lieutenant Bob Knowland; Warrant Officer JGP Billing; Sgt J Turner; Jim Ellis.
Australian War Memorial 019300

Tawiri, Laha, Ambon, December 1945. A Japanese working party at Mass Grave No. 4, which includes the remains of men executed after their surrender in the vicinity of Laha airfield in February 1942. *Australian War Memorial 030388/06*

Lieutenant-Colonel WJR (Jack) Scott at Bakli Bay prisoner-of-war camp, Hainan Island, August 1945. Having volunteered to lead Gull Force in January 1942, Scott suffered a breakdown during captivity and resorted to disciplining men by handing them over to the Japanese for punishment. *Australian War Memorial 030359/06*

The latrine squad in the prison camp on Hainan, I Fishwick (left) and Danny Noonan (right). The excrement was removed each day from troughs to fertilise gardens. In the background is an open-sided section of an accommodation hut, which linked the latrine and the sleeping quarters. This hut was used by the Australians as the officers' mess. *Australian War Memorial 030365/06*

The Bakli Bay prison camp, August 1945.
Australian War Memorial 030365/02

Lieutenant Sam Anderson tends to a crop of kankhon, an edible green weed
also known as water spinach, at the Hainan prison camp. The poor soil
and heat hampered the prisoners' efforts at gardening, which they did to
add nutritional value to the inadequate rations provided by the Japanese.
Australian War Memorial 030357/01

8
CATASTROPHE, 1944-45

The last year of captivity on Ambon was catastrophic. The aerial attack of August 1944 ushered in a final period of unremitting suffering. With rations reduced to starvation levels, and working parties acquiring an almost demonic quality, rates of illness soared, until only 121 of the 528 Australians left on Ambon in October 1942 were still alive. If the war had continued for even a few more months, perhaps all of Gull Force on Ambon would have died. Two, in fact, died after the force was liberated.

ILLNESS AND DISEASE

The health of the prisoners at Tan Tui was already debilitated as 1945 began. The first deaths on Ambon, in 1942 and early 1943, had been almost all caused by violence: battle, executions and the bomb blast of February 1943. However, from mid-1943, disease took over as the dominant cause of death. Beri-beri, which is caused by insufficient vitamin B1 in the diet, was first noted early in 1943 and spread until almost every man in the camp was suffering from it to some extent. Together with malaria and dysentery, beri-beri accounted for 16 deaths by the end of 1943.[1] Malaria did not necessarily kill, but it produced an incapacitating cycle of shivering, chills, high fever and sweating. As Stuart Swanton recorded in his diary for 1–2 July 1943, he woke up 'feeling very wretched and feverish ... Had a dreadful morning for my head was splitting ... In the evening I staggered down [to the doctor] and was put straight on quinine. Had a very rotten night. Still have splitting head and back ache. Spleen is painful.'[2]

From March to May 1944, an outbreak of bacillary dysentery claimed 37 lives: this, despite the Japanese providing 'reasonable quantities' of disinfectant and the medical officer Ehlhart introducing a temporary ban on private cooking in an attempt to curb the dysentery's spread.[3] A further 28 Australians fell victim to illnesses associated with malnutrition in the final seven months of the year. A plethora of other conditions battered the prisoners' health, among them dengue fever and enteritis.[4] An epidemic of conjunctivitis early in their captivity left some men with corneal ulcers and perforation. Stomatitis, or inflammation of the mouth, caused immense discomfort. Swanton recorded that he had great difficulty eating and sleeping at night for the pain of his swollen mouth and tongue.[5] Tinea was as maddening, given that it developed in sensitive parts of the body, such as the scrotum and the fingernails. Reg Brassey never forgot the pain as the doctor cut and ripped off his affected fingernails without anaesthetic. Ken Widmer remembered the agony of tinea:

the scrotums became raw flesh, and the only treatment was to recline on [a] bunk in the hospital and an orderly would go along them in the hospital

dabbing iodine or formalin on the exposed raw
flesh. A following orderly would follow with a
slouch hat fanning furiously to try and alleviate
the immediate sting.

At times, tinea necessitated circumcision.[6]

Perhaps worst of all were the tropical ulcers. From small
scratches these excruciating lesions grew, eating away tendon
and destroying bone. They stretched, in some cases, from the
ankle to the knee. Pieces of bone broke away.[7] The simplest
movement became an agony. Even a blade of grass touching
an ulcer could 'hurt like hell', Jim Wilson said. The hospital
had no resources with which to treat ulcers, apart from a
small supply of Australian Army field dressings, which they
had conserved, and the occasional issue of 'a few grains of
iodoform'. The foul-smelling putrid flesh of the ulcers had
to be cut away with scissors.[8] 'You could hear the screams
as this was being performed,' the Dutch prisoner Waaldyk
later said.[9] Then, the ulcers were treated with hot foments,
'vaseline' (actually, lubrication grease stolen from Japanese
garages) or salt water.[10] Charles Crouch recalled how he
would stand in the sea water and 'let the little fish nibble all
the putrid flesh … quite a tickly sensation until they got to
the real flesh and that used to hurt a little and draw blood,
but that kept my ulcer clean and I didn't lose a leg like a
few of the blokes did'. The ulcers almost always returned,
however, since the diet and condition of the men was so
poor that the tissue in their legs very quickly broke down
again. One prisoner, (Sergeant) Jack O'Brien, in July 1945,
had to have his leg amputated above the knee. Ehlhart used
a butcher's knife and saw. There was no ether and only a

small quantity of chloroform. Incredibly O'Brien survived the operation, despite his weak heart.[11] He lived for many years after the war.

Personal hygiene was very difficult to maintain. The Japanese never issued any soap, although individual guards occasionally donated pieces, and soap could be stolen.[12] Many Australians kept up shaving, if they had retained their razor or had bought one from another prisoner by trading cigarettes.[13] But on various occasions, the Japanese cut off all fresh water in the camp for bathing. Salt water from the bay was found to be a 'very unsatisfactory substitute' for personal washing, although it was missed when the Japanese decided to prohibit access to the sea.[14]

The medical personnel responsible for the camp's health faced almost insuperable challenges. The 'hospital' was a primitive hut, with a septic latrine that could hardly cope with the numbers of ill. The beds were improvised: Dutch camp stretchers, hospital beds reconstructed after the bomb blast and some makeshift wooden structures. When conditions became crowded in 1944, men seeking treatment had to bring their own old bags and blankets with them for bedding.[15]

Medical instruments were limited to those salvaged from the bomb blast, while medicines themselves were in short supply, especially after 1943.[16] The Japanese were willing to give assistance when the prisoners' illnesses threatened them, as did the various dysentery outbreaks. 'Up early this morning', Swanton recorded on 25 September 1943, 'for examination by the Japanese doctors for dysentery … We all lined up and had a swab taken of our bottoms.'[17] The Japanese also provided a coal tar preparation, which acted as a 'quite satisfactory' disinfectant.[18] But, for the most part, the Japanese did nothing to staunch the growing medical crisis. Each month Marshall and Ehlhart would requisition the supplies they needed, only to be abused or threatened. Requests for milk for a case of gastric haemorrhage met the response that they should use cat's milk.[19] At no time did the prisoners on Ambon receive any Red Cross parcels. When they asked about these, they were told by Ikeuchi that the Red Cross and international law no longer existed.[20]

Increasingly, then, Marshall and Ehlhart improvised or stole: for example, to supplement the supplies of quinine, which were halted after February 1943.[21] When supplies of plaster ran out, they constructed a range of splints, from wood, tin and iron bars, to manage the fractured limbs that resulted from Japanese beatings. The shortage of bandages (at one stage the Japanese issued one bandage in a month when about 200 men were suffering from tropical ulcers) was met, but only partially, by tearing up clothing such as pyjamas. The original field dressings of the hospital were washed and rewashed until they fell to pieces.[22]

In the battle against beri-beri, Marshall experimented with making yeast, a source of vitamin B, until the shortage of carbohydrate in the rations issued by the Japanese stopped this. Crops of soya beans were grown until the soil became so depleted, and the men so weak, that the results were too poor.[23] For the worst victims of conjunctivitis, Marshall made sunglasses from celluloid cut from anti-gas goggles and the stain used for malaria smears. The glasses were satisfactory at first, but their colour soon faded in the sunlight. As for dental hygiene, a dentist's engine was created from an old bicycle wheel connected to a drill attachment by a series of wires and smaller wheels. Some dentures were fashioned from aluminium. They performed well enough, although wearers could get a shock when drinking something hot. Ultimately, in the last days of the camp, only extractions could be performed.

Ehlhart and Marshall's ingenuity was fully taxed when dysentery patients needed saline and blood transfusions, and when major operations were required. Several of these were performed, for appendicitis, gastric ulcers, a ruptured gall bladder and, as mentioned, amputations. There was little in the way of anaesthetics, and the surgical instruments were kitchen utensils and hacksaws. Several of the patients survived – only to die later of malnutrition.[24]

Through all this suffering, Ikeuchi did his best to destroy the morale of sick and dying men. In Marshall's words: 'One patient who was dying from TB would have to listen to a recitation of all the good food that he should be getting, given by the interpreter. The interpreter would finish by saying, "You cannot have this food, therefore you will die."'[25] Ikeuchi also insisted that Marshall and Ehlhart falsify the prisoners' death certificates. If the words 'debility', 'starvation' and 'malnutrition' appeared on a death certificate, Ikeuchi would be enraged. In his eyes, the only acceptable cause of death was beri-beri, from which the Japanese troops also suffered to some degree.[26]

In April 1945, the Japanese made one, albeit dubious, medical intervention by conducting some experiments with vaccinations. Their reasons were unclear. Marshall thought they might be trying to measure the increase in immunity in a debilitated body given a typhus vaccine, by introducing additional foodstuffs such as cod liver oil, vitamin B, protein and carbohydrate.[27] The Japanese surgeon Nakamura Ryosuke said the program was intended to test the potency of some typhoid vaccine in the Japanese stores, which was past its expiry date.[28] Those men who volunteered for what they called 'the guinea pig parades' were given extra rations for a time and had blood tests taken to assess the effect of the vaccine. Since very few of the men survived for the duration of the course, the conviction grew among the Australians that the injections were contributing to their deaths.[29] This was almost certainly not the case; but neither did the injections do anything to improve the prisoners' health – which continued to collapse in the last year of captivity.[30]

'THE LONG CARRY'

Very few men were in the physical state required to endure the exceptionally gruelling working party that the Japanese introduced in November 1944. 'The Long Carry', as the prisoners called it, involved carrying 40-kilogram bags of cement and 113-kilogram bombs, suspended between two poles, up and down precipitous jungle paths between two villages about 13 kilometres apart on the south-east coast of Ambon.[31] The loads were so heavy, and the paths so steep, that sometimes the men could proceed only on their hands and knees. The Japanese maintained that this cargo could not be transported by sea because of the Allied air attacks and the dangerous reefs off the coast.[32] But it seemed that the 'Long Carry' was a vindictive attempt to destroy the Australians' remaining health. To quote van Nooten:

The party left camp by motor truck at 0630 for Batocgon [Batugong]. They seldom returned before 1930 hours. On returning to camp many of the men were so exhausted that they had to be lifted out of the trucks … some died after having been admitted to hospital … I feel certain that the track was specially designed as a form of torture. The cement and bombs were never used and I don't think there was any necessity for them to be moved.

Van Nooten tried to select only the fittest men in the camp for this 'torture', but the Japanese demanded 120 men each day. Many supposedly fit men had to work four or five days without a break. Eventually, the size of the party shrank from 120 to 80 or fewer, but always the Japanese demanded ten or 15 men more than the camp could reasonably supply. When the numbers were too low, Ikeuchi stormed into the huts and hospital to find more workers. To quote Jack Panotie, Ikeuchi would 'go through the hospital where the blokes were dying like flies, and he'd say, "You get out of bed! You get out of bed! You're all right, nothing wrong with you!" And all that sort of thing. The mongrel bastard.'[33] In Ikeuchi's opinion, the men who were too weak to work were just 'living corpses'.[34]

The 'Long Carry' lasted about six weeks and was the harshest work demanded by the Japanese. Its importance in later memory was attested to when historian Hank Nelson named the chapter on Ambon in his 1985 book, based on interviews with ex–prisoners of war, 'The Long Carry'.[35] But other working parties continued to be onerous. Work on the wharves declined as the Allied blockade isolated Ambon from the outside world, but prisoners were then assigned to building defensive installations. Those digging tank traps worked, without shoes, for long hours, knee-deep in mud and water. They had to cut and carry heavy coconut logs long distances to revet these traps. Many men also continued to dig tunnels, until this work ended about June 1945. On 14 April, one man, LH (Leonard) Cartwright, died from shocking injuries in an explosion when the Japanese supervisor ordered him to blow charges on the face of the tunnel.[36]

VIOLENCE AND EXECUTIONS

Through all this, the levels of gratuitous Japanese violence continued. Late in 1944, ERA (Edwin) Tait was caught stealing, from an air-raid shelter, some binoculars that he presumably intended to trade for food. He was beaten by the guard in charge of his working party, and then brought back to the camp. Under the supervision of Ikeuchi and Uemura Shigeo, the camp commandant, he was beaten with pick handles. In the words of an eyewitness, Verdun Ball:

> He was knocked unconscious two or three times; then the Commandant threw water over him and when he came to he was beaten again. In the end, he was left lying in the rain for about half an hour. Our officer tried all the time to have him removed and eventually he was taken away to hospital on a stretcher.[37]

The following morning, according to van Nooten who witnessed the scene, Ikeuchi 'beat Tait with a heavy walking stick and ordered him to lie on the concrete floor with one blanket'. Tait survived this assault but died about six months later of malnutrition and beri-beri, his poor health having been almost certainly aggravated by his beating.[38]

This incident was followed in March 1945 by the punishment of two Australians who risked escaping rather than dying of starvation. One of them, FN (Frederick) Schaefer, was recaptured and brought back to the camp to explain to the Japanese the route he had taken. Though he did not seem to have been maltreated at that stage, he was subsequently executed, on 30 April. On learning of this six months later, his wife would write to Australian authorities, seeking to know why:

> I will be so thankful if at any time you could possibly
> find out what he was doing for them to behead him.
> Some his mates might know if he was lucky enough to
> get one of my letters & what sort of health he was in
> it does make one more satisfied to know these kinds
> of things & I will be so grateful if you could find out
> some time. One thing we know now he is out of his
> suffering from the Japs.[39]

The other escapee, JF (James) Elmore, was recaptured around 22 May in an Ambonese hut after wandering in the jungle and hills of Laitimor Peninsula. According to the Japanese, he soon died of bacillary dysentery.[40]

Then, on about 18 April 1945, the Japanese discovered that certain warehouses in the vicinity of Lateri had been pilfered. They searched the camp and, finding signs of consumed tinned salmon, threatened to punish the whole of the party that had been working in the area unless the culprits confessed. Four Australians volunteered, encouraged by Ikeuchi's promise that they would save the rest of their party from harm and would suffer only light punishment. Instead, they were taken away on 25 April 1945 with their hands tied and executed the following day.[41] Lieutenant Kawahara Kiyomune, who supervised the executions at Paso, stated later that (Corporal) J Solomon, T (Thomas) Wadham, R (Ronald) Simpson and J (John) Morrison were individually blindfolded and bayoneted or, in three cases, beheaded with swords.[42] Kawahara claimed, at his later war crimes trial, that he and five others involved had been told by their superior officer that the executions were lawful because the Australians had been convicted in due process at a court martial. But all in the execution party were ultimately held accountable. Kawahara, and Sub-Lieutenants Ueda Kōsei and Kakinuma Morio were executed in May 1946, while others were given prison sentences.[43]

Soon after these executions, on 11 July 1945, another Australian, WF (William) Boyce, was caught stealing Japanese rations. Suspected of being one of Tan Tui's best scroungers, he fell into a trap laid by the Japanese. Once arrested, Boyce was beaten, tied up in front of Japanese headquarters, and then placed in solitary confinement. He was allowed only one meal a day and little medical attention for the foul tropical ulcers from which he was suffering. Van Nooten told the War Crimes Board of Inquiry in 1945:

He was tied in the way peculiar to the Japanese. They tie the wrists together behind the back, pull them up behind and then tie around the throat, leaving a length hanging, so that when they pull it, it pulls back on the throat. He was locked up for a period of about a fortnight … it looked as if he was going to get out of it fairly well, because the Japanese hated to go near him because of [the] overpowering smell [of his ulcers].[44]

Eventually, Boyce broke out one night in search of food, only to be recaptured. On 24 July he was taken away on a truck with shovels and executed. In this, the last of the executions of prisoners on Ambon (see Table 8.1), Petty Officer Kakuda Iwao described how Boyce was made to kneel in front of a hole:

When I received the orders to kill the prisoner, I had the feeling as if my own body was being torn apart. However, there was no escape … At the instance the platoon commander gave the 'Stab!' orders Superior Rating Tanaka stabbed the prisoner first on the right chest. I followed by stabbing him on the left chest. These were repeated four times when the platoon commander ordered the 'Halt'.[45]

Kakuda, in fact, was found not guilty of this crime after the war; he and another of the executioners, Tanaka Shōichi, were considered too junior to have known that Boyce had not been tried in a court martial. But three others, Shirozu Wadami, Lieutenant Miyazaki Yoshio and Sub-Lieutenant Shimakawa Masaichi, were held accountable and condemned to death (see chapter 12).[46]

Table 8.1: Australians executed on Ambon,
November 1942 to July 1945
(excluding those executed at Laha, February 1942)

	Date of death	Age	Charge
RA Bennett	22 November 1942	21	Outside the camp at night
GW Brown	22 November 1942	27	Outside the camp at night
AJ Collins	22 November 1942	25	Outside the camp at night
DA Evans	22 November 1942	25	Outside the camp at night
JF Kelly	22 November 1942	23	Outside the camp at night
AW King	22 November 1942	33	Outside the camp at night
NG Leary	22 November 1942	30	Outside the camp at night
PJ O'Donoghue	22 November 1942	21	Outside the camp at night
S Rainsbury	22 November 1942	n/a	Outside the camp at night
W Ripper	22 November 1942	34	Outside the camp at night
CE Tucker	22 November 1942	31	Outside the camp at night
J Morrison	26 April 1945	30	Pilfering of warehouse
RA Simpson	26 April 1945	n/a	Pilfering of warehouse
J Solomon	26 April 1945	29	Pilfering of warehouse
TFJ Wadham	26 April 1945	25	Pilfering of warehouse
FN Schaefer	30 April 1945	40	Escape
WF Boyce	24 July 1945	25	Stealing Japanese rations

SOURCE AWM 54 1010/9/2.

STARVATION

For all the horror of such executions, the threat to most prisoners was now starvation. From October 1944, the Japanese reduced the quantities of the rations – a move that could not be justified by reduced numbers in Tan Tui, since nearly 450 of the Australians were still alive at the start of 1945.[47] Nor was there, as the Japanese claimed at their later war crimes trials, a critical shortage of food on Ambon.[48] To be sure, Ambon was blockaded, and the Japanese relied on local food production, which was far from plentiful.[49] But the Japanese guards, so far as the Australians could see, were eating 'fairly well' and not showing any signs of malnutrition.[50] When the war ended, so one Japanese source said, substantial quantities of rice were stored on the island.[51]

In the three months after the August 1944 bombing, the Japanese issued the prisoners only 28 grams of rice per man per day, plus 140 grams of tapioca flour.[52] The tapioca, when mixed with water, made a glutinous substance that resembled the paste used to hang wallpaper in Australians' homes. It looked and tasted revolting. Nothing that the prisoners added to it could make it remotely palatable. Things improved slightly during the 'Long Carry', with rations of about 110 to 140 grams of rice per day and irregular supplies of sweet potato. When sweet potato was not available, the rice ration was increased to 280 grams. But after about three months the ration shrank back to a consistent 100 grams of rice per day, with the ubiquitous 'greens', potatoes of various kinds and bananas.[53] The rice was often sweepings from the floor of warehouses that contained grit and dirt.[54] Arthur Rogers later said that his evening meal, 'if you could call it that, could be fitted into a matchbox'. Desperate with hunger, men ate anything they could lay their hands on: cats, dogs, rats, frogs, lizards, snakes and grass (which gave them severe enteritis).[55]

On this diet, the heath situation spiralled out of control. Up to 250 men appeared on the daily sick parade, which started by the light of a hurricane lamp burning on coconut oil at 0500, and ended, after the long day's work, at 2230.[56] Beri-beri was endemic, and tropical ulcers sapped both physical strength and the will to live. The death toll began to soar. Two deaths were recorded in January 1945. But in May the deaths totalled 53. In June, 74 died; in July, 92.[57] As Marshall said later, the hospital was 'only a staging point for the cemetery':[58]

> many men were suffering from ancylostema infection [hookworm]. At this period the camp hygiene had completely broken down, due to the fact that the men did not have the strength to go to the beach latrines and even when deep trench latrines were constructed immediately outside the door of the huts, their debilitated condition and their enteritis did not allow them to reach the latrine. Very few men in the camp possessed footwear and so infection spread rapidly.[59]

Still, the Japanese drove the men out to work. Hobbling on crutches or sticks, they were hunted out of the huts almost every day. In one sweep, the Japanese guards pulled the blanket off a man and started to bash him, before realising that he was dead.[60] Any man who showed signs of faltering was viciously punished. To quote John Culton:

About two months before the surrender … Pte
Alford was in a working party of which I was a
member and we were coming home from the job.
At the time Pte Alford was very sick and could not
keep up with the party and was lagging behind. It
was then 'The Blob' attacked him with [an] iron bar,
which was a steel bar for reinforcing concrete works
and about half an inch in diameter and about three
feet long. He gave him about a dozen hits, Pte Alford
fell to the ground and then 'The Blob' kicked him
in the mouth and in the face. Pte Alford was semi-
conscious and bleeding slightly from the mouth and
we had to help him home.

Culton himself had his tropical ulcer jabbed by the spade
of 'The Blob' for no other reason, apparently, than that 'the
thought of jabbing me with a spade just occurred to him as
he was passing'.[61] Waaldyk recounted:

There were a number of working parties leaving camp
each morning and a number of sick men remained in
the hut, these men were frequently suffering from four
or five complaints at once, ulcers, beri-beri, dysentery
… They were merely skin and bone. Ike Houchi [sic]
… would hunt these men out of the hut kicking away
their crutches. I recollect a particular case of Jack
Knight [who] … was on crutches suffering severely
from ulcers and in a feeble condition. Ike Houchi
kicked away his crutches, lashed at his ulcers with
a stick and sent him off on the Galala Farm Party.
[Petty Officer Kuwahara Masuji] drove into camp

each morning on a bicycle … He took charge of the party, marching it out of camp, striking those who could barely walk, hastening those who were carrying prisoners who were incapable of walking.[62]

Van Nooten recorded another example of gratuitous cruelty in these last months of the war.

[Pte JF Smith] was hunted out on to the camp road to join a work party, He struggled along with the help of a pole or stick. He was very weak suffering from beri-beri, malnutrition and a huge tropical ulcer. Ike Euchi asked him what his illness was. He told him that his main trouble was his ulcer. Ike Euchi then knocked him down, deliberately kicked his ulcer and beat him with a heavy walking stick. He continued this for a few minutes and proceeded to drive him down the road for a distance of about 300 yards. Smith then collapsed. Ike Euchi bashed him again and waited for him to recover sufficiently to stand up. He then excused him from the out of camp work party but forced him to hoe grass in sight of the sentry … throughout the day in the hot sun.[63]

The prisoners could do little to protect themselves. Verdun Ball used to try and 'ride the blows, thereby easing the impact'. But a guard effectively stopped this by placing a fixed bayonet sitting in a rifle butt on the ground in front of him, its point poised some inches from his throat.[64] It became common to see working parties coming back at the end of the day, carrying the body of someone who had been left lying until the scheduled time for the party to return, or supporting someone who was so ill that he died soon after.[65]

By August 1945, those men still alive had every reason to despair. Ambon was being targeted by air raids, up to ten times per day and six per night.[66] Allied victory might be imminent, but if the July rate of deaths continued, the whole camp would be dead within two months. Every day they buried more and more of their mates. George Williamson remembered later:

> I was on nearly every burial party. We'd go out and dig the graves, and then bury them. And by the time we got back from one there'd be another one ready to go out, and so we'd just have to start again. You couldn't keep up with it. You'd wake up through the night and you'd hear them, you'd hear the death rattles going on. Not only in the hospital, but in the huts themselves. … Funny part of it was, I think it was comical anyway, this chap, you couldn't shut him up. He died, and we took him up to bury him. When we were lowering him into the ground, with the ropes around him, he bent, the wind came out over his sound box, and as he was going down he went 'Oooorrr'. One of the chaps then said, 'You can't even shut the bugger up when he's dead.' Yes, you used to think to yourself, I wonder if I'm going to be next.[67]

Men were buried in their blankets and a short service was read over their graves by van Nooten, there being no padre after Chaplain Patmore's death in February 1943.

LIBERATION

If the prisoners did not die of starvation, they feared that they might be massacred when the war ended. One of the petty officers at the Japanese headquarters told Walter Hicks, who was employed there, that this was probable, and those without this intelligence knew enough of the Japanese to believe that prisoners might not be allowed to live to tell their story of captivity.

It was, therefore, with a sense of disbelief, and intense excitement, that the prisoners received the news that the war had ended. The information came again from Hicks, whose Japanese informant gave him a copy of the imperial rescript in which the Emperor Hirohito announced the surrender of Japan.[68] The Japanese forces stationed on Ambon did not admit defeat until six days after the surrender, on 21 August. On the insistence of the prisoners, however, working parties ceased, and daily rations were increased to an incredible 765 grams of rice supplemented by meat, fish and fresh vegetables.[69] In addition, the medical supplies that Marshall and Ehlhart had requested over so many months were handed over.[70] The Japanese also presented van Nooten with a cheque for 7.9 million yen, drawn on the Bank of Tokyo, as payment for the officers and warrant officers, for the full period of their captivity. Van Nooten tore the cheque up and gave it back.[71]

All this came too late for some Australians. Three died in the next two weeks from the accumulated effects of malnutrition and overwork. When, on 10 September, four ships of the Royal Australian Navy, HMASs *Glenelg*, *Junee*, *Cootamundra* and *La Trobe*, sailed up to the wharf of Ambon town, only a small band was there to greet them. They had cobbled together 'quite smart uniforms for the occasion' and the regimental sergeant major, 'his voice undiminished by captivity, and his flow of language unimpaired, made the men "fall in"'.[72] But they seemed a 'pathetic remnant of what had been a battalion at full strength', a 'pitiful sight'. As one of the crew of the *La Trobe* wrote to his parents, the majority were

> mere skin and bone ... many of their mates, rather
> than make a show of themselves, receded to the
> seclusion of shrubs as we sailed into the harbour
> ... The prayer of all the boys on the way down [to
> Morotai] was answered for our return journey was
> very calm. An act of god comparable to Dunkirk.[73]

For the prisoners and naval personal alike, it was an emotional occasion. One prisoner told his mother by telegram, they were 'safe and well – released from Hell'.[74] There was 'hardly a dry eye amongst the ship's company of Latrobe'.[75] One of the medical officers wrote:

> It is singularly moving to see a grossly emaciated
> man weighing about 4½ st. [29 kilograms] quite
> philosophically arranging his head more comfortably
> on his pillow by the simple expedient of grasping his
> forelock with a thin wasted hand and moving by this
> means his head into the desired position.[76]

Embarkation of the stretcher cases began as quickly as possible.[77] They included acute sufferers of beri-beri, scurvy, diarrhoea and malaria. The average weight of these men was about 7 stone (44.5 kilograms), some being a low as 5 stone (32 kilograms). Three of the ulcer cases were 'particularly bad'.

> One patient had an infected unhealed stump of his left leg after amputation four weeks [earlier] following a large ulcer. The stump was almost indescribable having 1½" [3.8 centimetres] of unhealthy protruding femur, receding unhealthy muscle and skin, the whole being bathed in pus and emitting an unpleasant stench. This patient's spirit was unquenchable despite this great disability.[78]

In all the emotion of reunion and attention to the sick, however, Ikeuchi was not forgotten. He was conducted under guard to the *Cootamundra* where he was interned in a potato locker. Reportedly, he 'did not approve'.[79]

HOW HAD THEY COPED?

The Australians on Ambon suffered one of the highest death tolls of any group of prisoners of war held by the Japanese. Their captivity had a particularly unremitting character, in that they were confined for the whole period to a single location. Moreover, that environment was progressively degraded, not just by Japanese gross maltreatment and regulation but by Allied bombing. Prisoners on Singapore used to chant, 'You'll never get off the island.' In fact, most did, but the men on Ambon did not.

How, then, did they cope with this trauma, individually and collectively? It is hard to answer this question. Many of the prisoners did not live to recount their personal strategies of survival. Few kept diaries chronicling their daily struggles in captivity and the memoirs they wrote after the war reveal little about their mental health or the social dynamics of the POW camp. The focus of these accounts was largely on the practicalities of survival: food, work, health and Japanese punishment. The official records, too, were often silent on the question of the cohesion and resilience of Gull Force in captivity. Scott, as we have seen, was an exception, dwelling in his 1946 reports on the problems of Gull Force's discipline, as he saw them. Much of the other official documentation about life on Ambon was collected in the immediate aftermath of war with the aim of exposing Japanese brutality for the war crimes trials that followed.

The interviews with Gull Force survivors conducted in the 1980s had the potential to reveal more, but in the event, they offered a diverse range of opinions. Some former prisoners maintained that the battalion weathered the stresses of captivity well. 'I was really proud to be an Australian after I came out of that camp (despite some things that happened),' Dick Brown said. Bob Nowland likewise reflected:

> The average Australian is a pretty good fellow. He'll do practically anything for his mates. He is prepared to – most of them are prepared to – work for the common good. I can't say that for the other races I struck. In fact I feel that we are so far ahead of the Dutch, the Americans and even the English that it's unbelievable.

Jim Wilson meanwhile stated, 'We were very close knit. We stuck together well.' On the other hand, some survivors told a more dissonant story. Captivity brought out the worst as well as the best in men. Or, as one man said, the lesson of captivity was that 'men were animals'.[80]

The sincerity of those with positive memories of Gull Force cannot be doubted, but as already noted, the memory of the past is often filtered through contemporary public debate and cultural representations. In the early 1980s, a strongly affirmative narrative about Australian prisoners of war was emerging in the Australian public sphere, with the publication of Stan Arneil's diary and the release, on ABC radio and in book form, of a powerful series of interviews, conducted by Hank Nelson and Tim Bowden. While acknowledging tensions within the POW camps, and the resentment of the officers by other ranks, these works also celebrated Australian mateship. No man died alone; 'at the hour of their deaths, there was always a comrade there to hold a hand, smooth a brow or say a prayer', wrote Arneil in his retrospective introduction.[81] Nelson also promulgated the popular belief that Australian prisoners of war were distinguished from other national groups, such as the British and Dutch, by their group cohesion.[82] Possibly, then, men's positive memories of Gull Force in the 1980s were shaped by this dominant discourse of Australian mateship and by the associated rituals of remembrance, commemoration that elevated narratives of unity over those of division.

The reality of Gull Force was probably somewhere between two poles of memory. Some prisoners did 'stick together well', drawing strength from the emotional and functional support that their syndicates provided. They forged relationships that had an edge and a quality rarely, if ever, encountered in civilian life. These friendships lasted for the rest of their lives, cemented by almost annual pilgrimages to Ambon when the political situation allowed.

However, the stresses of captivity also fractured Gull Force. The contemporary record shows that stealing, from gardens and chicken coops, was widespread as starvation increased. The circle to which a prisoner owed loyalty contracted as the struggle for resources intensified. Notably, mateship seems to have excluded the officers, at least as a collective. The anger that had been triggered by Gull Force's defeat was fuelled over time by the mismanagement, as some men saw it, of food, work and discipline. The distribution of food, so critical to survival, was an especially sensitive matter. Two of the American prisoners interned with the Australians at Tan Tui alleged after the war that food had been distributed unequally, and that the camp staff did not give the men their full share. The staff were 'a closed corporation', whose primary purpose was 'their own welfare' and 'saving their own skins'. When the Australian Army Advanced Land Headquarters at Morotai in October 1945 set up an inquiry to investigate these allegations, it concluded that Quartermaster Ryan had used flat cooking trays to produce meals in an easily divisible form, so each man could see that he got the same quantity as others. But it also noted that 'on the orders of the Japanese', from late 1944 a small additional daily ration was given to key personnel of the Australian administrators of the camp, Westley, van Nooten, Ryan and the medical team, Ehlhart and Marshall and his assistant.[83] This might have been a cause for envy, but given the size of the Japanese rations, it could not have made much difference to these officers' chances of survival.

The greater privilege that the officers enjoyed was their exemption from manual labour outside Tan Tui. At some time in the later months of the war, NCOs assumed the role of supervising the men on working parties. Van Nooten attributed this arrangement to the Japanese, who suspected that the officers were making contact with the Ambonese population.[84] Westley claimed it was because the officers were thought to be boosting the men's morale.[85] Hence, the officers, at least in the last 12 months of captivity, worked on internal camp maintenance: constructing several large air-raid shelters within the prison camp, digging graves (sometimes daily), and venturing into the jungle to fell, saw and later split the wood for all cooking fires in the camp. This work was not necessarily easy. The graves might hit hard coral and the officers themselves had ulcers and illnesses such as malaria and dysentery.[86] But the officers seemed – at least in the memory of some men interviewed later – to be sheltering in Tan Tui, socially aloof, living in separate quarters. More critically, the officers were spared the relentless exhaustion of the 'Long Carry' and the bashings that occurred on other working parties.

This made the difference between life and death.[87] If we exclude from officers' deaths those killed in the bomb blast of February 1943, their death rate was about 23.5 per cent (four of 17). The other ranks, in contrast, suffered a death rate (excluding accidents, deaths from bombing and executions) of 73.5 per cent.[88] In this respect, it should be said, Ambon was little different from the Thailand–Burma railway, where even in the worst situations, such as F Force, officers died at a much lower rate than the other ranks.[89]

The officers' exemption from the working parties not only improved their chances of survival; it also denied many of them the authority and respect that came from visibly defending the men's interests through interventions with the Japanese. As Harry Williams said, of an incident in which he was caught stealing sugar and bashed across the face by the Japanese guard:

> I'm not tall but I was looking down on this thing and I thought, 'I can put my fingers around you and choke you to death', and yet I had to stand and take that. And Lieutenant [Graham] Pullin came up … and he talked him out of bashing me. He couldn't do no more. He done that [sic].

Lieutenant R (Ralph) Godfrey, when supervising a working party, also took the brunt and received two bashings so severe that he required back surgery in 1962.[90]

A further challenge to the officers' authority was their need to mediate between their men and the Japanese – a role from which it was difficult to emerge with any credit. Forced to promulgate the Japanese punitive regulations, Westley and van Nooten were at risk of being seen as their agents. When meeting the Japanese demands for working parties, van Nooten faced a devil's choice. He could refuse to supply the number of men demanded, but Ikeuchi and other guards would then comb the huts and the hospital for workers. Or van Nooten, the Regimental Sergeant Major and the medical officers could make the decision themselves as to who was 'fit' enough to go on the working parties, a task that could be construed as collaboration. The Americans who instigated the postwar inquiry claimed:

> The constant concern of the camp staff was meeting the daily demands of the Japanese for work parties, irrespective of the physical condition of the men. The Adjutant and the RSM frequently pulled Australians who were too ill to go on work parties out of their bunks and compelled them to go on work parties, using physical violence where necessary to achieve this purpose.[91]

However, the inquiry rejected this accusation, concluding that the Americans seemed to be motivated less by a concern for the truth than by their own sense of grievance at being excluded by Westley from the position in the camp to which they thought their rank entitled them.[92] The other 12 Americans in the camp, if we can judge by Weiss's later account, felt no particular hostility towards the Australian officers. The Australians, for their part, seem to have tolerated the Americans, although their bragging about the United States' military prowess was sometimes irritating.

That said, the grievances that the Americans articulated found their echoes in the oral history 40 years later. While many survivors conceded that van Nooten faced an impossible task, which he performed with considerable courage in the face of regular physical harassment from the Japanese, others were critical of the fact that, with the apparent acquiescence of the Australian command, very ill men were sent out to work. The implication was that with different leaders – perhaps those who died in the bomb blast of February 1943 – the rights of the prisoners might have been more effectively protected.

Such judgments take little account of the inflexibility of the Japanese with whom the Australian command had to deal, but they reflect a widespread disenchantment with the man most responsible for the defence of Gull Force's interests on Ambon, Westley. This hapless major found himself in a situation for which, in terms of temperament and personality, let alone rank, he was manifestly ill equipped. Originally an estate agent who had served with Roach in the militia, Westley had apparently been a competent staff officer. However, from the time of the 2/21st Battalion's days in Darwin, he had become the butt of jokes. He was nicknamed the 'Swamp Ghost', a possibly apocryphal reference to the occasion when he had got his company lost while on manoeuvres outside Darwin. Another title was the 'Roan Steer', a reference to Westley's habit of tossing his distinctively coloured hair.

It was Westley's misfortune that the fighting on Ambon had not given him the opportunity to establish his reputation as a combat officer. The company he commanded, A Company, was stationed at Eri and saw no action before the surrender. Westley, therefore, assumed command on Scott's departure for Hainan with his competent authority unproven. In terms of personal authority, he was also hindered by the fact that, like Scott, he found it difficult to fraternise with his men. He thus failed to provide the leadership expected of him at Tan Tui – something he conceded in an awkward interview many years later. In the alien and harrowing situation of captivity, he withdrew into himself and left the camp's administration to van Nooten and, in the case of food distribution, to Ryan. The dentist and doctor conducted many of the battles with the Japanese over medical matters.

In thus delegating responsibility, Westley claimed that he was acting in the prisoners' best interests. The Japanese, so he maintained at the inquiry after the war, treated him like a 'naughty child', losing no opportunity of humiliating him in front of his men. They even struck him before a parade of all prisoners. His subordinates, in his opinion, had a better chance of improving the prisoners' conditions. The postwar inquiry agreed that this claim had some substance, but it concluded that, while van Nooten and Ryan had done all they could to improve the conditions in the camp and deserved to be recognised for their efforts,

> [Westley] might have acted with more vigor [sic] in his relations with the Japanese and made more use of his rank and seniority. He does not appear to have kept contact with his men, to the extent expected of a Commanding Officer in the circumstances in which the prisoners were situated, nor does he appear to have discussed his difficulties with those under his command. To this extent there was a lack of leadership displayed by Maj Westley.[93]

The issue which more than any other alienated the men of Gull Force from Westley was that of discipline. In trying to control behaviour, such as stealing, that threatened the collective good, Westley operated a regimental orderly room and threatened the men with assignment to harsher working parties or disciplinary action on their return to Australia.[94]

But these sanctions carried no weight. So, Westley asked the Japanese to make available to the Australian camp staff a guard room used by them for camp headquarters. The Japanese refused and instead directed the Australians to build their own detention centre. The resulting structure, made to Japanese specifications, was an open cage, constructed of 'native materials', approximately 2 metres square, situated within the camp.[95] Initially men held there were exposed to the elements – although they could take their ground sheet, great coat and a blanket for protection. After a few weeks the cage was roofed.[96]

The 'boob', as it became known, was used to detain a number of prisoners, usually those caught stealing. 'Sentences' were served at night, that being the time when bandicooting of gardens normally occurred. No men held in the cage were ever denied food, and their medical problems were monitored by the doctor. If, in Elhart's opinion, they were unfit to complete their sentences, they were released. Later, when the Japanese commandeered the boob for their own disciplinary purposes, these controls over its use were lost, but then van Nooten ensured that food was smuggled, under the cover of darkness, to the detained men.

No part of Gull Force's history proved more sensitive than the use of the boob as form of discipline. When I conducted the interviews for the first edition of this book, some ex-officers denied the boob's existence. Van Nooten insisted that it was 'a complete and utter figment of the imagination'. Westley said he remembered it only 'dimly', and then, when presented with documentary evidence of the cage's existence, claimed it was 'a Japanese thing'.[97] Other officers, with one exception, conveyed the impression that the boob had existed, but again they implied that it had been built by the Japanese. The survivors from the other ranks, however, were more than willing to reveal the cage's existence and explain how it had been part of the disciplinary procedures used by the Australian command on Ambon. The records of the postwar inquiry, held now in the National Archives, confirmed their testimony.

It might be asked if the cage was a tolerable form of discipline in the desperate situation on Ambon in 1944–45. Something had to be done to control the stealing and the normal methods of military discipline were ineffectual. Facing starvation, few prisoners feared losing their rank. Extra duties and a reduction in rations were life-threatening. Corporal punishment was repugnant when prisoners were already weakened by malnutrition and disease, although van Nooten resorted to it on one occasion, when two Australians were discovered, twice within a few weeks, stealing food.[98] Handing men over to the Japanese for punishment was also an unacceptable option, as Scott was to demonstrate on Hainan Island (see chapter 10). Though some survivors suspected that Westley handed men over to the Japanese, no evidence survives to support this view.

Of the radical options for deterrence, the cage was probably the least injurious. It was a form of punishment that, with appropriate controls, did not cause significant harm to the individuals involved. As it happened, the command at Ambon were not the only Australian officers to resort to some kind of 'prison' within a POW camp. Colonel Albert Coates, an Australian medical officer in Thailand, when faced with problems of discipline at Nakom Paton in July 1945:

applied to the Japanese authorities for permission to have a hut set apart in our hospital compound for the detention of any [prisoners] who might get out of hand … The Japanese agreed and, in place of the ugly guard room cells in which men had been put previously, under the surveillance of Japanese who used to torment them with bamboo sticks, deny them water and practise other grosser forms of torture, we had a 'prison' but segregated and guarded by our own men. I visited the men detained and saw that their ulcers and any other diseases were attended to daily and properly.[99]

Civilian internees at Muntok prison, late in their captivity, also set aside a special room within the jail for detaining men who were caught stealing food, clothing or other items.[100]

Yet, if the use of a cage might have had a logic in 1944–45, it was incompatible with the values of the AIF. As the men saw it, Australian officers should lead by example, not force. If Gull Force was not united in captivity, this was an indictment of the officers' leadership. Anzacs were supposedly only poorly disciplined when badly led. The fact that Westley acted to stem the individualism that challenged the collective good was not the point. The norms of a more inclusive form of mateship, and a preference for informal over formal sanctions, were the standards by which officers were judged. Australians should not turn on each other when they needed to be united against a cruel and vindictive enemy. Westley's authority, already fragile before the boob was built, never recovered from the controversy this sparked. He did not attend postwar reunions or pilgrimages.

The Australians on Ambon thus had to endure the worst and most desperate months of their captivity, in one important respect, leaderless. Yet, for all this, nothing in the archival record and later testimonies suggests that Gull Force ever became a rabble. The hierarchy of the battalion was never overthrown, nor seriously challenged. The ravages of starvation and overwork in the last year of captivity were possibly so debilitating that they precluded any coordinated opposition to the camp staff. Beyond that, Gull Force remained unified in their hatred of the Japanese. With one ambiguous exception, no prisoner betrayed the group by overt collaboration with the Japanese.[101] Against the enemy, at least, Gull Force presented a united front.

PART V

PRISONERS ON HAINAN, 1942-45

9

CRISIS ON HAINAN, 1942-43

The 267 Australian prisoners who left Ambon in October 1942, under the leadership of Scott and his second-in-command, Ian Macrae, escaped the catastrophe that unfolded on that island in 1943–45. But they could hardly have predicted this when they set sail. They were travelling to a destination that was unknown and, for all they knew, might turn out to be worse than the tropical Ambon. In the event, their new place of internment was Hainan Island, off the coast of southern China, which the Japanese had occupied in early 1939 because of its strategic importance and potentially useful resources. First impressions of the new POW camp were deplorable, and living conditions on Hainan were nothing like the convalescent camp the Japanese had promised. By mid-1943, many of the men who had been included in the contingent leaving Ambon because they were sick had succumbed to beri-beri and other illnesses. Only a change in Japanese personnel later in 1943 pulled the POW camp back from crisis – for a time.

GETTING THERE

The sea journey from Ambon to Hainan Island, 24 kilometres off the coast of China, lasted 11 days. The Japanese freighter the *Taiko Maru* was certainly no passenger liner. At night the prisoners were crowded into the holds where conditions were distinctly unpleasant. Seasickness compounded the problems of dysentery. The weaker prisoners struggled to use the latrines, which were a primitive platform suspended over the stern of the boat.[1] It was like 'being on the big dipper at Luna Park when you were squatted there', RK (Bob) Allen recalled.[2]

However, during the day the prisoners were allowed on the deck, and, in a pleasant contrast to Ambon, their Japanese guards seemed reasonably cooperative. The regulations were minimal. The food, too, was relatively good, since the Japanese provided some tinned rations as well as rice, all of which was cooked on deck. Many men, however, lost their appetite when heavy weather set in for several days while they were crossing the South China Sea. For the good sailors this was a bonanza. They got the rations that their mates could not stomach – and even some of the Dutch meals, too – but only if they were able to bridge the communication gap. As Stuart Campbell recounted:

> It was pretty rough one day on deck and a Dutchman was standing next to me on the rail and he had a plate full with some bully beef and a biscuit on it, which was like a complete Christmas dinner to me. He obviously was going to be seasick and he held the plate over to me and I said, 'Thank you'. I didn't realise that 'Thank

you' in Dutch is accepted as 'No, thank you'. I should have said 'please', And he tipped the plateful into the ocean. I nearly wept.

Drinking water was readily available on the ship and the prisoners were able to douse themselves with seawater, which gave them some relief from their tinea. Compared with the nightmare voyages that many other Australian prisoners endured as they were transported around the extremes of the Japanese empire in the Asia-Pacific, the men from Gull Force had a relatively easy voyage.

Most importantly, they were not torpedoed by US submarines. Four months earlier, the men of another Australian island force, Lark Force, had been sunk by the USS *Sturgeon* when travelling from New Britain to Hainan on the Japanese transport ship SS *Montevideo Maru*. Some 1060 military personnel and civilians were lost. In the remaining years of the war, a further 18 160 Allied prisoners and Asian labourers would be sunk by 'friendly fire'.[3] At no time during the war did the Japanese – or, for that matter, the Allied powers – agree to mark ships carrying prisoners with any protective symbol, such as the red cross that identified hospital ships.[4] Had Gull Force travelled later in the war, when the US Navy dominated the South China Sea, they would have had a high chance of drowning.

Land came into sight on 4 November 1942, and the ship's captain summoned the Australian adjutant, John Turner. 'There is the island of Hainan,' he said, 'where there is much hard work for you all.' When Turner noted that the Australian contingent had, on the specific instructions of the Japanese, included many sick men who were unable to work,

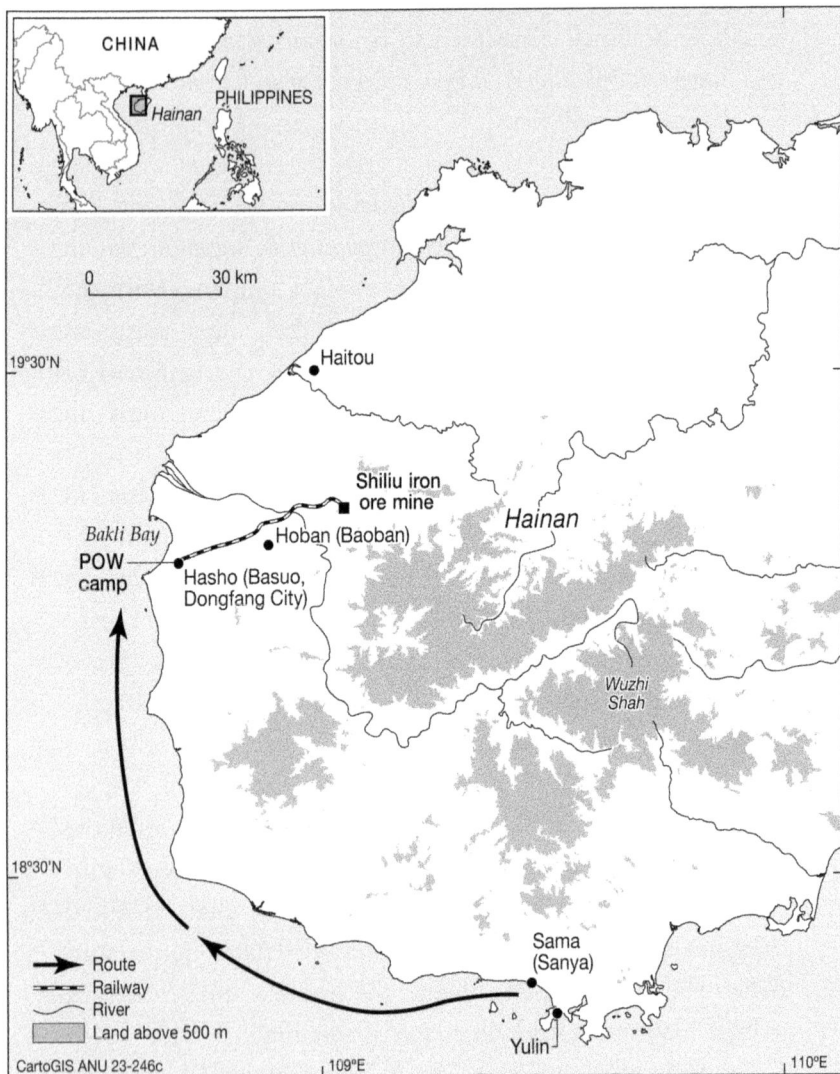

Map 9.1: Hainan Island, key sites

the captain and his first officer collapsed into laughter.[5] Later that day, the transport anchored in the Bay of Sama where the prisoners were vaccinated against cholera and typhoid before they set sail again, in a north-westerly direction. Reaching Bakli Bay on 5 November, they disembarked and marched to their camp around 3 kilometres away, the sick men all carrying their kits.[6]

BAKLI BAY CAMP

The new environment made a terrible impression. In Scott's words, 'The outlook was deplorable – a barren, sandy island with nothing but a little cactus here and there, a hot wind.'[7] The men described it as 'the arse end of the earth', 'shocking, just wide open spaces and sand', 'bloody desolation' and 'heartbreaking'.[8] The camp in which they were to live covered about 4 hectares, surrounded by a low barbed-wire fence.[9] Within this area a few small buildings served as storerooms and the Japanese guard house, while several huge wooden huts, measuring about 60 metres by 9 metres, were the prisoners' quarters. Originally occupied by Chinese labourers, these buildings were constructed of scrap iron and timber, and offered little protection from the weather. At floor level they had open louvres. Above these were ill-fitting wooden shutters, which took the place of windows. AT (Tom) Pledger was to comment in his diary some months later, 'It is raining and we have been trying to dodge the drops as this roof is one mass of holes. When the sun is shining you can lie on your bed and watch it from sunrise to sunset and it is never out of your vision.'[10] When the winter winds started to blow, it was just as bitter inside the huts as outside.[11]

Within these huts two 3.6-metre-wide wooden platforms, raised about half a metre above the dirt floor, flanked a central aisle. On these *bali balis*, as they were known, the prisoners had to sleep. Conditions were at first very crowded, as all Australians were housed in one hut. A third large hut provided sleeping quarters for the Dutch prisoners. Privacy was impossible, although within a month the pressure was relieved a little when another hut was vacated by Chinese labourers and was assigned to the Australians and the Dutch as a hospital.[12] The only partition within the Australian hut was that which separated the officers' quarters from those of the men (see Figure 9.1).

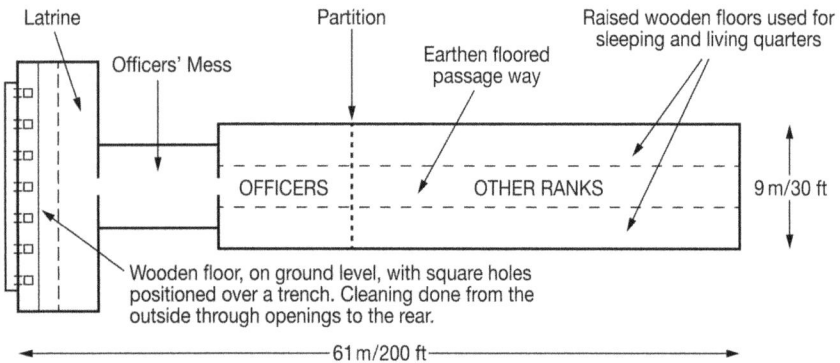

Figure 9.1: Accommodation hut, Bakli Bay POW camp

For bedding, each man was issued with a thin straw sleeping mat and two worn blankets. Some Australians later turned their mats into hammocks strung between poles, but otherwise they slept on the hard boards of the *bali balis*.[13]

The Japanese at least provided mosquito nets. The camp was only 400 metres away from a swamp into which the refuse of a Chinese labourers' camp drained, creating a breeding ground for malarial mosquitoes. Nothing in the way of cleaning materials or implements was supplied to rid the huts of the other insects with which they were infested.[14] The prisoners had to reconcile themselves to sharing their beds with cockroaches, rats, lice, fleas, bed bugs, ants and the flies with which the district swarmed.

The kitchen was no better. It, too, was not weatherproof and was situated within 90 metres of a low-lying patch of ground into which all camp drainage ran and stagnated. Four large coppers for cooking were set into brickwork, which often collapsed. The concrete floor also quickly broke up, providing a breeding ground for rats. Meals had to be taken at tables in the open air, often under mosquito nets to ward off the flies. The officers did have a 'mess', but this was located next to the latrine. Since this was simply a wooden floor with holes, mounted over a trench, which had to be emptied daily by wooden baskets on poles, the atmosphere in the mess was often foul.

For their hygiene, prisoners had two bathhouses, one open and one covered in, which contained three or four wooden troughs and one long concrete trough. The wooden troughs eventually rotted, leaving only the concrete one, at which men washed by throwing cold water over their bodies. Fortunately, water itself was not in short supply, given the presence of two deep wells in the camp, but it had to be carried to wherever it was needed and boiled before it could be drunk. Over time this would become increasingly difficult, as firewood was often in short supply.[15] All in all, it seemed that these men of Gull Force had drawn the short straw when exchanging fertile Ambon for the wasteland at Bakli Bay.

WORK

Hainan was undeveloped, but the Japanese saw its potential in mineral resources, tropical agriculture and related industries.[16] In their six and a half years of occupation, they strove, with mixed success, to develop not only iron and tin mining, but also forestry, a range of tropical crops and light industries based on agricultural products; for example, cotton, paper, tobacco, soap, fish and meat canning, and brick and tile production.

These plans were contingent, first, on the pacification of the island. The local population was potentially hostile and several thousand Chinese communist and nationalist guerillas operated in the island's interior, as Gull Force would discover later. Second, the transport infrastructure was primitive. The Japanese had to extend the port facilities and the system of roads (all of which were unpaved in 1939) while creating a new railway network. To achieve these objectives, they conscripted Chinese labourers, many of whom were killed after the construction of the more strategic sections of railway. They also shipped in prisoners of war, not just Australian and Dutch but also Indian.

In late 1942, Hainan was under the command of Japanese naval forces, and the prisoners of war were controlled by the Yokosuka no. 4 Special Naval Landing Party.[17] It was the commander of this unit, Captain S Kondo, who greeted the

Australians and Dutch the day after they arrived with the words:

> Now Japan is establishing NEW ASIA, in which
> every race is equal in opportunity. You are not our
> enemy since you have surrendered, ceasing your hostile
> action against Japanese Forces. So you can get along
> and serve your duty here without any need of anxiety.
> Henceforth you are good co-operator to us, I am sure.
> We feel very much sympathy with you, and treat as
> well as our regulation permits, but … even a small act
> of opposition must be severely punished.[18]

The same day, the Japanese adjutant, Captain Ida, told Scott that the prisoners would be expected to do manual work, regardless of their poor health. Scott and the Dutch commander, Kapitz, were also pressured around 19 November to sign an undertaking that the men under their command would collaborate with the Japanese Navy in developing a New East Asia. Though threatened with execution, Scott at first refused to sign, until the fear of reprisals against the whole camp forced him to give way.[19]

Working parties for the Japanese began on 10 November 1942. The first task was roadbuilding, but this was soon extended to a range of tasks connected with Japanese defence needs and with the exploitation of the island. Building airstrips and a large viaduct for unloading iron ore; pushing trucks full of sand for defensive positions and harbour reclamation; siting anti-aircraft guns and preparing anti-aircraft batteries: these were typical of the tasks the Australians found themselves employed on over the next three years. As on Ambon, they were also required to help unload shipping, in this case in Hasho harbour where ships had to berth some distance from the coast and be unloaded by lighters.[20]

Almost all the work involved hard labour, for perhaps ten hours or more a day.[21] In the summer months, temperatures soared to the high 30s Celsius in the shade, with a strong hot wind.[22] Modern equipment was often scarce. The carrying of dirt was done by two men at either end of a hammock slung between poles.[23] Roadbuilding meant relentless physical exertion, relieved only by the humour that the Australians somehow managed to display. To quote Bob Allen:

> The Japs produced a big iron roller, about six feet high with shafts and ropes. About a dozen of us were pulling this roller over the coral on the road for a couple of days. It was tough going. On the second day, Freddie Williams yelled, 'Whoa'. We all stopped pulling and Freddie said, 'I'm working like a bloody horse so I'm going to look like a bloody horse', and he pulled out a certain part of his anatomy and we continued pulling the roller. However it wasn't long before a Jap guard saw Freddie and did not like it at all and Freddie soon carried on as normal.

As on Ambon, the officers were exempt from manual work, although this seems to have been a reluctant concession. According to Scott, the camp commander, Naval Lieutenant Takai Toshijiro, announced on the day that working parties began that officers were expected to work, since this would be good for their health and character. 'They must live a simple life like the Japanese and be earnest and diligent.' Scott, to the surprise of some of his officers, did not immediately object to this. He even assigned some officers to working parties. But then he went over Takai's head and protested to Kondo, who as area commander, was his superior. If the Australian officers and NCOs were forced to work, Scott argued, they would lose authority in the eyes of their men. This would have serious implications for discipline within the POW camp. Rather than risk this, it would be preferable if the officers accompanied working parties as supervisors, 'to assist … in any way possible'. If the Japanese conceded this, Scott undertook that the officers would agree to maintain a garden, which would not only keep them fit but also provide food for the camp community.

Scott won the argument. Kondo agreed that Australian officers and sergeants should not have to do manual work, although they would still supervise working parties. They were also permitted to establish a garden outside the perimeter of the camp. But in going to Kondo, Scott had caused the camp commander to lose face, and from then until he relinquished command of the camp in mid-August 1943, Takai was extremely hostile to the Australians.[24] Soon known by the prisoners as 'The Black Snake', he seemed much more antagonistic to the Australians than to the Dutch prisoners.[25] 'A real slave driver of the worst type', Takai demanded ever larger working parties, and took the lead in driving sick men to work harder.[26] On 8 April 1943, when a group of prisoners were sitting by the side of the road waiting for instructions from the Japanese in charge of their party, Takai suddenly appeared:

apparently in a furious rage he started shouting in
Japanese. All the men got up and started to move
up the road as his gestures seemed to indicate. Takai
struck several men on the back with a stick and threw
some to the ground. He threw Pte Woodward and
Pte Stevens down and proceeded to kick Woodward
as he lay on the ground; at least two kicks were aimed
at Woodward's head. Takai was wearing boots with
hard soles.

When the Australian officer supervising the working party,
Ian Macrae, intervened to stop the kicking, Takai struck
him on the face, grabbed him by the neck of his cape, and
seemed intent on throwing him to the ground. For some
reason, however, Takai thought better of this and walked
away.[27] Later, after Scott had protested to Takai, Macrae was
offered an apology.[28]

Some weeks later, in June 1943, Takai approached
four men who had been allowed to rest during a working
party because they were suffering from malaria. He struck
each of them in the face and ordered them back to work.
On yet another occasion, on 28 July 1943, he assaulted an
Australian whose offence was to have slipped while carrying
heavy sandbags up a steep railway embankment to anti-
aircraft gun positions.[29]

Other camp personnel were no more sympathetic. The
interpreter, a Chinese man called Chen Tze-Ping, emerged
as one of the more malign influences in the prisoners' lives.
Remembered by Ron Green as a 'Formosan, of small and
slight build, with slightly slanting eyes, neatly dressed,
[and] particularly vain and effeminate about his personal

appearance', Chen had poor language skills and went out of his way to obstruct the Australians' negotiations with the Japanese.[30] However, despite this hostility on the part of Chen and Takai, physical attacks on the prisoners seem not to have reached the proportions in 1943 that they did in the later years.[31]

KEEPING FED

The major concern for the prisoners in the first year on Hainan was the deterioration in their diet. The Japanese originally promised to provide food that was typical of the Japanese diet: rice, fish, miso and seaweed. But as 1943 progressed, rice became dominant, at the expense of foodstuffs rich in protein and vitamins. The fish and meat rations were often bad, or soon went bad, given the lack of refrigeration in which to store several days' rations. Vegetables became scarce and finally disappeared from August to October 1943.[32] According to Tom Pledger, a prisoner could look forward to a breakfast of only one cup of rice and a cup of soup, and to a lunch and dinner of the same. Twice a week there was rotten fish, sometimes grass ('greens'), and once a month, fresh meat.[33]

The quantity of the rations issued by the Japanese was also less than promised. In the opinion of Gull Force's quartermaster, (Captain) PP (Philip) Miskin, it was obvious that 'we were getting foodstuffs which had been picked over by the Japanese at all points between the Hokurei issuing depot and our camp, and also that our share of the rations were [sic] being freely looted at every Japanese guard house the ration truck passed'.[34] The Japanese also failed to provide any cooking utensils or materials from which some could be made. Scraps of iron and sheeting retrieved from roofs around the camp were adapted to serve as saucepans.[35]

Complaints by Miskin about the situation were dismissed brusquely. Eventually, in June 1943, when the effects of malnutrition were becoming evident, Scott decided to again go over the head of the local commander and protest to the Japanese headquarters at Hokurei. The letter that he ordered the Australian doctor, Bill Aitken, to write to the Japanese doctor at headquarters triggered a violent response. According to Miskin, the camp commandant, Lieutenant Hachialla:

> came into Australian officer's [sic] quarters in a very hostile frame of mind, and abused Capt Aitken and myself. He tore up the letter and thrust the pieces down the neck of my shirt and keeping up a tirade of abuse in Japanese, struck me repeatedly and forcibly in the face. He only paused in this treatment of me to mete out similar treatment to Capt Aitken. He pointed out that we were prisoners, and indicated that he could do what he liked with us, threatened severe chastisement or execution and then left our quarters.[36]

Despite this outburst, the Japanese did partially restore the food cuts. It seemed to Miskin that determined and persistent complaints to the Japanese could have a positive effect, whatever the physical cost to the individuals who made them.[37]

The increased rations, however, were still inadequate, and at no time did the prisoners receive any parcels from the International Committee of the Red Cross.[38] As on Ambon, the Australians did everything they could to supplement their diet. Gardens soon sprang up and although the soil was poor, many syndicates managed to grow tomatoes, pumpkins and various green vegetables. Often the seeds were provided by the Japanese. The produce from the gardens, however, was seasonal, and in the hot months, the yield of the gardens was very low.[39]

Gardening also demanded physical effort from the prisoners. Rainfall was unreliable in this part of Hainan; water had to be drawn and carried to the gardens from the camp wells. If fertiliser were required, excrement had to be retrieved from the latrines.[40] For some Australians, the burden of maintaining their gardens became too great. Stealing from the Japanese once more became a popular means of supplementing food. While road and railway building gave little access to food supplies, the prisoners sometimes worked in the port or near Japanese stores. Here they could pilfer items ranging from sugar to skimmed milk and rice. A favourite tactic was to sit next to or crawl under a Japanese storeroom (depending on the building's construction). With the aid of some improvised funnel, like a piece of piping, the prisoners could siphon off rice.[41] Or other stratagems could be used. As Frank Biddiscombe remembered it:

Behind this shed was the stable where they used to keep [the Japanese captain's] horse. We were working on a gun pit and at rest time we'd all sit around this hut … The stable [for the horse] was behind that.

> We knew that the horse was fed each day, and it was
> fed on rice and bean shoots. So we used to take it in
> turns. We had little bags and we'd knock off the food
> from the horse … and eventually it died of starvation
> … because there wasn't a blade of grass for it to eat
> around the place.

Beyond scrounging was trading. In contrast to the situation
on Ambon, the Japanese on Hainan connived at the prisoners
trading with the local population, the Taiwanese guards
who were sometimes on duty at the camp, and even with
the Japanese themselves. While prisoners were sometimes
punished severely when caught trading, some Japanese
personnel, and the interpreter, Chen, were complicit in the
trading.[42] A flourishing trade, therefore, developed between
the prisoners and the local community. Chinese men,
many of whom were from Hong Kong and able to speak
English, would loiter around the working parties. When the
opportunity arose, they would exchange cigarettes, sugar,
rice, eggs, peanuts and a variety of other commodities,
including medicines and alcohol, for any marketable goods
the Australians could offer.[43] Watches and clothing were
always in demand. In one notable incident, recorded in the
diary of Alan Murnane:

> One of the lads had occasion to go to the scrub from
> the ack-ack road job. He met a chow who offered him
> 20 eggs for his shorts. He promptly took them off and
> sold them on the spot then cooled his heels and things
> in the bush 'til he could attract the attention of one
> of his cobbers who peeled off his underpants for the

Trader to finish the days [sic] work and go home to barracks.[44]

Woollen clothing seemed popular with the Chinese and Sikhs who were employed on the island, and the Japanese guards. When trading their greatcoats, scarves, socks and singlets for food and medicines, the prisoners took the risk of suffering when the harsh winter winds swept down from the Gobi Desert. They were provided with very little clothing by the Japanese: only 100 cotton shirts, 99 pairs of shorts, one pair of sandshoes per man (which did not necessarily fit) and 66 pairs of part-worn boots were issued for the Australians.[45] Scott therefore prohibited the trading of clothes.[46] But the men ignored this. Their logic was summed up by Tom Pledger who wrote, when he had traded his sweater for 250 vitamin B tablets to help stave off beri-beri, 'it is better to be cold for a few months than for good'.[47] Indeed, trading was probably one of the reasons why many of the Australians survived their years of captivity on Hainan. At the height of the beri-beri crisis, for example, Alan Murnane was able to buy a small bottle of vitamin B from a Dutch prisoner who purchased it from the Japanese stores.[48]

If conditions on the working parties were too risky for trading, the Australians waited until night. In the darkness they slipped out under the two strands of the barbed wire fence to rendezvous with their Chinese contact. Alternatively, they simply 'bandicooted' some unlucky villager's garden.[49] But, after six Dutchmen had escaped in February 1943, the Japanese headquarters told Scott that he, his officers and sergeants would be held personally responsible for any further escapes.[50] Certain individuals, therefore, emerged as middlemen, willing to take the risks of trading on other people's behalf. Every commodity soon had two prices: one inside and one outside the camp. When the supply of goods for trading became scarce, some prisoners resorted to IOUs, which they promised to redeem after the war.[51]

To counter the problem of smuggling the goods back into the camp, eggs were buried in buckets of manure being brought into the camp to fertilise gardens. Rice was hidden in trouser legs tied around the ankle.[52] When subterfuge failed, bravado sometimes worked. Ron Leech found himself and his mate in an awkward situation after a successful sortie outside the camp in search of alcohol:

> we were blind drunk and we're coming back with these kerosine [sic] tins full of grog on a stick. We passed an open area and all our guards were sitting there getting drunk, and we had to go past them because we couldn't have got there [otherwise] before the roll call. So we just walked past and nobody looked up ... We got to where we got out, and there's a guard posted over the hole. So, what are we going to do? There's only one way. We've got to walk through the front gate. So we went up to the front gate with the two kerosine [sic] tins full of grog, put them down, bowed to the guard. He bowed back and we walked in. I guess we should have been dead a lot of times!

HEALTH CRISIS

Despite the trading, scrounging and gardening, sickness mounted in 1943.[53] In November 1942, there were 13 cases of beri-beri; in December, 40 cases; and in January 1943, 22 cases. For several months thereafter the incidence of beri-beri declined, because the Japanese supplied the hospital with 'fairly good' quantities of vitamin B. But in May and June, these supplies halted. When they resumed in July and August, the quantities issued were very small. The number of men with serious symptoms of beri-beri rapidly increased, until more than half the Australians were afflicted. The situation, as Aitken put it, was 'scandalous'. By August 1943:

> Five men (5) had died and many more were dying. The hospital was full of men with ataxia [loss of power controlling movement], paralysis and oedema [swelling] – some able to stagger about and others could not. Every bed held a man with complete oedema of the whole body and gasping for breath. Others in the same condition were being nursed on the floor, propped up against the wall and boxes with kit bags etc.; everywhere one looked in the camp one saw men with oedema of the legs and almost every man in the force had the disease to some extent. Japanese were insisting on 120 men going to work and the work party consisted partly of ataxic and oedematous men, scarcely able to stagger to work at which they were flogged and kicked. Every night saw several cases being carried or helped home as best their companions could and then their medical examination continued up to 2200 hours.

Tom Pledger's account of his own condition in July 1943 was equally graphic:

> my weight increased from about 10 stone, 10 lb. to
> 12 stone 8 lb. in 6 days, this consists of fluid in the
> tissues ... I was the same thickness from the top of the
> head to the shoulders and everywhere you have a joint
> it just cracks open. My testicles were the size of a small
> football and every time you walked you carried them
> in your hand.

Many men with beri-beri also suffered from dysentery and diarrhoea, illnesses that were particularly prevalent in the first seven months on Hainan. Of the 594 cases recorded by Aitken, 305 occurred in this period. Three Australians died during an outbreak of bacillary dysentery in December 1942. Diseases of the eye also reached serious proportions at this time. Although conjunctivitis, from which many prisoners were suffering when they arrived on Hainan, disappeared after they became acclimatised to the new environment, other eye complaints, such as night blindness, blurring and dimness of the vision, became common.

Then there was malaria. Many of the men suffering from this disease when they arrived on Hainan began to improve, because the Japanese supplied the requisite drugs (quinine, Atebrin and Plasmoquine). But after June 1943, the Japanese provided only quinine, irregularly and in small quantities. Many men relapsed, and suffered the side effects of repeated malarial attacks: anaemia and enlargement of the spleen.

When the beri-beri outbreak was at its height, the Australians made yet another formal complaint, and several

Japanese visited the camp. Among them was Kikuchi Ichiro who, as the chief medical officer of the Yokosuka no. 4 SNLP, was theoretically responsible for the prisoners' health.[54] To Aitken's fury, the Japanese reacted to what they saw with 'intense amusement'. The victims of beri-beri they seemed to see as the 'fat ladies of the circus'.[55] In late 1943, however, the attitude changed. Possibly this was due to the departure of Takai, who left 'unwept, unhonoured and unsung' in August 1943.[56] He was replaced, in quick succession, by two commanders of the camp who were more sympathetic to the prisoners. The deaths of two Australians in August, and the startling decline in the number of men who were fit to work, seem to have stirred the Japanese into action.[57]

Within days of Takai's departure, the prisoners noticed an improvement in their diet. Meat and eggs were supplied several times a week.[58] Then on 1 September 1943, Kikuchi and the chief intendance officer, Captain Yajima Mishima (who had overall responsibility for food, clothing and pay), visited the camp and undertook to increase the supply of food further – a promise which, in contrast to the many made earlier in the year, was honoured within days. Not only did the rations improve in September (beans, dried peas and some unpolished rice), but the Japanese also resumed supplies of medicines and vitamin B. They also agreed that men suffering from beri-beri should no longer be forced to go on working parties.[59]

This change of policy came too late, however, to save a number of prisoners whose beri-beri was so advanced that their bodies could not respond to the improved diet or even massive dosages of vitamin B. In September, a further nine Australians died, in what became known as 'beri-beri month'.[60] Many of these victims were older men, in whom beri-beri affected the heart. It was 'very hard', wrote Tom Pledger, who worked in the hospital as a medical orderly, 'to sit there and see them grasping [sic] for breath, for about 24 hours before they pass[ed] away'.[61] In October and November the deaths continued, although at a diminishing rate, until in December they finally stopped.

BETTER DAYS?

Conditions for the prisoners improved in other ways under Takai's successors. Concerts, which had been banned in March 1943, were resumed in October.[62] The Japanese were among the most enthusiastic in the audience. They loved the dance tunes played by the battalion band, which had been included in the Hainan contingent, and were enchanted by the improvised costumes and scenery that the Australians managed to create. Thanks to the supplies of clothing brought to Hainan by the Dutch and the creativity of some of the prisoners, the performers managed to appear in anything from dinner suits to Cleopatra's pantaloons. Scenery was improvised out of cement bags and colouring extracted from brick dust.[63]

Sporting activities were also resumed late in 1943, with the support of one Japanese commander, First Lieutenant Chusamara, who was soon given the nickname of the 'sports master'. In December, there was an 'International Sports Day' in which the Australians competed for prizes against the Dutch and the Taiwanese, Sikh and Japanese guards. Diplomatically, the Japanese commander was allowed to win all the events in which he participated keenly. If he seemed to be losing, a false start was declared![64]

More significantly, in November 1943, the Japanese announced that they would pay the officers each month, something which had not been done at any previous stage of Gull Force's captivity. This money was hardly riches. Rates of pay ranged from 85 yen per month for a lieutenant to 220 yen a month for Scott. All officers lost a proportion of their salary in a compulsory deduction to cover the cost of the rations the Japanese supplied. The Japanese rationalised this as a form of compulsory saving, since the money was supposedly held for the officers in the Bank of Taiwan at nearby Hokurei. Despite protests to the Japanese, the officers had to content themselves with the balance of their pay, which did at least give them liquidity for several months. The other ranks never received any pay but were notionally credited with 10 to 25 yen for each day worked. According to the Japanese, the cigarettes and other 'amenities' they sometimes provided for the ranks were given in lieu of pay.[65]

With the pay the officers received, they were able to fund the acquisition of medicines for the hospital and to buy extra food from the Japanese and others with whom they traded. Any additional foodstuff was shared with the troops 'in varying proportions'.[66] At Christmas time in 1943, the Japanese allowed the officers to purchase two pigs that they then shared with the rest of the Australians in the camp.[67] Christmas was thus a reasonably happy celebration. A half-holiday was declared, and many prisoners spent weeks making sure that they had a banquet to smother the homesickness and melancholy that their second Christmas in captivity and their third away from Australia generated.

The king's health was toasted with prickly pear juice.[68] Tom Pledger's syndicate managed by trading some surplus clothing to accumulate two tins of pineapple, two bottles of sugar, four bottles of Chinese whisky, two bars of chocolate and 30 packets of cigarettes. As he said, all they needed was 'a Christmas pudding and few old faces to finish it off'.[69]

LEADERSHIP ISSUES

Such moments of contentment were short-lived and not universal. Scott, for one, was experiencing problems of mental health by late 1942. The evidence on this matter is thin, but according to his own official report, by this time Scott's health had become the cause 'for the gravest concern'. He wrote in 1946:

> The duplicity of the Japanese in sending all the sick men to such a dreadful spot, the total absence of facilities and drugs for the treatment of urgent cases, lack of proper food, bitter resentment and complaints from the men who faced a dreary future of hard manual labour under appalling conditions, all took toll [sic] mentally.[70]

Possibly, the shell shock Scott suffered in the First World War predisposed him to depression in captivity. It is axiomatic now that if post-traumatic stress remains untreated – and Scott seems not to have received any support from Repatriation in the interwar years – it can last longer, and recur in an even more intense form when further traumatic events are experienced. Scott was also confronting the full consequences of his hasty choice in January 1942 to volunteer to lead Gull Force. If captivity on Ambon had seemed unheroic, life in the wasteland of Hainan was even worse. He was trapped in a situation over which he had no control. The Japanese took no notice of him and humiliated him by ignoring his constant complaints.

Progressively Scott withdrew into himself, becoming even more remote from the rest of the camp than he had been on Ambon. Trying to prevent his 'complete breakdown', Aitken and Macrae secured from the Japanese permission to build a small hut, separate from the main barracks, in which Scott could live. This arrangement lasted only a month before the Japanese resumed control of the hut, but according to Scott's later report, this 'brief respite ... [was] sufficient to allow an improvement in his health'.[71] This account, incidentally, was dismissed decades later as 'a lot of rot' by Macrae, who said that the separate hut for the commanding officer was a privilege not a necessity.[72] However, there seems little reason to reject Scott's version of these events. Why would he have recorded a narrative of his own mental frailty that was so unflattering?

It seems that most of the prisoners had no idea of Scott's mental struggles.[73] He rarely spoke to the men but wandered the camp, always in the company of Lieutenant DW (Denis) Smith. The 'bottle and the cork' they were nicknamed, and it is clear from all the reports Scott later wrote that Smith was the confidant on whom he came to rely.[74] Although he played cards regularly with a select group of officers, chain-smoking if his supply of cigarettes allowed, he had a particular bond with Smith. His batman, W Johnson, also formed a deep attachment to Scott, which lasted until the latter's death in 1956.[75] Few other Australians on Hainan, however, felt this way. To them Scott appeared simply remote – and authoritarian.

Undoubtedly this was because of the disciplinary policy Scott continued to pursue on Hainan. Soon after prisoners arrived at Bakli Bay, he called a parade of all ranks to upbraid them for the criticisms that were being levelled against the cooks and the quality of the food: 'everyone', Scott said, 'should be thankful for what [they] were getting because before the war ended things would be much worse'. The men should 'remember that they were Australians and behave like men'. Then in January 1943, when the incidences of stealing and the selling of clothes and watches rose, and there was a case of sodomy, Scott reiterated the warning he had given on Ambon to a parade of all ranks: namely, that cases of stealing, refusing to obey orders and insolence to officers would be dealt with personally by him and he would take the offenders to the Japanese for punishment. He was determined, Scott said, 'to return the men under his command to Australia to be useful citizens for the future. They must retain their self-respect.' Subsequently he assured his officers that he would take responsibility for this disciplinary policy and would accept any repercussions on his return to Australia. He argued: 'It was no use threatening men with punishment when the war was ended. Crimes had to be stopped at once and the type of man who would not respond to appeals for honesty and decency must be ruled by fear.'[76]

In the months that followed, Scott lived up to his threat and handed a number of men over to the Japanese. Their offences were stealing, trading clothing and refusing to obey commands. For their punishment, some men were made to stand to attention throughout the day, holding a dish of water in their hands. Others were given electric shocks – a punishment that the Australian command itself seems to have trialled by placing a wire connected to a dry cell telephone battery on the offender's foot.[77] One of the men who endured such punishment maintained that it was severe. The shocks, as he recalled them, were applied to the whole body and were strong enough to knock a man off his feet.[78]

Scott's reputation among the men plummeted. Alan Murnane's diary entry for 6 June 1943 read: 'Colonel Scott very unpopular with everybody, main reason – his handing over to Japs of our boys for trivial offences.' Like Westley on Ambon, Scott was resorting to formal rather than informal sanctions, and worse, surrendering control over these to the Japanese.[79] Moreover, he was doing this at a time when, in the opinion of many survivors of Gull Force, disciplinary problems were not acute. Although there was a certain amount of stealing among the prisoners, the consensus in later interviews with survivors of Hainan was that generally the discipline within the camp was satisfactory. Like the true Australian digger, so the retrospective narrative went, the men on Hainan disciplined themselves. Why, then, would Scott resort to abandoning his men to an enemy that was known to be cruel?

10

VIOLENCE, AMBUSH AND DIVISION, 1944

The improved situation on Hainan in late 1943 did not last for long. In 1944 living conditions deteriorated again, and 19 Australians were lost when a working party came under attack by Chinese guerillas in April. With this, the prisoners came under intense strain, physically and emotionally. Nonetheless, relations between the ranks in the prison camp generally remained reasonable, with officers and men working together to maintain an underground trading organisation that ensured the supply of vital drugs. The exception, as ever, was Scott. His draconian approach to maintaining discipline, and willingness to hand men over to the Japanese for punishment, erupted in a dramatic incident in August 1944 that marked a complete breakdown in his authority as commander of the prisoners of war. For a brief time, the men themselves took control of dealing with behaviour that threatened the collective good.

THE TRADING ORGANISATION

Japanese policy began to harden again when a new commander of the Bakli Bay camp guards, Fukunaga Tsuneyoshi, was appointed just before Christmas 1943. One of the first things Fukunaga did was to halt the walks that officers had been allowed to take outside the camp. Supposedly this privilege had been abused by officers going too far afield. Henceforth, Fukunaga ruled, only prisoners on working parties would be allowed out of the camp. He also insisted that the officers' gardens, which were beyond the confines of the camp, should be moved inside the wire. This decision restricted food production, since the officers had to recreate their gardens and compete for space within the camp where the soil was becoming exhausted. Confined to the camp, the officers also had fewer opportunities for trading with the local population or scrounging food. On one occasion, Ron Green and some fellow officers had managed to catch a wild pig while outside the camp. The Dutch leader, Kapitz, attempted to protest to Japanese headquarters at the implications of the new regulations, but Fukunaga beat him severely in view of all ranks in the camp.[1]

A few months later the conditions under which officers were paid – itself a recent concession by the Japanese – also changed. Instead of part of officers' pay being available to spend, all of it was compulsorily deposited in the Bank of Taiwan. In theory, the officers could order food from the Japanese to be credited against their accounts, but in practice these orders were never fulfilled. When a Dutch officer, Commander Jaeger, protested at this new system by refusing to sign for the pay which he had notionally received, he was punched in the face by the senior Japanese NCO in the camp.[2]

This hardening in Japanese attitudes threw the prisoners even more on their own resources. Many men kept their gardens going and actually managed to increase their crops in their second year of production.[3] However, they sometimes lost their vegetables to thieves within the camp.[4] As (Sergeant) KE (Ken) Lupson recalled:

[Our] pumpkin came on and it grew and it grew and it grew. The syndicate wanted to pick it but I said, 'No, we'd better leave it there for as long as we can. The longer it's there, the riper it gets, the more vitamins it will have.' We used to argue about this for ages and eventually we said, 'Okay, tomorrow morning we'll pick it.' So we went out and it had gone!

However, if the assurances of many survivors are to be believed, the stealing of vegetables did not reach major proportions on Hainan.

Even more important in sustaining health in 1944 was the securing of medicines from the outside world. The medical officer, Aitken, although only 28 years of age in 1943, was by all accounts a man of extraordinary drive and dedication, as well as passionate temperament. When the Japanese consistently failed to provide medications, Aitken agreed with Quartermaster Miskin, and other officers, to purchase drugs from the Chinese men outside the wire. This trading was funded by using surplus Q (quartermaster) supplies, such as clothing and blankets, as well as any marketable commodities available within the camp.[5] Miskin, who coordinated the purchase and sale of goods for trading, kept accounts of the transactions, which were audited each month by Smith. This official monitoring was intended to quash any suggestion that members of the trading organisation were commandeering Q supplies for their own benefit. Inevitably, however, such accusations were made, given that few of the prisoners knew of the trading organisation and the purposes to which the supplies were being put. Nor did they know of the risks being taken by the individuals involved in the organisation. Some trading took place when the men were on working parties or when the officers were able to work on outside gardens, but many transactions took place at night. The traders slipped under the wire, when the back of the guard patrolling the fence was turned. Even if the guards condoned the trading, as the Taiwanese tended to do, there was always an element of risk. Ron Leech had one lucky, if amusing, escape.

> [A guard] wanted a pair of officer's riding pants, and he had atebrin … I remember putting him in the riding pants, and they came up under his arms (he was only a little fellow). He started to scream and he said, 'These are no good.' I said, 'The trouble with you is you don't understand horse pants.' I got him there, buttoning the fly around his neck! Got his atebrin, gave it to Miskin and took off.

Through the efforts of such men – in all, five officers and 21 other ranks (see Appendix V) – the Australians on Hainan were kept supplied with vital drugs until the end of their captivity. The medicines thus secured included 685 grams of quinine, 22.7 grams of Atebrin, 5685 grams of vitamin B powder, 300 ampoules of vitamin B injections, 12 000 yeast tablets, 24 cubic centimetres of quinine solution, 20 ampoules of emetine and 82 grams of sulphanilamide. These drugs not only kept beri-beri at bay in 1944, they also enabled Aitken to contain most cases of amoebic dysentery and malaria.

In addition, the trading organisation purchased food that sick prisoners needed: for example, eggs, powdered and condensed milk, and oil.[6] It was an inestimable advantage that prisoners on Hainan had over those men left behind on Ambon.

This trading was possible only because certain Chinese people living nearby were willing to collaborate with the Australians – something they did in the face of brutal Japanese intimidation. In one terrible incident, 17 July 1943, 120 Chinese civilians were brought to the prison camp with their hands tied behind them. There, in Scott's words:

> They were crowded into the back of several lorries.
> Waiting for them in the camp was a lorry load of young
> Japanese soldiers with fixed bayonets. Also present were
> a number of Japanese Staff officers and Major Kakuchi
> [sic] … All these officers had drawn their swords and
> were practising various cuts in front of the Australian
> and Dutch prisoners. On the arrival of the Chinese
> prisoners the officers and guards mounted their lorry
> and a procession was formed. The lorries went out in
> front of the Camp and just over a rise.[7]

An hour later the Japanese returned alone, clearly having bayoneted the Chinese prisoners. On other occasions, Chinese civilians were tortured, many of them in the Japanese military police headquarters at Hokurei, others in the POW camp itself where Chen dispensed electric-shock treatment.[8] Often they were humiliated in front of the prisoners. To quote JE (James) McDougall:

In the case of women one of the most popular pastimes was the undressing of the offender and making her stand naked in a position where passersby could view her at the same time placing mud crabs on her body. Japanese coolies would flock around and the women became almost hysterically insane under their insulting looks and remarks.[9]

Another Chinese woman, who failed to remove her headdress and bow as she passed the camp guard room, was knocked to the ground and jumped on, even though she was obviously six or seven months' pregnant.[10] Not only Australians, then, took risks in maintaining the trading between the prisoners and the outsiders.

VIOLENCE

From February 1944, Hainan Island began to be subjected to Allied air raids, and working parties became almost exclusively focused on the preparation of Japanese defensive positions.[11] In contrast to Ambon, the POW camp itself was never attacked. Possibly this was because, on 13 February 1944, a US bomber flew low over the camp at the very moment that the Australians were playing that unmistakably Anglo-Saxon game, cricket. Although the Japanese quickly herded the Australians with their rifle butts into the huts, the crew of the plane had time to see what was happening on the ground. The machine gun that was trained downwards was withdrawn.[12] The camp only suffered damage from fragments of shells aimed at nearby defences.[13]

The rest of Hainan, however, was now a target and the prisoners were driven hard to help improve Japanese air defences. For the first two months of 1944, many men were employed on building a 12-metre-high mound for the siting of a sound-detection locator, used in conjunction with anti-aircraft batteries. In April, some of them were relocated to work at an airfield, digging out gravel from pits. Then, for most of the next ten months the majority of Australians was assigned to constructing batteries to accommodate anti-aircraft guns.

Conditions on all these working parties progressively deteriorated. For several months in the later part of the year, the Japanese stopped giving the prisoners any rest days, or yasmes, as they were known. Earlier, at least one, two or even all Sundays had been free, and occasional special holidays had been allowed, but from July until mid-October the Australians worked ten weeks without any break. Similarly, there were no holidays in the first two and a half months of 1945. As Clive Newnham later said, 'it was just "speedo, speedo"', as the Japanese demand for men to work became ever more insistent. They reduced the number of prisoners allowed to remain in the camp for cookhouse and hospital duties, regardless of the impact on the wellbeing of the camp.[14]

At the same time, the violence that was an intrinsic part of prison life under the Japanese continued. Any minor accident on a working party, and any infringement of Japanese regulations, even if unintentional, was punished summarily. On 26 February 1944, the trucks being used to cart sand up the mound for the sound-detection locator hit each other. No serious damage resulted, but the senior NCO in charge of the prisoners, Tajima, apparently concluded that the Australians were negligent. He lined up 16 men and struck each of them heavily with a shovel handle.[15] Work on the mound became so dreaded that men were not told in advance of their being allocated to this party, lest they have a sleepless night in anticipation. Nor were men assigned to this work by the adjutant for more than one day at a time.[16]

On another occasion in April, a small group of prisoners were halted by Fukunaga as they made their way back to the camp carrying some old bottles that they had scavenged to use as water containers. Even though the Japanese guard under whom they had been working had allowed them to take the bottles, Fukunaga stood them to attention and ordered a Japanese sergeant to punch them all in the face. The rest of the Japanese garrison looked on, laughing.[17] Later in the year, a particularly vindictive Japanese guard, Otsuki Shigetada, made life miserable on the working parties that he supervised. The prisoners nicknamed him 'Gordon Coventry' because his ability to kick rivalled that of the record-breaking Victorian Football League (Collingwood) player.[18]

If the Australian officer or NCO supervising the working party tried to intervene on his men's behalf, as often happened, they too were bashed. Ken Lupson, for example, went over the head of the marine in charge of his working party one day to ask a Japanese sergeant for a rest time for some of his men. The sergeant agreed but when he left, Lupson found himself attacked by the marine wielding a stick with a nail in it.

He kept on striking me and then I made off towards
the barracks to see the Japanese Sjt [sic]. He followed

me and when we arrived at the barracks he ordered
two more Japanese marines to seize me … Two of
them held my hands up and the third bashed me with
a stick. They took it in turns to hold and hit. While
this was going on, the Jap Sjt was watching through
the window and laughing.[19]

The Japanese seemed not to appreciate that their violence
was counterproductive, in that it reduced the prisoners'
efficiency. One group working on a battery of guns on the
beach near Hasho were harassed in a seemingly irrational
way. In Sergeant F (Francis) Elliott's words:

After lunch, I was detailed with about seven men
to carry a heavy anti-aircraft barrel and its parts to
a position on top of a rock. It was a steep climb of
about 150 feet. Steps had been blasted in the side of
the rock. We had to negotiate this steep climb on a
narrow track. The marines did everything to impede
our progress, such as purposely wobbling the load,
and pulling back on the rear man. It was extremely
dangerous as we were skirting the edge of a dangerous
cliff … Throughout the afternoon the men carrying
these loads were bashed with sticks, punched, kicked,
pushed about … After the gun was in position heavy
ammunition cases had to go up, two men to a case.
There was one odd man, Pte Woodward, and he was
made to carry a case on his own. A marine waited for
him in a bend of the track and flogged him with a
stick all the way to the top … When we returned to
camp everyone was thoroughly exhausted. No one had

any boots, but had been forced to walk over broken rocks all day and everyone was badly bruised.[20]

THE HOBAN AMBUSH

Given the poor working conditions and the dreariness of camp life, some Australians welcomed the chance in March and April 1944 to go on a working party that was stationed at Hoban, a Japanese outpost in the hills some 24 kilometres from Bakli Bay. The work there would be much the same as normal – building a road and a fort, and chopping wood – but at least it would be a change of environment. The food might also be better.[21]

However, soon after the prisoners arrived at Hoban, the commandant of the Japanese garrison there, Warrant Officer Okabishi, warned Ron Green, who was supervising the working party, that there were hostile Chinese guerillas operating in the area. For some months they had been setting fire to stores and raiding Japanese barracks.[22] Now, Green was told, they might come down from the hills.[23] He protested at his men being placed in such danger, but Okabishi laughingly assured him that his guards (some 30 to 40 men) would guarantee the prisoners' safety. All Green could do was advise his men to be alert and be ready to take cover, should any trouble eventuate.[24]

On 8 April, 24 of the Australians were assigned to work on the road being constructed through dense scrub from Hoban to another village 8 kilometres to the north. Another ten prisoners were directed to chop wood just near Hoban. Three prisoners, including Green who was suffering from an attack of diarrhoea that day, remained in the camp. At about 9 am, the road party left Hoban in a truck, accompanied by 15 Japanese and Taiwanese guards. When they were some 2.5 kilometres from the camp, they heard firing. The truck stopped, and the driver jumped out and raced down the road, leaving the Australians to face a full-scale armed attack. Whether they were nationalist troops, communist guerillas or some other armed band is unclear. J (John) McMahon later stated:

> At the sound of a bugle, fire was opened up at a rapid rate from the scrub on both sides of the road. Some of the guards, and some of our men were hit at once … Some of our men jumped off the truck, three got underneath, and some ran to the side of the road and took cover behind trees. I remained in the truck. I had no choice, as I was wedged in by dead Jap. guards. There was a lull in the firing and then another call on the bugle. I looked over the edge of the truck and saw about 100 Chinese charging at the truck, from a ravine. I ducked my head and the next thing I knew they were all over the truck. They stripped the dead Japanese guards and took their arms. I lay quiet beside Pte Cornell and pretended to be dead. They went through Pte Cornell's pockets and took his cigarette tin … I closed my eyes. There was a shot right beside me and I felt Pte Cornell stiffen out. I lay still while they pulled my water bottle from around my neck. Another bugle call sounded and they all left.[25]

Another Australian, FA (Frederick) Hillier, also lay with McMahon in the truck. His boots, socks and water bottle were taken off him and, then, as a guerilla stood on his buttocks, he was bayoneted three times in the back. Incredibly, the wounds he suffered were only slight and he survived the attack.[26]

During the attack, some other Australians decided to make a break for safety. They raced along the road only to be confronted as they came over a rise by four or five armed Chinese men lying in the middle of the road. One of the Australians, CG (Cyril) O'Donnell, was shot in the shoulder. Another, Alan Murnane, managed to escape unharmed into the scrub. It was, as he wrote in his diary, a 'miraculous escape'.[27]

The immediate death toll from this ambush was nine Australians, as well as a number of Japanese and Formosan guards. Some prisoners were killed in the initial volley of bullets; others, at close range, by blows or stab wounds.[28] The guerillas did not discriminate between the Japanese guards and their prisoners. Three other Australians were wounded, one fairly seriously, and were taken to the Japanese hospital at Hokurei. The dead were placed in another truck and taken to Hoban, where one of their surviving colleagues washed them, laid them out and rolled them in blankets.[29]

Another ten prisoners disappeared.[30] What happened to them we do not know. According to JH (John) Nelson, who was captured briefly after the ambush, they were taken hostage by the Chinese guerillas and invited to join forces with them.[31] Nelson himself was left at a Chinese village with two other wounded, AH (Arthur) Chenoweth and EM (Ernest) Ratcliffe. As these men were 'too stiff' to walk further, Nelson made his way back alone to Hoban.[32] Chenoweth and Ratcliffe were never seen again. Likewise, the other eight Australians vanished. Despite an extensive postwar search (more of this later), their remains were never found.

In the days that followed the ambush, Green pleaded with Okabishi to be allowed to mount a search party to search for the missing men. The Japanese assured him that they were doing this themselves, a promise which they seemed to fulfil, albeit in a dilatory fashion.[33] By 13 April it seemed that the missing men must have left the district entirely, and Green persuaded the Japanese to allow what remained of his working party to return to the camp at Bakli Bay. Initially, Okabishi planned to bring more Australians to Hoban to replace their casualties, but Green pre-empted this by writing to his superior officer, the commanding officer of the district.

The ambush at Hoban cast a pall over the Australian prisoners, given that almost as many men were dead or unaccounted for as had died in the previous 12 months.[34] Furthermore, they been killed by Chinese soldiers who should presumably have been on the Allied side.

SCOTT'S LEADERSHIP CRISIS

Despite this tragedy, morale among the Australians seemed to have been at reasonable levels for much of 1944. Scott, almost predictably, would have us believe otherwise. His 1946 report on Gull Force depicted the prisoners as disintegrating into feuding individualism under the pressures of captivity as early as January 1943. By that time 'most of us [were] in a low mental state bordering on despair' and stealing was becoming prevalent.[35] This negative version of events, however, is not entirely confirmed by other contemporary records or the recollections of survivors in the 1980s. Aitken agreed in his postwar medical report that many prisoners did become depressed, given the bad food, the trying climate, the lack of news and tobacco, the hard and monotonous work, the boredom, the many minor and unnecessary restrictions and 'the continual pestering' by the Japanese on working parties.[36] Tom Pledger, too, wrote in his diary on 10 October 1944:

> there are moments when you wonder if you can really
> carry on, the monotony of it all, nothing to see but
> faces you know off by heart, you know just what
> they'll say and you feel like screaming at them and
> having a go at the Japs by yourself, but then comes
> the despair, what good will it do you, you'd only get
> belted to death and so reason takes its place and you
> start to dream.

Such moods were accentuated by the fact that the prisoners received only one batch of mail from home in the three years on Hainan, in June 1944, and at no time were they allowed to write to their families.[37] As it was, the Japanese on Hainan were cut off from mainland Japan from late 1944 and might not have been able to receive or forward mail from that time. The celebration of Easter and Christmas was also obstructed by the Japanese.[38] But, on balance, Aitken concluded that 'most men maintained a cheerful outlook and occupied themselves well, and it was usually found that these men maintained a better standard of heath and recovered more quickly from disease than those who were depressed'.[39]

On the individual level, it would seem, many prisoners managed their mental health by talking to their mates, dreaming of home, fantasising about food, and doing much the same things as their colleagues on Ambon did: playing cards, gambling, reading what books were available in the camp, planning their future, and listening to the occasional 'educational' talks given by those with expertise – and sometimes those without![40] Depression also was kept at bay by the friendships within syndicates, and the small but costly acts of generosity, like sharing rations with a sick mate or scrounging extra food for his birthday.[41]

It seems that Scott presented an unremittingly negative view of the Australians' morale not just because of his own depression, but because he needed to vindicate his practice of handing men over to the Japanese for punishment. Already controversial in 1943, this policy caused a mutiny in the camp in October 1944. Private LHG (Lewis) Roy was discovered using the bathhouse at a time when the 'showers' were reserved for the use of the officers. Egalitarianism on Hainan, it seems, had its limits. Roy exchanged words with (Lieutenant) AB (Alan) Growes, accusing him, so one source later claimed, of cowardice during the fighting on Ambon.[42] The matter was referred to Scott, who then handed Roy over to the Japanese. The only account we have of Scott's motivation is from Smith, who wrote at the time: '[Scott] considered it his duty to maintain order. He owed a responsibility to the whole force, but in particular to his officers, and he must protect them if the welfare of the whole camp was to be considered.' Scott was also influenced, Smith maintained, by the way that the Japanese consistently undermined Kapitz's authority, by releasing men he had stood to attention on the parade ground. In Scott's eyes, this made Kapitz a laughing stock within the camp.[43]

Scott did not anticipate, however, that the senior Japanese NCO in the camp, Akiyoshi Hideo, known to the prisoners as 'Heavy Harry' because of his harshness on working parties, would beat Roy severely. According to the adjutant Clive Newnham, who witnessed the punishment, Roy was suspended by his hands from a special stand and then beaten on the back with a heavy pick handle. After a fairly lengthy period, Akiyoshi handed the stick over to three other guards who continued the punishment. Roy was rendered unconscious but was revived with water to be beaten again. By the time the punishment was over, his back, buttocks and legs were covered with bruises, and he required hospitalisation for some two weeks.[44] Roy, in fact, survived this beating and the war, but his postwar medical record notes that he was admitted to hospital in November 1945 with 'old injury back'.[45] He died of malaria in January 1946 and was buried in Springvale cemetery with the inscription on his grave, 'His duty bravely done for his country. In God's care. RIP.'[46]

The effect of Roy's beating on Australians of all ranks was explosive. Scott himself was shattered by the severity of Roy's punishment and, so Smith thought, was for a short time in danger of losing his reason.[47] The ranks, however, spared Scott no sympathy. Seeing him as 'the old man who could not see fit to punish [Roy] in a white man's way but handed him over to the little yellow bastards for punishment', they despised him with an intensity that would last well after the war.[48]

Australian officers, too, were livid. Some of them had already had serious disagreements with Scott about the administration of the camp. Aitken, for one, had quarrelled bitterly with him over the question of whether Japanese demands for working parties should always be met fully. In the doctor's opinion, men who were approaching exhaustion, but were not technically ill, should be allowed a few days' rest in the hospital, which would enable them to build up their reserves. Scott apparently thought that such a scheme risked infuriating the Japanese unnecessarily. As Aitken saw it, Scott's general policy was:

> selfish, weak and nearsighted, his attitude to the
> Japanese conciliatory, and generally marked by a
> readiness to temporise and to accept and pursue any
> course that would obviate his personal conflict with
> them, even in matters of the utmost importance. ...
> Although he often stated that he would accept the full
> responsibilities for his actions (presumably after return
> to Australia) he was always ready and willing to pass
> on and did pass on to others this responsibility for any
> course of action. It was pointed out to him, in vain, by
> myself that his later acceptance of responsibility was of
> no value to sick or dead men, and that the extra work
> and worry resulting from some of his actions fell on
> other shoulders.[49]

Aitken also resented Scott's attitude to the trading organisation. At first, it was claimed, Scott took little interest in it.

Then he interfered in its operations in a way that limited its effectiveness and reduced the amount of drugs it acquired.[50] Miskin, too, who had crossed swords with Scott on many occasions before late 1944, thought that Scott protested too little to the Japanese about the prisoners' conditions. Instead he left it to more junior officers, whose rank the Japanese seemed to respect less, to play this role.[51]

Scott, for his part, maintained that the impact of his protests would have been devalued, had he pestered the Japanese continually over minor matters. It was a better strategy 'to keep himself aloof until such time as something was really needed urgently'. He conceded that some of his officers would not understand this approach. They would come to him with 'many requests of minor importance and could not see the point when he would not take the matter up personally'. But in time, he claimed, he was vindicated in that when he went to the Japanese authorities for a personal interview he was 'always treated with respect'.[52]

The day after Roy's beating, some of the officers confronted Scott. According to Smith's account of the meeting, Aitken and another officer dissociated themselves from the disciplinary policy that Scott had adopted, while the other officers, in more temperate language, urged that the policy be abandoned. To this Scott agreed.[53] Certain officers considered going further, wresting control of the camp from Scott by certifying him as insane. Such drastic action, however, required the evidence of two doctors, and although there were several Dutch doctors operating within the camp, Aitken does not appear to have been willing to break Australian solidarity to the point of seeking their cooperation.[54] In any case, the plan to depose Scott almost certainly did not have the approval of Macrae. To the last, he remained conscious of his duty to obey his commanding officer. Although he was appalled at what had happened to Roy, Macrae did not wholly disapprove of the policy Scott had pursued, believing that it had had some effect in maintaining discipline within the camp.[55] When Roy asked Macrae to intervene for him before he was handed to the Japanese, he was told 'that he richly deserved whatever he would get'.[56]

The officers may have held their hand, but the troops did not. Shortly after the beating of Roy, some of the men decided to establish a vigilance committee within which the men themselves would decide how to deal with instances of stealing. Memories of this committee vary considerably but it seems to have consisted of between six and 12 men. According to two accounts, it was elected by popular vote. At least one of the committee had been a victim of Scott's disciplinary policy in the past. He had endured the pain of electric shocks administered by the Japanese and was adamant that anything was preferable to this. Almost certainly the committee dealt only with the offence of stealing and the 'sentences' it meted out were mild. A number of strokes on the buttocks seems to have been the most common punishment; and, despite some lurid retrospective accounts of men 'screaming' while being hit and dying later from their injuries, it seems unlikely that anyone suffered serious injury. Aitken, who viewed the whole experiment with some ambivalence, would have ensured that the punishment was strictly controlled. It was not so much the pain as the public humiliation of the beating and the ostracism that often accompanied it, that were meant to stop the offenders from repeating their crime. In this, the activities of the vigilance committee seem to have had some success, and after only a limited number of 'cases', it was disbanded.[57]

Not surprisingly the vigilance committee was controversial, given that the use of even mild physical punishment was repugnant when men were afflicted with hunger and illness. Apparently many within the camp disapproved of its activities.[58] Yet, the vigilance committee never aroused the passion that the cage on Ambon did, even though, like the cage, it was a form of punishment administered by Australians against Australians. Perhaps the difference was that the committee was probably formed by the men themselves, although by some accounts Scott knew or approved of it.[59] Its activities were, therefore, not tainted by the sense of 'them and us' that might have destroyed any similar effort at discipline had it been initiated by the officers. In other words, even though the committee was not universally approved, it was in some ways a kind of democratic sanction, congenial to the values of the AIF.

The tensions that these events of late 1944 and early 1945 created in the camp on Hainan were fortunately contained by the fact that, while Scott's standing within the camp was destroyed, relations between the men and the rest of the officers seem to have remained reasonable. As on Ambon, some officers were not popular, but a solid core of officers retained the respect and confidence of their men. Perhaps this was because the stresses of captivity on Hainan, even at their worst, were less intense than on Ambon. The officers were less identified with failure, with all that that implied for their claim to competent authority. On the basis of the oral evidence, it seems also that certain officers on Hainan manifested the personal authority that was essential in captivity. Aitken was clearly one: his extraordinary capacity for work, his ingenuity in tackling new medical problems, his obvious distress at losing a patient, his rebellious streak that made him take on Scott as well as the Japanese, with whom he was fearless, and his wild but lovable nature ('He could fight like a thrashing machine'): all these qualities seem to have endeared him to the Australian prisoners.[60]

Macrae, too, was a strong personality who commanded respect, even from those who did not like him personally. His forthrightness, his 'guts' and his willingness to suffer physical punishment with obvious fortitude were qualities remembered years after the war.[61] As the gulf between Scott and the men widened, Macrae was able to fill the vacuum of leadership to some extent. So far as the other officers were concerned, it was those who risked their own safety to battle for their men's interests and were seen to act as 'one of the boys' in the camp who emerged from the experience of captivity retaining their men's respect. An officer like Ron Green, who was beaten viciously while supervising a working party in March 1945, was admired many years after the event.[62] So, too, were other young lieutenants like Sam Anderson, Colin McCutcheon, and GW (Geoff) Sutcliffe.[63] The fact that other officers figured less prominently in the memories of survivors may not, of course, tell us much about their competence or their personal qualities. The quartermaster Miskin and the adjutants, Turner and Newnham, for example, had many confrontations with the Japanese that required great physical and moral courage, but they were less visible and rarely in the public eye.

11
SURVIVING TO THE END, 1945

In the final year of Gull Force's captivity on Hainan, conditions deteriorated even further. While the Japanese stopped demanding working parties, they reduced food rations erratically, and the whole POW camp was threatened with malnutrition and starvation; 26 Australians died. In contrast to Ambon, however, the prisoners could still access supplies from outside sources and, since they did not have to perform exhausting manual labour, the majority survived until liberated by the Americans at the end of the war. Six prisoners, led by Macrae, even managed to escape in April, and joined Chinese Nationalist forces with the aim of assisting any invading Allied forces to liberate the camp at Bakli Bay.

AN END TO WORKING PARTIES

The year 1945 began much as usual, with working parties on ammunition dumps at anti-aircraft batteries, at the Japanese barracks at Hokurei and even at Hoban, to which wood-chopping parties continued to be sent after the disaster of April 1944. In February, construction focused on the building of roads, railway sidings and anti-aircraft machine-gun pits. In a sign of the changing war situation, the pits were now even inside the POW camp. The working day often lasted from 7:30 am to 8 or 9 pm, depending on the transport available to take the men to and from the worksite. For nearly three months the Japanese allowed no free days, while continuing to demand at least 90 men each day. When Newnham protested that, in order to meet the Japanese demands, sick men had to be included in working parties, the Japanese proposed, yet again, that the numbers employed on camp duties should be reduced. This time, they suggested that the latrine squad, which included fairly healthy men, should be dispensed with.[1]

In March 1945, the main work was constructing pill boxes and defence works on the beach near Hasho. This was the scene of some especially violent incidents. On 13 March 1945, HW (Harold) Beamsley, who was struggling to carry a heavy load of coral, was attacked by a number of Japanese guards. Eventually reduced to unconsciousness by their blows, he was revived with water, only to be beaten again. His arm was broken. When he was left to lie at the edge of the worksite, several Japanese soldiers made a point of pulling and twisting the broken limb.[2] Similar attacks occurred on other Australians working on the beach party in this same week. Green, the supervising officer, tried to intervene and stop the Japanese mistreatment of his men, but he was set upon by two guards who assailed him with blows which eventually brought him to the ground.

The vicious beating of Beamsley provoked Scott and Newnham to protest strongly to the Japanese lieutenant then in charge of the prisoners, Yoshida Tomonobu ('The Boy Wonder'). In response, Yoshida, who was living some distance away, visited the camp on 16 March. After seeing Beamsley and hearing details of the other beatings, he apologised for the treatment of the Australians in the preceding week. He promised the camp a long overdue three-day holiday.[3]

As it turned out, the respite from work was to last until the prisoners were liberated late in August.[4] For these six months they were confined to their camp, surrounded by a new electrified fence erected on 16 March 1945 to replace the previous barbed-wire barrier.[5] This exemption from work – a stark contrast to the 'Long Carry' at Ambon – almost certainly helped many Australians to survive, but it reduced the opportunities for trading with the local population, at the very time that Japanese food rations were shrinking. The electrification of the fence also increased the risk of slipping under the wire at night. Several prisoners continued to do this, and the secret trading organisation functioned until the end of the war. But the dangers were made clear when Scott was injured on the fence on 2 May 1945. Noticing one of the Q staff, Sergeant N (Norman) Finn, outside the fence, checking rations in the rain, Scott tried to throw him a waterproof cape. His arm touched the top wire of the fence, and he was thrown heavily, breaking his arm as he fell. Given the lack of plaster or splints, his arm had to be set, without anaesthetic, with a piece of old galvanised iron from a roof.[6]

ESCAPE

Soon after the fence was electrified, several Australians escaped. This was the first escape attempt by Australians on Hainan. Not only was this camp a far greater distance from

Australia than Ambon, but the penalty for escape was known to be dire. In February 1943, six Dutch prisoners had escaped, only to be captured within a few days and apparently executed. Scott had been told by the Japanese headquarters that he and his officers would be held personally responsible for any further escapes from the camp.[7] It was also clear that, without good contacts outside, it was very difficult to escape on Hainan, which was infested with bandits, few of whom spoke English.[8] The difference in physical appearance also made it impossible for Australians to pass as local people.

By February 1945, however, it was clear that the war in the Pacific had turned against the Japanese. One Dutchman and one Australian, who had learnt to read Japanese, provided prisoners on Hainan with information about the progress of the war, gleaned from stolen Japanese bulletins.[9] Early in 1945, friendly Taiwanese guards also told the prisoners that an American landing on Hainan was expected daily and that, should this eventuate, the Japanese planned to execute their prisoners at once.[10]

Scott, therefore, gave his permission to a group of Australians to escape, in the hope that they would be able to assist any invading forces to rescue the other prisoners immediately. For reasons of security and practicality, the numbers in the escape were small: only six, including Macrae. As the senior officer, he made detailed preparations for the escape, slipping under the wire at night to contact local villagers who might provide guidance to the headquarters of the Chinese nationalist troops on the island. Green accompanied Macrae on one of these forays and later stated:

we walked for what seemed like hours across the
plain without finding the village he wanted; and
then by the position of the moon we knew it was
time to get back to camp if we wanted to be there
before sunup. It was still dark when we got back to
the wire fence around the camp; and I remember as
we lay on our bellies just outside the wire watching
for the Jap sentry he whispered, 'I'll go first'. 'No,
I will.' It seemed that whoever went first stood the
bigger risk, but the Major 'pulled rank' and silenced
me with 'I'll go first, you wait, and that's an order.'
So we both duly slithered under the wire and
returned to our quarters without mishap.

On 17 February, however, Macrae was caught trying to leave
the camp at night. After being interrogated by Akiyoshi,
he was forced to stand to attention in front of the guard
house for 72 hours. During this time, he was allowed no
food, except what was smuggled to him by the prisoners.[11]
However, on a quick visit to the latrines he contacted Green,
who hid incriminating papers in Macrae's quarters before
the Japanese could discover them. Eventually Macrae was
released, possibly because of the way he conducted himself
during this ordeal and the reaction of his fellow Australians.
To quote Green again:

as each of our work parties left the camp in the
morning, and returned at night, they perforce had
to pass the guardhouse – and the Major. As they did
so, the officer or NCO in charge of each work party
would order the party 'March to attention–party, eyes

left (or right)'. And the men going past saluted the Major, and in doing so, scorned the Japanese.[12]

Hence, planning for the escape party continued, encouraged by the fact that on 24 February 1945 and early in April, two groups of Dutch prisoners escaped, apparently successfully.

Finally, on the night of 16 April, after the moon had set, Macrae and five other Australians stole out of the camp.[13] As they did so, US aircraft started to attack the area. Ron Leech, who was a member of the escape party, later recounted:

> Just as we got out ... the Yanks came over and dropped phosphorous flares. Campbell and I were outside the fence, and the other three were still inside. We were only ten yards from the fence, and the Japs ran up to the fence and started shooting at the planes over our heads. I think the only reason they didn't see us was because of the blinding flare, and when the light went out, it was pitch black.

Once clear of the camp, the escapers set off on a supposedly well-planned course, but when morning dawned, they found themselves, to their horror, sleeping under bushes that were only 45 metres from a Japanese post! They had to lie all day in the heat, unable to move for fear of drawing attention to themselves. Several times they thought they heard the bushes around them being beaten. But it was only the goats the Japanese had let out to graze.

When darkness came, and the moon had set, the party moved off again in an easterly direction. The small quantity of rice and water they brought from the camp soon ran out, so when the next day dawned, two men went to look for further supplies. Returning a while later, they found the others (in Macrae's words) surrounded by 'twelve picturesque characters – each with a dirty piece of cloth tied in a piratical bow on one side on his head. They were armed with muzzle loaders and bows and arrows [and] did not look [the] least like coastal Chinese.' These men took the Australians to a village where they were marched between two rows of Chinese men each pointing a Luger gun at them. Fortunately, however, the village was sympathetic to the Chinese Nationalists, and the Australians were provided with rice, poultry and vegetables – luxuries after the diet at Bakli Bay. Then, after an 'interminable' wait, the local headman arranged for them to be taken to the Chinese nationalist headquarters.

A guide appeared, reminding Macrae of those 'professional gamblers as portrayed in western movies'. With him in the lead, the six Australians, together with ten Chinese soldiers, ten local bearers and one Dutchman, who had foisted himself on the escape party at the very last moment, set off. For 14 days they made their way across Hainan. Their route was wildly circuitous, presumably because they had to evade both the Japanese and local bandits. Overnight they sheltered in Chinese villages, witnessing the kind of rural life that had not changed in centuries: gambling at fan-tan, labour-intensive rice cultivation and flocks of ducks following their leader down to the village pond. Once the party stopped for some days at a kind of recruitment and training centre. There, the Australians had to stand like statues as the soldiers sang an endless dirge which, for all the visitors knew, could have been the Kuomintang national anthem or a bawdy army ballad.

Eventually the party reached the villages of the indigenous peoples of Hainan and the rugged mountains at the centre of the island. By now Macrae was so weak with dysentery that he had to be carried on horseback. The horse lost its footing and slipped, together with Macrae, into a fast-flowing mountain stream. On another occasion, it became stuck when crossing what had seemed to be a dry paddy field. Macrae almost expected to spend the rest of the war in that mud. But if the journey was exhausting, the mountain scenery was magnificent and a joy after the semi-desert around Hasho.

On 30 May 1945, the Australians finally arrived at the Chinese Nationalist headquarters, where they met the commanding Chinese general and his troops – and also the Dutch prisoners who had escaped from the camp some weeks before them. The headquarters had a markedly non-military atmosphere given the presence of women, children and fowls. Here these Australians spent the rest of the war. One of them, M (Myles) Higgins, died in June of cerebral malaria. The other five gradually recovered their strength with the aid of Chinese medicine and food. They asked to be given weapons and to be included in some offensive operations, but there was little action against the Japanese. The months were whiled away in drinking rice spirit (which was as close to methylated spirits as anything Macrae had ever tasted) and in consuming the good food and coffee the Chinese provided. The thought of what might be happening to their fellow prisoners back at Bakli Bay always troubled them.

HUNGER

They had reason to worry, since conditions in the POW camp continued to deteriorate. Even before the Australians escaped, the Japanese controls had tightened. On 27 March they sprang a surprise search of the camp, confiscating goods ranging from food to sheets and air cushions from the hospital. New irritating regulations were announced, including a ban on movement between the various huts in the camp at night, even for medical personnel like Aitken.[14]

Most alarmingly, the food ration was cut in March 1945 to 300 grams per man per day. The Japanese issued only two pork chops for the 211 Australians in the camp. The decision was taken to raffle them, an event that caused considerable hilarity.[15] But hunger soon returned. Daily meals were cut to two per a day: one at 10 am, the other at 6 pm, each consisting of a mug of rice. Meat, fish and vegetables were no longer issued. According to Aitken, the prisoners were receiving only 1470 calories per day. Even firewood, to cook meals and boil water, was in very short supply.[16]

Then, on 8 April the daily rice ration was cut to 200 grams, and finally, on one day early in May, fewer than 170 grams of rice were issued for each man. The Japanese NCO responsible for issuing food, Corporal Obara Naoji, often issued less than even these small rations. The 'rice', too, included the sweepings from the floor. Once the Australian kitchens sifted 7.7 kilograms of sand from their rice ration. Another time they found, in the rations, pieces of rope, straw, stone, rat droppings and cigarettes. To pre-empt complaints about the quantities he was issuing, Obara confiscated the

Australian Q store's scales on 18 April. The quartermaster's task of dividing the two days' rations into meals of equal size became almost impossible. All protests to the Japanese were met with laughter or blows.[17]

The prisoners tried to maintain their gardens, but this took a physical effort that many could not manage on such a poor diet. In any case, the soil within the camp was almost exhausted after two and a half years of cultivation.[18] Rats, then, which the Australians had considered vermin when they first arrived, became a delicacy. Pledger recorded in his diary on 3 May 1945, 'nearly everybody has a rat trap. We cook them with onions, tomatoes from out of our garden and they taste like beef stew.' Snails, too, were highly prized. '[I]t is funny,' Pledger wrote, 'to see grown men down on hands and knees chasing snails, horrible slimy things but still protein.' Frogs, wood grubs and geckos were also devoured in these hungry days.[19]

During this food crisis the hostility between Miskin and Scott erupted again. Sometime in April or May, Scott decided to partially suspend Miskin from his duties as supervisor of the Australian kitchens. He claimed that a different officer might have a better chance of improving the Australians' diet. Miskin, in turn, claimed that over the years he had developed many techniques for maintaining hygienic conditions in the kitchens and extracting the maximum food value from the Japanese rations. Vegetables were steamed for the minimum period necessary; food was served as soon as it was cooked; vegetable water was recycled as 'soup', and all water was boiled for at least 20 minutes. In Miskin's and, more importantly, Aitken's opinion, many of these practices lapsed when the supervision of the kitchens changed.

Late in May, as deaths from malnutrition mounted, Aitken confronted Scott. A tense argument ensued, after which Scott agreed to Miskin's resuming responsibility for drawing up menus and issuing instructions as to how to prepare food correctly. He insisted, however, that Miskin should deal with the kitchen staff through Scott himself.[20] This rather clumsy arrangement continued until, under growing pressure from officers in the camp, Scott agreed to Miskin's complete reinstatement.[21]

By this stage the worst of the food crisis was over. In early May, after Scott and other officers had bombarded the Japanese with complaints, the Japanese warrant officer in charge of food, Hirata Sadao, visited the camp. There he was confronted with a 'skeleton parade' of about 30 men who were so emaciated that their ribs and other bones protruded clearly. Ashamed at what he saw, Hirata, who could speak English comparatively well and had tried in the past to do what he could for the prisoners, promised the Australian and Dutch commanding officers that the food situation would improve.

Like so many of Hirata's previous promises, which had been negated by the obstruction of his superiors and Obara, this undertaking was only slowly and partially fulfilled. But from 10 May onwards, a gradual and slight improvement in the prisoners' rations occurred. The rice rations remained very low, but some sweet potato (fresh and dried) was provided to add to the diet. This had the effect, when it was issued in lieu of rice for three weeks, of producing painful intestinal fermentation in many of the men. After further complaints by Aitken and Miskin, and another two visits by Japanese personnel on 8 and 10 June, milk, fat and small quantities of vegetables, meat and fish were included in the prisoners' rations. The scales that Obara had confiscated were returned to the Australian kitchens.[22] These changes almost certainly helped to limit the death toll on Hainan. But still, in July the daily intake of calories was 1180 per day.

ILLNESS AND DEATH

On this diet most of the camp was unwell. Beri-beri again became prevalent. From seven cases in January 1945, the number of sufferers rose to 26 in June and 32 in August. As before, the Japanese provided little vitamin B – only 75 grams in the first three months of the year, none at all in April and May, and an inadequate amount after supplies resumed in June. Thanks to the trading organisation, Aitken did have some additional sources of vitamin B, but the amount required to counter the disease in each patient's case was higher than in 1943. Eventually, six of those suffering from beri-beri in 1945 died.[23]

Many prisoners continued to have dysentery. They, too, often failed to respond to treatment, given the lack of medication and nutritious diet. Pneumonia and other respiratory infections were also common, as were skin complaints. The lack of vitamin C meant that most men developed impetigo, while sweat rashes, tinea, dermatitis and boils testified to the dirt and lack of soap in the camp. Many workers had infections and wounds of the feet because the Japanese had provided very little footwear since 1942. Finally, from March to May 1945 another outbreak of paratyphoid fever erupted. Even though the Japanese had stopped giving inoculations against this disease after June 1944, this episode proved less severe than the first epidemic a year before, which had claimed a number of lives. Fortunately, tropical ulcers, even though they occurred, never became as prevalent and horrific a problem as they did on Ambon.

Over seven months in 1945, the average weight of the men in the camp dropped from 57 kilograms to 50 kilograms – and many of these men were swollen with fluid as a result of beri-beri.[24] Everyone felt weak, listless and lacking in energy. Simply to get up from the *bali bali* or to stand on parade required so much effort that some Australians blacked out.[25] In order to conserve men's strength, the official rising time was extended until later in the day. Aitken wrote after the war:

> Most of the men presented a ghastly picture walking
> around like skeletons with pot bellies and oedematous
> legs and faces and with various sores and boils
> etc. dressed with any old scrap of rag. We were all
> extremely weak and I don't think a single man was
> capable of running 100 yards and it took the greatest
> effort to carry out the normal functions of life, let
> alone any extra duties.

For many prisoners the agony of hunger was compounded by their having roundworm. In Aitken's estimation, 15 Australians died directly from starvation in the six months between March and August 1945. Complaining at first of weakness and a mild swelling of the feet, these men usually developed rapidly spreading areas of wet gangrene over the feet and lower legs. Then after a few days of diarrhoea, they suddenly and quietly became comatose. Death came within a couple of hours.[26] Despite these symptoms, the cause of death could never be recorded as starvation. Like Ikeuchi on Ambon, the interpreter Chen would not allow this.[27]

Aitken seems to have performed miracles in these most difficult of circumstances. His 'hospital' was one of the most primitive huts in the camp, which the Australian medical personnel shared with the Dutch.[28] The roof was full of holes, and patients ended up wet when it rained. Infectious cases could not be isolated, and the bedding was improvised out of whatever the prisoners could find. Most items for maintaining hygiene – soap, nailbrushes and towels – remained unavailable. Very rarely was electricity supplied, and for the greater part of the time, the Japanese forbade even kerosene lamps and candles.

As for the chronically scarce medical equipment: the Japanese issued only two glass syringes, four thermometers, one old pair of scissors and two suture needles. The one microscope, which they supplied in December 1942, was taken away 12 months later. Plaster was rarely supplied, so fractured limbs, like Scott's, had to be set with improvised metal or wooden splints. Even though there was a large and well-equipped Japanese hospital only 8 kilometres away at Hokurei, the Japanese never provided facilities for examining blood or urine. They admitted only a few of the very serious surgical cases among the prisoners. One of these, it seems, they accepted simply because the Japanese medical officer, Kikuchi, happened to be showing some of his friends around the camp on the day the man became ill with appendicitis. On another occasion, Kikuchi ignored Aitken's pleas to admit to Hokurei hospital an Australian suffering acute intestinal obstruction. In desperation Aitken operated, using chloroform anaesthesia, but the patient died.

The occasional Japanese officer did show some interest in the prisoners' health. Apart from Hirata, the most notable case was Commander Abe, who helped Aitken in 1944 by supplying equipment, food and considerable assistance in the diagnosis of diseases. His aid, however, was limited by the indifference of Kikuchi, who, after showing some interest in the prisoners in late 1942, failed to be concerned about them. His successor, Kano, who arrived in 1945 when the health of the prisoners was at its worst, was conspicuous by his failure to appear at the camp at all.

While coping with these difficulties, Aitken was the Australians' dentist as well, (since Marshall had stayed on Ambon). He had no dental equipment and the 'treatment' he offered was limited to extractions with forceps and no anaesthetic. In nearly three years on Hainan, the men received only one toothbrush and one packet of tooth power. Surprisingly, however, their teeth seem to have survived comparatively well.

Aitken himself was far from well and he could only maintain these efforts with the help of his medical orderlies.[29] They, too, were grossly overworked, since their numbers were reduced on Japanese orders from 14 to six in August 1944, when there was an average of 100 patients in the hospital. Often ill themselves, they continued to work, assuming complete responsibility for large numbers of patients and tending them with cheerfulness, energy and devotion. Captivity again, while it reduced some people to a ruthless concern with their own preservation, brought out in others extraordinary qualities of selflessness.

Between January and August 1945, 26 Australians died, all but one of them in the months after May. The dead were buried in a cemetery some 3 kilometres from the camp. The coffins had to be carried on poles slung beneath them supported by six to eight men. The Japanese very rarely provided a truck. At times they even withheld supplies of wood for coffins and, until the war ended, they ignored the Australians' attempts to replace the crosses that had rotted away. On one occasion, to the fury of the padre, VE (Vincent) Cochrane, they even insisted that two bodies be stripped of the thin blankets in which they had been wrapped.[30]

LIBERATION

Despite everything, more than two-thirds of the Australians in Hainan were alive, if not well, when the war in the Pacific came to an end. The prisoners had known for some time that the war in Europe had ended and that the Japanese were nearing defeat. Allied aircraft appearing over Hainan could only have been operating from aircraft carriers nearby. But it was hard not to despair. Tom Pledger wrote in his diary (which he addressed to his family), on hearing the news of Germany's surrender on 8 May 1945:

> It must be great news to you, but it is marvellous to us, but now every minute counts as we are living on plain rice and the hot winds are ruining our gardens, so although a couple of months does not mean a thing to you it means life and death to us.

And on 1 July:

> Each time I write I say I will be seeing you soon and
> I say it again as it must shortly come as by the law of
> averages we have overdone our turn of suffering and
> it must break soon, God willing.

The prisoners did not learn of Japan's defeat until some days after its capitulation. But they took heart from some unusual attention from their captors. The medical officer visited the camp on 17 August, senior officers apologised for the poor state of the food, and on 19 August, Kano even offered to transfer the sick prisoners to a Japanese hospital at Hasho. On 22 August, the Japanese provided more drugs than the Australians had seen for years, the first cigarettes they had had for eight months, and a pig. Then on 25 August 1945, a Japanese fatigue party arrived in the camp and painted the letters PW on the roof of the hospital hut – the first time this had been done during the prisoners' three years on Hainan. Later that day a US aircraft flew over the camp and dropped leaflets.[31]

Finally, the Australian and Dutch adjutants were called to the Japanese guard house. Green, who had taken over from Newnham as adjutant a few months earlier, gave this account of what then followed.

> We were not in the guard house for long. Speaking
> in Japanese, one of the officers (not the commandant,
> who was sitting with his head bowed, in a most
> dejected fashion) said, without preamble 'The war is
> finished' … I think perhaps a little stupefied, we asked

for a repeat, and he said it again … We said we didn't
believe him, and asked the Jap when the war had
finished. When he replied '15th August', we said,
'But that was ten days ago. If that is true, why
haven't we been told before?'

It was not until the Japanese had produced one of the leaflets
that the US aircraft had dropped, which said that US troops
would be arriving at the camp by parachute the following
day, that Green and the Dutch adjutant were convinced.
They raced out of the guard house to spread the news. In
Scott's words, the scene was 'indescribable. Everyone shook
hands, many were silent, as if unable to realise that it meant
life and freedom, and some broke down completely.'[32] As
Green remembered it, most men had one priority, to break
the news to their sick mates, and a stream of men made for
the hospital.

Liberation came soon.[33] On 27 August 1945, nine American parachutists were seen dropping from the sky some
distance away. They did not appear at the camp, but the
following day Scott, Kapitz and their adjutants were taken in
a Japanese lorry, still guarded by soldiers with fixed bayonets,
to the hospital at Hokurei.[34] There, in Green's words:

We were directed to a hut, and when we entered I saw
a tableau that is burned on my brain until the day I
die. There was a long table, and on the far side of it,
and at the ends … were nine magnificent looking men,
seated … Sitting around the wall were several dozen
Japanese officers, some of senior rank up to admiral.

The Americans, headed by Major Jack Singlaub, explained that they were members of the US agency, the Office of Strategic Services. They had come to Hainan with the objective of liberating the prisoners in the Bakli Bay region. However, the hostility of the Japanese, many of whom were still armed, was forcing them to tread warily at first. Hence their failure to appear at the POW camp the previous day.

Within a day or two the Americans returned to the prison camp, bringing with them not only concentrated food, medicine and the coveted Chesterfield cigarettes, but also the astounding news of the atomic blasts that had ended the war and, many prisoners believed, had saved them from dying of starvation. The attitude of the Japanese in the camp, who until then had still been somewhat truculent, changed perceptibly. The electrified fence was dismantled, the prisoners' cemetery was tidied up and a film show, in Japanese unfortunately, was staged the night the Americans appeared. More truckloads of Japanese food and medicines started to arrive. On 29 August, the Japanese even went so far as to produce the pay that the Australian officers had notionally been credited with over the last 14 months but had never received. Somewhat to the Japanese paymaster's surprise, Miskin, with the approval of Scott, refused to accept the money. As he pointed out in an outburst of anger, that money could have saved many Australian lives if it had been made available when it was due.[35]

The following day, 30 August 1945, all the prisoners, except for a few who were so ill that they could not be moved, were taken to the Japanese hospital. From there they set off, on 31 August, by train for the port of Sama. Maddeningly, the train was derailed by Chinese guerillas still active on Hainan. In Green's words:

> As we rattled over rickety looking bridges across deep
> ravines in the lonely countryside, I thought that any
> hostile Chinese really could do a job on these trains
> as they crossed the bridges; but thank heavens it
> happened on a flat plain. The train was derailed, as our
> carriage jerked to a stop we spotted a few Chinese in
> the scrub a few hundred yards away – and I spotted
> something else; Rocky Ned [a survivor of the Hoban
> ambush] had leapt out of the train and was sprinting
> away into the scrub … no doubt remembering that was
> the way he had saved his life at the Hoban ambush.

Word was sent back to the railhead for another locomotive, which hauled the train back to Bakli Bay. There the prisoners, suffering an acute sense of anticlimax, had to spend another four days.

The journey to Sama was again attempted, and successfully completed, on 5 September 1945. From there, six days later, Singlaub's unit located and rescued Macrae and his escape party. On 12 September, Scott and a select number of Australian, Dutch and Indian ex-prisoners left for Hong Kong in the Royal Navy destroyer HMS *Queenborough*. At the British colony, Scott and Smith dined at Government House with Rear-Admiral CHJ Harcourt, the recently appointed commander-in-chief of Hong Kong. The rest of the Australians arrived in Hong Kong on 18 September, and later that day the whole contingent set sail for Australia. Tom Pledger wrote to his fiancée, Jessie, from the hospital ship.

Well love at last we have said goodbye to that land of bad memories. Land fit only for Asiatics not white men. One [British nursing] sister started to cry & believe me, I couldn't stop crying myself as the nervous strain is too great. But just think of it dearest one of that day when we will be together once more after all these years of separation ... I won't sleep tonight because we have nice mattresses & just think sheets, white sheets & pillow, it seems a shame to get between them. ... my memory of you & my folks has often been the only thing which kept me going thro' these last 3 years.[36]

Stopping briefly at the US base at Manus Island en route, the now ex-prisoners reached Sydney on 3 October. The final leg of the journey home for the many men who came from Victoria was completed by train on 4–5 October. They were at last reunited with their families and could do the simple things they had dreamed of for more than three years. Green, for one, went to the local corner store and bought a pound of broken biscuits. Then he walked around the family garden, smelling, picking and even eating the flowers.

THE LOST

However, many of the survivors, not only from Hainan but also, and especially, from Ambon, faced the pain of meeting the families of those men who had died in captivity. For the past three and a half years, these families had been in a state of suspense, hoping that their father, husband, brother or son had survived. The Japanese never supplied complete lists of the Allied prisoners they held, and the Labor Prime Minister John Curtin was reluctant to allow families to broadcast messages through the Australian Broadcasting Commission. As he saw it, the prisoners of war were being exploited by the Japanese as 'propaganda bait' and messages would play into the enemy's hands.[37] In time, the government did agree to allow some outward broadcasts and telegrams through the ICRC, but inward mail from prisoners of war was infrequent and confined to relatively uninformative standard postcards. Nothing was known of the situation on Hainan and very little of Ambon. The brother of one of those men who seemingly disappeared without trace later wrote: 'As the months and years went by without knowledge of her son's welfare, but with constantly recurring reports of Japanese brutality in other theatres of war, I watched my mother's health deteriorate, both physically and mentally.'[38]

Now, with war's end, it was clear that hundreds of Gull Force men were never coming home.[39] This news often came after an agonising period of waiting. Families saw friends getting an official notification of death and jumped to the conclusion that their man was alive, when he was not. A statement regarding the losses at Laha, to the effect that these men were presumed dead, was not made until December 1945. As the daughter of Horton Newbury, the senior officer at Laha who was bayoneted or beheaded in February 1942, wrote: 'It must have been a very long wait for my mother. I was seven at the time and as we lived near the Middle Brighton pier used to imagine a large ship stopping to let him off on its way up to Port Melbourne. It was not to be.'[40] One Gull Force mother had to wait until late March

1946 for official notification of her son's death. She was so traumatised, her daughter recalled, that she did not speak for three weeks.

> The thing that hurt her most was never knowing.
> You bring a child into the world, and there's an abyss
> for so many years ... She couldn't believe that she had
> been cheated of ever seeing her son after waiting and
> hoping. ... Everyone who was touched by Ambon has
> a crying heart which will never leave them. So little
> was said and so much damage done.[41]

THE ELEMENTS OF SURVIVAL

Some 66 of the 267 Australians sent to Hainan died during their three years on the island, most of them of disease.[42] Each of these deaths was an individual tragedy, but the losses on Hainan were far fewer than on Ambon. How do we explain the difference?

This question raises a broader one: why is it that certain individuals survive the profound trauma of being a prisoner of war when others do not? This is a complex issue, given that many of the factors that ensure physical and mental resilience cannot be readily measured. Nor can we attribute personal resilience to one variable alone. It commonly results from a mix of variables, and that mix, being specific to individuals, defies generalisation. Among those scholars who have written on prisoners of war, there is no consensus about what determines the chances of survival.[43]

The members of Gull Force interviewed 40 years after

their captivity similarly expressed varying – and sometimes contradictory – views on this question. Some suggested that older men were more resilient than younger; they had some experience of life and a greater degree of self-awareness with which to confront the challenges of captivity. Others thought that younger men survived because of their greater physical strength. Some claimed that married men had a greater will to live because they were sustained by the thought of their wives and families awaiting their return. Others, to the contrary, thought that it was a liability to be anxious about the safety, welfare and even fidelity of families at home.[44] Perhaps, it was also suggested, a prisoner who was educated and had superior intelligence had an advantage when planning strategies for survival. But, possibly individuals with less formal education were able to weather the emotional storms of captivity with greater ease.

On certain questions there was some agreement. Men with larger frames, it was thought, died more rapidly because of their need for extra food (a conclusion with which JE Nardini, writing about American prisoners in the Philippines, in some respects agreed, although in his opinion it was the tall men with thin, delicate frames who were less resilient than the thick, stocky individuals).[45] Many survivors also emphasised the importance of their state of health before they became prisoners. For yet others, survival was a matter of luck and chance: their number simply 'wasn't up'.

Almost universally, Gull Force survivors noted the importance, in the struggle for survival, of will and mental outlook: a sense of humour, an unquenchable optimism, and a fierce determination to live. Aitken wrote shortly after the war about the men on Hainan:

depression was very difficult to combat, and when [it was] present the patient rarely did well and men often gave up the battle for life and allowed themselves to drift away. Once this sort of hopeless despair set in they never seemed to respond to any mental or material treatment but simply died, no matter what disease they had, or how serious it was. On the other hand a number of seemingly hopeless cases … determined to live and keeping a most cheerful outlook on life and by hard battling either recovered or kept themselves alive for no other apparent reason than this mental effort.[46]

Some of these impressions are consistent with observations made about prisoners of war in a variety of other places.[47] But none can be proved empirically. No systematic medical research was conducted immediately after Gull Force's return to Australia, and the medical examinations conducted when the men of Gull Force enlisted in 1940–41 seem not to have survived in their entirety in the national archives. The attestation forms that the men of the 2/21st Battalion and ancillary units completed when they volunteered for service are of some use, but the information they provide is partial and at times unreliable. For a variety of reasons, men sometimes falsified their age and the details about their personal lives.

So far as they have any value, these attestation forms do not suggest any strong correlation between the deaths in Gull Force and the variables of age, marital status and prewar residential status.[48] As already noted, the only factor that can be said to have influenced survival was rank. While nine officers on Ambon died, five were the victims of Allied bombing, and four died of other causes.[49] On Hainan no officer died of any cause.

The survival of officers need not be the subject for moral judgment. Their exemption from manual work, which was of inestimable value in the struggle for survival, was enshrined in the Geneva Convention of 1929. Innumerable other officers, in prison camps throughout the world during the war of 1939–45, enjoyed this right and other privileged treatment, including being interned in separate camps.[50] But in the dire circumstances that Gull Force faced, we might ask why officers did not offer to substitute for sick men on working parties, if only to give them temporary relief from the manual labour that was destroying their health. Perhaps the Japanese would not have countenanced any kind of rotation system, but it seems not to have been considered as an option.

What of the higher survival rate on Hainan as opposed to Ambon? The explanation surely lies not in any differences between the individuals who formed the two cohorts of Gull Force but in the different treatment meted out by the Japanese. The conditions on Hainan were harsh, and the death rate high by the standards of POW camps throughout the Far East, but at times of severe medical crisis at Bakli Bay, the Japanese relented. They provided just enough extra food and medicines to prevent the catastrophe that occurred on Ambon. Moreover, the Japanese authorities tolerated, if only unofficially, the trading between the prisoners and the outside world that ensured that some drugs were available to treat the sick. And in the last year of the war, when rations were low, the Japanese did not force the men on Hainan to perform manual work. Scarce calories were not wasted on exhausting physical labour.

On Ambon, none of this applied. In the last year of the war, the Japanese authorities failed to provide the food or medicines that might have arrested the mounting death rate. They cut rations, banned the private production of food, and prohibited contacts between the prisoners and the local population. A trading organisation was never possible. Even if it had been, it is unlikely that supplies of medicine on blockaded Ambon would have been readily available. Ikeuchi and Shirozu claimed as much in their self-defence when being tried as war criminals after the war. To quote Ikeuchi:

> That so many POWs died one after another in the latter part [of the war] was really deplorable [sic] thing, but this was solely due to the complete blockade by the Allies plus intensified aid raid causing the dearth of provisions, medicines etc. Therefore, this was not caused from our intended mal-treatment nor from our intrigues.[51]

Predictably, Ikeuchi's protestations of innocence persuaded no one, and he was executed by shooting on 25 September 1947. But the remoteness of Ambon no doubt contributed to the appalling death toll there. As the Allies advanced across South-East Asia, the Japanese themselves became prisoners, of the Allied blockade and aerial bombardment. Isolated and remote from their homeland, where US bombing was laying waste to their cities, their homes and their families, they vented their fury on the nemesis within their reach, the prisoners of war in Tan Tui.

PART VI
AFTERMATH

12

JUSTICE AND BURIALS

By late 1945 all survivors of Gull Force were home, but for many of them the war 'never ended'.[1] So far as they could, these men resumed the civilian lives that had been disrupted in 1940. But the memory of their captivity stayed with them, and many struggled to achieve what is now popularly called 'closure'. If such a state is possible – and on that a healthy scepticism is surely warranted – it was facilitated by a number of processes: the bringing to justice of those responsible for the atrocities inflicted on Gull Force; the burial of the dead of Gull Force in a culturally appropriate and sensitive manner; the creation of a purposeful and stable personal life after the war; and the participation of veterans in rituals of remembrance and commemoration that invested the losses of the war years with some meaning.

WAR CRIMES TRIALS

First, the search for justice. It was a high priority for all Australians – not just the surviving prisoners of war but also the government and the public – to bring to account the Japanese responsible for war crimes.[2] This was far from easy. Some presumed war criminals had already died. One of the more vicious commanders at Tan Tui, Ando Noburo, for example, committed suicide on 15 September 1945 by drinking a cup of coffee containing potassium cyanide while on a ship at Surabaja Harbour.[3] The senior officer thought to be responsible for the mass executions at Laha, Rear-Admiral Hatakeyama Koichiro, had been killed in action in China.[4] The identity of other war criminals could not necessarily be proven conclusively. Even though the liberated prisoners filled out questionnaires and made sworn statements about Japanese brutality, the names they gave the Japanese were often nicknames, some of which were assigned to more than one guard. The details provided were not always helpful: of one possible criminal it was said he had 'several good teeth – prominent teeth – very effeminate, tall ... Walked round with shirt out. Very screechy voice'.[5] Few Australian prisoners remained long enough at their camps to identify their Japanese captors. On Ambon this task then fell largely to the Dutch warrant officer, Waaldyk, who remained on the island because he was married to a local woman. Able to match nicknames with some individuals and to demonstrate some of the torture methods used on the prisoners of war, Waaldyk would become a witness at the later war crimes trials. However, he was not familiar with all Japanese personnel charged with war crimes. The Australian officer who immediately started work in anticipation of the trials on Ambon, (Captain) John M Williams, had to extract from the local Japanese headquarters the details of all the officers and men of the unit responsible for guarding the prisoners of war.

The trial of some Japanese began on Ambon, in January 1946, but the court soon moved to the island of Morotai.

Ambon had to be returned to the control of the Dutch colonial authorities, and it was feared that Australian guards close to the sites of their compatriots' suffering might assault some Japanese. Or, to the contrary, there were some reports of fraternisation, such as the exchange of cigarettes or liquor, between the guards and their charges. Morotai was not only more distant from the place of the prisoners' suffering; it also offered more of the infrastructure for court proceedings. While very humid and prone to malaria, it had become, during the war years, one of the largest Allied bases in the south-west Pacific, serving as a staging post for assaults such as the attack on Balikpapan, Borneo, in July 1945. A range of army personnel were still based there, and could serve as the guards, clerks, stenographers and cooks needed to support the war crimes trials. Morotai would thus host some of the major trials about Ambon, although Rabaul, New Britain, and Manus Island and other venues were used, for example, for the trials relating to the Laha massacres.

Once the accused Japanese had been transferred from Ambon, they were crowded into an enclosure nicknamed 'PW Cage Morotai'. Ikeuchi, now at the receiving end of punishment, found much to protest about. He later claimed that on his arrival he was stripped naked, searched and robbed of many of his possessions: his purse containing some 150 yen, his fountain pen, uniforms and two suitcases containing personal effects.[6] Then, at 'the concentration camp' in Morotai, he was interned with a hundred other accused Japanese in a hut with a dirt floor. At early dusk they were ordered to put up mosquito nets and retire to bed. The dim light, Ikeuchi asserted, made it impossible 'to spell out the necessary documents of evidence' and prepare his defence.[7] Beyond that, Ikeuchi complained about the poor rations – he said he was already suffering from beri-beri – and alleged that he was beaten several times. To cite his complaint to the authorities:

> Notwithstanding that my whole body was out of order
> on account of blows inflicted by Indian guards and
> especially severe lumbago made me [sic] hard to walk,
> I was forced to go to the working place at double-quick
> every morning. … Whenever [Sgt Churchill] saw me
> limping along he gave me hits almost every day on
> my hip, buttock and thighs still aching with bruises.
> Moreover, with a heavy sand bag on our shoulder, we
> were compelled to make pits for latrine and for waste
> water of bath, digging the ground mixed with reef with
> pick-axe and shovel down to the depth of 16 feet or
> until water vein was found.[8]

Ikeuchi further alleged that in September 1945, one Australian, Private Williamson, punched him, breaking five teeth: 'the blood flowed out of my mouth copiously. I sank to the ground owing to distress and severe pain'.[9]

Few Australians had any sympathy for Ikeuchi, especially as he showed no signs of contrition. According to a report on his trial in the Melbourne *Sun News-Pictorial*, he 'glared defiantly as Captain Williams unfolded the sorry story of Japanese brutishness', while another of the accused, Nakamura, 'hung his head'.[10] But Ikeuchi's allegation about his beatings could not be ignored after he wrote to his wife, Ikeuchi Kotoko, in a letter smuggled to Japan by a repatriated Japanese man, Takata Haruo, and soon circulated in Japan and the Australian press. The Australian authorities, therefore, ordered a medical examination.[11] This concluded that Ikeuchi did lack seven teeth, but that this might have been the result of gum disease rather than an assault. Ikeuchi's body and face bore no scars to corroborate his claims that he had been continually beaten.[12] To verify this – or was it humiliate Ikeuchi? – his naked body was photographed from all angles. These images remain on the archival record, attesting, at this distance in time, to the humanity of even this man.

The war crimes trials that brought Ikeuchi and the multiple other Japanese personnel to account were criticised, both at the time and later, as being potentially unfair, a victors' justice motivated by revenge.[13] Certainly, politics always played 'a conspicuous part' in the prosecutions of the Japanese, and the processes and procedures of the trials were established when public emotions about Japanese atrocities were at their height.[14] The Australian media seemed to take guilty verdicts as given. They assiduously reported the details of atrocities on Ambon – the 'Dutch garden party', the 'Long Carry', the beating of men with tropical ulcers, the dismantling of picric acid bombs and the starvation rations of 1945 – and denounced the 'bestial sadism' of the enemy and the 'murderous villain', Ikeuchi.[15] Furthermore, the court proceedings were conducted in English, and the accused struggled to follow their cases, given that few interpreters were available. Notably, too, one trial of Japanese personnel from Ambon had 91 defendants.[16] Its huge scale caused William Simpson, the Australian Judge Advocate (a lawyer appointed to assist the court on matters of substantive and procedural law) to register an 'emphatic protest' in early 1946. Finally, the normal rules of admissibility of evidence were relaxed. Hearsay evidence was admitted, as were the sworn statements by prisoners of war written after their liberation. Since these men had returned to Australia, the defence counsel had no chance to cross-examine them and test whether they had exaggerated the extent of their mistreatment, as some of the accused Japanese would complain.[17]

Yet, in defence of the trials, the Australian legal personnel conducting them displayed integrity and an acute awareness that justice had to be seen to be done. Moreover, the charges against many Japanese were conventional war crimes, not the more novel and controversial charges used at the Nuremberg and Tokyo war crimes trials, of crimes against humanity and crimes against peace. The procedural regimes employed were also consistent, and although the Japanese accused were not familiar with the Australian legal system, they were assigned legally trained, independent counsel. Some Japanese defendants even thanked these counsel for their efforts. Most importantly, there was no presumption of guilt. One in every three of the Japanese accused in the Australian trials was acquitted. Leading scholars have thus concluded that 'no systemic abuse occurred in the trials'; and that it would be 'wrong ... to say that politics trumped justice in Allied dealings with Japanese war criminals'.[18] That said, the rate of successful petitions against the courts' findings or sentences was not high and there was 'a glaring problem' of significant disparities in sentencing.

In the trials held at Morotai, members of the Japanese 20th Garrison Unit (Marines), who managed the Australians at Tan Tui, were charged with executions, physical beatings and torture, forcing sick prisoners to go on working parties, and denying them adequate food and medicines.[19] That such crimes were committed was never in doubt, but it was more difficult to establish legal culpability. At what level were orders issued? Could junior soldiers claim that they had only been obeying orders? Ultimately, only a few of the Japanese on Ambon were condemned to death. Among them were Shirozu Wadami and Ikeuchi Masakiyo, the managers of Tan Tui; Hatakeyama Kunito and Tsuaki Takahiko, two of the executioners at Laha; Kawahara Kiyomune, Ueda Kōsei and Kakinuma Morio, the killers of Simpson, Morrison, Solomon and Wadham in April 1945; and Shimakawa Masaichi and Miyazaki Yoshio, executioners of Boyce in April 1945. The prison terms given to other guilty Japanese personnel ranged widely, from one to 20 years.

Ikeuchi's death sentence was handed down on 15 February 1946, but it was deferred because he was needed as a witness against other alleged war criminals. This gave him time to petition for the mitigation of what he claimed was an 'unjust and unreasonable' sentence. He was, he argued, only the camp interpreter, obeying orders from above; and he had spared no effort to help the prisoners. Evidence to the contrary, for example, from Waaldyk, van Nooten and Westley, was unreliable. The suffering of the prisoners in the last year of the war was a result of 'the perfect blockade from the sea, and air by the Allies'.[20] To bolster his case, Ikeuchi wrote to one of the American prisoners in Ambon, Clyde A Rearick, asking him to testify that he 'devoted [himself] to the welfare of PW and never did [he] commit an awful ill-treatment to PW'. To his own wife he wrote:

Preparing for the worst I have enclosed my hair
as a substitute for my ashes. I thank you for your
companionship and love. I ask you to take care of
the young children. I know you must be suffering
under economical and spiritual hardships in post-war
Japan. You must not hesitate to ask support from the
Government when you find it too hard.[21]

His wife, in turn, petitioned for a retrial, saying that Ikeuchi's sentence 'shocked me almost to death'. He was merely a language interpreter. He 'has been always considerate and sympathetic for others'.[22] His siblings, too, also attested that Ikeuchi was very kind and only a subordinate obeying orders.[23] Two of Ikeuchi's professional colleagues in Japan claimed that he was 'a man of straight-forwardness and righteousness, sympathetic toward the weak and the powerless and always ready for public services and full of love for his home'. His family 'are spending gloomy days and nights worrying over the fate of their beloved loved one. We see another war victim here too.'[24]

This was not the man that any survivor of Gull Force recognised. On 25 May 1947 Ikeuchi was executed by firing squad. So, too, were Shirozu and Miyazaki. Kawahara, Kakinuma, Ueda and Shimakawa had all been shot in early May 1946.[25] Tsuaki Takahiko was executed in 1951. Hatakeyama Kunito's sentence, however, was reduced to 20 years and remitted on 11 May 1956 when the policy of interning Japanese war criminals was reviewed in the light of Japan's value to the West as a Cold War ally. The testimonies in his file noted that Hatakeyama's family suffered during the atomic bombing of Hiroshima, in which they lost their property, and that his relatives were now living in poverty.[26]

The Australians imprisoned on Hainan had to wait until 1948 before the Japanese responsible for their maltreatment faced justice. These trials were conducted in Hong Kong where the British were themselves holding war crimes trials.[27] Once more, experienced Japanese defence counsel were in short supply. Those recruited by the Australian court had to learn Western courtroom procedures and war crimes law as they went. The Japanese defence counsel were also reportedly in great financial distress. Their allowances had been paid to their dependants in Japan and the monthly allocation of £10 in Hong Kong had been suspended when the Australian authorities took over responsibility for them (from the British) in December 1947. Though the Australian Government, for some reason, starved the Australian court of resources, the Australian Army had to move to restore the counsels' allowances.

At the trials, which began on 5 January 1948, 17 Japanese soldiers were charged with inhuman treatment of the prisoners of war that contributed to their deaths, bodily injuries, damage to health, and physical and mental pain. The case against the Japanese relied on the normally inadmissible evidence used on Morotai – sworn written statements by former prisoners – but also included the testimony of three Gull Force survivors, Clive Newnham, Tom Pledger and Colin McCutcheon, who travelled to Hong Kong to appear at the trial. In their defence the Japanese mounted similar arguments as at Morotai: they had been only obeying orders; the evidence of the prisoners was untrue or exaggerated; and the imminence of Japan's defeat placed severe strains on all personnel on Hainan.

All defendants were found guilty. Most were given prison sentences ranging up to 20 years. This included the medical officer, Kikuchi Ichiro; the camp commander, Fukunaga Tsuneyoshi; 'The Boy Wonder', Yoshida Tomonobu; 'Gordon Coventry', Otsuki Shigetada; and the NCO responsible for food distribution, Obara Naoji. Two of the more senior personnel, Aoyama Shiego, the Commanding Officer at Bakli Bay in the last six months of the war, and Kano Terutami, the chief medical officer over the same period, were sentenced to death.[28] Presumably this was because they had presided over the so-called 'starvation period' when 19 Australian and some 24 Dutch prisoners died of starvation or malnutrition.[29] As with Ikeuchi and others who were condemned, Kano's family petitioned on his behalf, his mother writing that her heart was 'torn asunder'. Her son was a Christian:

> It is unthinkable that such a gentle and loving son would deliberately commit the crime attributed to him. His being taken to Hainan Island under such adverse conditions and appointed to such a post was a great misfortune indeed. In a broad sense, it may be said that the responsibility for such acts lies with the entire Japanese nation.[30]

Ultimately, the death sentences of both Kano Terutami and Aoyama Shiego were commuted to prison sentences.

BURYING THE DEAD OF HAINAN

These war crimes trials served to comfort some survivors of Gull Force, although one interviewee later expressed dismay at the death sentence imposed on Ikeuchi. But equally important, for Gull Force veterans coming to terms with their trauma, was the knowledge that the dead in Ambon and Hainan had been given an appropriate burial. This process, like the search for justice, proved complicated.

It was assumed in 1945 that Australia's war dead would be buried overseas, as had been the practice after the First World War. Soon after Germany surrendered, the Australian Government agreed to the proposal of the Imperial War Graves Commission (IWGC) that Britain and the Dominions should once again bury their dead near 'where they fell', rather than bring their bodies home.[31] But the politics and geography of the Asia-Pacific region soon made it clear that it was not possible to replicate what had been done in France, Belgium, Gallipoli and Palestine after 1919.

First, in Hainan, the Chinese civil war that ended in Communist victory in 1949 complicated efforts to discover what had happened to the Australians missing after the 1944 Hoban ambush. A small detachment of Australians went the island in March 1946 to find out.[32] It was a high-risk operation, with Nationalist and Communist forces battling for control of the island and bandits still operating in the more rugged areas. As the Australian unit travelled almost completely around the island, it took pains to appear neutral to all contending parties. It conducted an extensive search but gleaned only incomplete and conflicting intelligence. The villagers of Hoban seemed afraid of reprisals if they said anything about the ambush. The Communist general, who might have been able to provide reliable information, could not be contacted. One hearsay report suggested that the Australians had been taken to a beach and shot, and their bodies thrown into the sea; another said that they had died from weakness and starvation; yet another surmised that they had stayed with the guerillas and continued to fight with them by choice, even after the war with Japan had ended. It was even mooted that the Australians had somehow managed to leave the guerillas and escape from Hainan, making their way by sampan or junk to French Indochina. None of this was ever proven and the leader of the investigating unit reported to Australia that the missing men were in all likelihood dead and buried in unmarked graves in an unknown location. There the matter rested until the 1980s.

Second, the political instability in Hainan made it impossible to create an IWGC cemetery at Bakli Bay, where the dead of Gull Force had been interned during the war. Instead, an Australian War Graves unit exhumed the bodies in early 1946, and shipped them to Hong Kong, then a British colony. Here the remains were reburied between 17 March and 2 April 1946.[33] However, given the obstacles to creating permanent war cemeteries in Hong Kong – the competition for scarce land, the steep terrain that required terracing, and some unanticipated construction difficulties – the military authorities in Melbourne decided almost immediately to exhume the bodies of Gull Force once more.[34] They opted then to rebury them in Yokohama, in Japan, a transfer that took place in mid-1946.[35]

Yokohama had some practical advantages. It was IWGC policy to concentrate graves, allowing 'economy in beautification and maintenance', and to locate them at sites that would be accessible to relatives. In late 1945, the Australian War Graves Service already had some responsibility for the Yokohama cemetery, and the remains of prisoners of war who had been held in Japan were to be buried there, as were any Australians who might die while serving in the British Commonwealth Occupation Force (BCOF). Bodies drawn from across the region could at least 'rest together'.[36] Moreover, it was not uncommon to bury Australian dead in the territory of their enemies. Gallipoli was the pre-eminent example from the First World War. Over a thousand Australians would be buried permanently in Germany after the Second World War.[37]

However, for Gull Force, Japan was different – abhorrent. On 28 September 1946, the Melbourne *Argus* published a letter from none other than Scott. Seeking, it seems, to redeem himself with Gull Force survivors by championing this cause, Scott claimed that it was 'an incredible insult' to bury in Japan the men who had died as a result of the 'incredible and fiendish brutality and bestiality, inhuman conduct and deliberate murder' of Japanese officers, medical officers and other ranks. The decision to move the remains to Hong Kong was understandable, given the problems of access and upkeep on Hainan but, Scott said, 'No words of mine can describe the horror' he felt at the proposed transfer to Japan:

To move these graves deliberately to Japan itself, to ask relatives to visit Japan and all that that country conjures up, to visit the grave of a loved one in such surroundings so far removed from peace and quiet thought, must not be allowed. ... The burial ground of Australian soldiers murdered by Japanese, by whatever means, should be found and cared for in any other place in the world, but not Japan.[38]

The families of Gull Force agreed and lobbied their members of parliament.[39] One WS Farrell wrote on behalf of his sister-in-law: 'I am quite sure that many other wives and mothers feel that this action is an insult to the memories of their dear ones. On looking at the map of the Pacific it is not such a great distance from Hainan to Australia where they should have been interred.'[40]

The wider ex-POW community also spoke out against the Yokohama burials. 'Weary' Dunlop, now president of the Australian Prisoners of War Relatives' Association, wrote to Prime Minister Ben Chifley on 11 October 1946:

We do not regard the Japanese as an honourable foe, and the action contemplated ... would be most distasteful to the feelings of relatives and friends, and, I venture to submit to the majority of Australians generally. ... the distance from Australia to Japan is so great as to make it impossible for many relatives to ever visit the graves of their men.[41]

The RSL, too, took up the cause, telling the former minister for the army, Forde:

After the treatment received from a vile enemy while in their hands, we feel it is repugnant to think that their last resting place should be in Japan, particularly when it needs two movements over long distances to achieve it. These brave boys did their best for Australia, and as a result gave their lives, and we feel Australia should do its best for them.

If bodies did need to be relocated, then they should be moved 'to the soil for which they fought and died, i.e. Australia, or taken and placed with their pals at Ambon where they were captured'.[42]

Faced with this outrage, Forde conceded that the transfer of Australian dead from Hainan to Yokohama was 'naturally repugnant to Australian national feeling … [and] offensive to the relatives and next of kin of the servicemen concerned'. He recommended to Chifley that the remains should be returned to Hong Kong.[43] However, the Cabinet decided on 5 November to leave the dead of Gull Force in Yokohama.[44] The incident, it admitted, was most regrettable, but it was not in the best interests of the prisoners' relatives that the remains of 'these unfortunate men' be further disturbed. Instead, they should remain in Yokohama close to the Australian dead of the war years and of BCOF.[45]

There, the matter ended. Only a few newspapers reported, without editorial comment, the Cabinet decision to leave the remains in Yokohama.[46] The veterans and the families of Gull Force acquiesced. It was not much of a consolation to have the assurances of the government that, in future, the next-of-kin of deceased servicemen would be consulted about such decisions; that, if the opportunity arose, the remains of all Australians buried in Japan would be reinterred; and that access to the cemetery land would be guaranteed in the forthcoming peace treaty with Japan.[47] In time, Yokohama would actually become one of the most beautiful of the IWGC cemeteries around the globe, but it would never be a major site of pilgrimage for Gull Force. The graves of the Hainan dead remain there to this day.

BURYING THE DEAD OF AMBON

On Ambon, the burial of Gull Force's dead faced different challenges. The most urgent and distressing task was actually reburial: that is, locating the bodies of the hundreds of Australians known or suspected to have been executed (including airmen who had been shot down). Nothing had been heard of the more than two hundred Australians deployed to the Laha airfield; and the grave sites of the men who had been executed near Tan Tui were unknown. With the aid of local intelligence and captured Japanese guards, who were set to digging, the Australian authorities soon found a number of mass graves. Four, near Laha, revealed a ghastly tangle of bones, skulls and personal effects – watches, a Bible, rings, lockets, engraved cigarette cases, even a newspaper clipping announcing a soldier's engagement. Alas, the exhumation was not well managed. Journalists wanted photos, curious onlookers were tempted to take souvenirs, and a monkey supposedly ran off with a watch.[48] But the human remains, sometimes identified, sometimes not, were taken across the bay to be reburied in the war cemetery being developed on the site of Tan Tui camp.

This cemetery's development, as it turned out, was protracted. Within months of the war ending, the businessman who owned the land on which the POW camp had been located offered to donate the site: 'when Australians come to Ambon to visit the graves of their sons', said TK Lim, 'I will help look after them'.[49] But the development of an official IWGC war cemetery at Tan Tui was stalled as the Netherlands East Indies erupted into a war of independence between 1945 and 1949. For a time, it was not clear who, on the Indonesian side, had the authority to negotiate with the IGWC. Then, Ambon itself became a conflict zone as Ambonese elements of the former Dutch colonial army took part in a rebellion aiming to separate the southern Moluccas from Indonesia. After the Indonesian national army landed on Ambon to suppress the secessionist movement, some 80 per cent of Ambon town was razed to the ground during two months of heavy fighting, Five of eight churches were destroyed, and practically the whole of the population rendered homeless.[50]

In this chaotic time, the graves of those buried at Tan Tui during the war were vulnerable. According to an Australian embassy official, the local Ambonese population respected the sanctity of the war graves, partly because they wanted to win Australian sympathy and partly because of their Christian background. The Ambonese reportedly sacrificed an excellent tactical position during the civil conflict in order to prevent damage or fighting over the cemetery. But when Indonesian military forces later occupied the cemetery, they set up an artillery unit, played football among the flower beds and graves, and used the cemetery flag to cover the seat of a despatch rider's motorcycle. In one instance, the cemetery crosses were used for target practice.[51]

Once the Moluccas rebellion was suppressed, the construction of the IWGC cemetery resumed, albeit with many logistical constraints and delays. The political situation remained volatile throughout the 1950s, especially when Australia, which headed the Pacific-region division of the IWGC, the Anzac Agency, colluded with the United States Central Intelligence Agency in 1958 to unseat the Indonesian President Sukarno by backing rebel movements in Sulawesi. Australia also irritated Jakarta by supporting the Dutch claim to retain control of Western New Guinea, which Indonesia regarded as an integral part of its territory.

A formal agreement between the Indonesian government and the now Commonwealth War Graves Commission (CWGC) was signed only in late 1962. Initially the Indonesians maintained that there should be only one CWGC war cemetery, in Makassar, and they were 'firmly against' granting any land in perpetuity on the already land-hungry Java.[52] But they were told that 'such importance [was] attached to the Ambon cemetery by the Australian people that a tremendous outcry would result from any attempt to remove it'.[53] Ultimately, Indonesia agreed to two CWGC cemeteries: one at Ambon, the other in Jakarta. Some five hundred war dead from Makassar and bodies from other sites in the region were moved to Tan Tui.

Again, political tensions intervened. From 1962 to 1964, British and Australian forces engaged in 'Confrontation', a small undeclared war with Indonesia over the creation of Malaysia, which Sukarno saw as a British attempt to maintain colonial rule behind the guise of independence. CWGC officials from Melbourne, who visited Ambon at the end of 1964, were confronted by Ambon Youth Front protesters and forced to leave. In subsequent diplomatic negotiations, the Indonesian Department of Foreign Affairs claimed that local authorities in Ambon were opposed to an Australian presence, in view of Australia's support for Malaysia and various statements of Australian ministers 'which they did not like'. When the CWGC officials later returned, they met further protests, some of their supplies had gone missing, and substantial damage had been done to the stones that were to be used for the Cross of Sacrifice that would sit at the heart of the cemetery.[54] Tan Tui itself was supposedly being used as farmland by people who lived nearby.[55]

Despite all this, by 1968 the CWGC cemetery at Tan Tui was finished. In the aftermath of a 1965 coup attempt, Sukarno lost his hold on power. The ensuing massacres of between half a million and a million communists or alleged communists were mostly played out, with Western support, in locations other than Ambon, most notably in Java and Bali. In 1966–67, the army leader Suharto emerged as the national leader, bringing some kind of stability and foreign policies that were much more to the liking of the anti-communist government of Australia.

The completed Ambon cemetery included not only the graves of Gull Force, but other Commonwealth war dead from the region, some 186 Dutch personnel and one American airman.[56] The cemetery's design followed the template of CWGC sites across the world: a towering cross of sacrifice, replete with Crusader sword, and individual graves inscribed with details of the dead soldiers and poignant messages from their families. Many graves held men 'Known unto God', while a shelter on the lower terrace listed another 450 Australian soldiers and airmen who had gone missing in the region and whose remains had never been found.

The formal dedication of the cemetery on 2 April 1968 was a carefully orchestrated public ceremony in which all the governments whose nationals were buried at Tan Tui were represented. Australia sent its minister for the interior, Peter Nixon, and a delegation from the Australian armed services. Gull Force was represented by nine veterans, including the sacked commander, Len Roach. The Indonesians, realising at last the potential for soft diplomacy in war remembrance, provided delegates from the central and local governments and the armed forces, a guard of honour, a band, a choir from a local teacher training college and a large crowd. Despite the threat of further disturbances and torrential rain in what was supposed to be the dry season, the ceremony was, so the CWGC thought, 'an outstanding success'.[57] It was also a very Christian occasion, replete with imperial overtones. The opening hymn, 'God of our Fathers', reads, 'Beneath whose awful hand we hold/Dominion over palm and pine'. The ode was, naturally enough, the English one, by Laurence Binyon, immortalised since the First World War.[58]

These Christian allusions were probably not offensive in 1968, given the religious adherence of much of the Ambonese population at that time. However, in the decades to come, the cemetery's association with Christianity would put it at risk. By the end of the 20th century, the demographics of Ambon had changed, and the population had become almost equally Christian and Muslim. In 1999 a mix of sectarian tensions and economic competition exploded in a bitter communal conflict, first in Ambon, and then more widely in the Moluccas. The arrival of a Java-based radical Muslim group, Laskar Jihad, fuelled the violence. Christian neighbourhoods suffered extensive damage, as did many churches. By mid-2001, an estimated 4000 people had died and over 500 000 had been displaced.[59]

Tan Tui cemetery fell victim to this violence. None of the graves were desecrated but the Cross of Sacrifice was smashed, reduced to a stump. The gardener at the cemetery managed to salvage the twisted metal sword formerly embedded in the cross. Arguably, it was not just its Christian symbolism that made Tan Tui vulnerable. Once again, the Australian–Indonesian diplomatic relationship was strained, this time by Australia's role in East Timor's independence struggles and referendum. In 1999, another memorial to Australia's war dead, on the other side of Indonesia in Balikpapan, was vandalised, and the Australian residents at that site had to be evacuated.[60]

For some years the Cross at Tan Tui cemetery remained in its ruined state and Ambon was closed to Australian diplomatic personnel from Jakarta and members of Gull Force.[61] Eventually, the CWGC chose not to replace the Cross. Instead, in 2013 it installed a less overtly Christian symbol, in the form of a stone of remembrance, as is commonly found in larger CWGC cemeteries.[62] As it happens, this stone, made from material quarried in Queensland, has its own potentially difficult cultural associations. The original was designed in 1917 by Edwin Lutyens, later the imperial architect of New Delhi, and its inscription, 'Their name liveth for ever more', was selected from the biblical book of Ecclesiastes by another quintessential imperialist, Rudyard Kipling. But these cultural references are obscure, and the stone at Tan Tui has remained undisturbed to this date. Now surrounded by mosques, and the expanding Ambon town, the war dead of Australia and other nations are wakened at dawn, even on Anzac Day, by amplified Muslim calls to prayers.

13
LIVING WITH THE MEMORY

The war crimes trials and the burial of Gull Force's dead took place in the public sphere. For the individual survivors of Gull Force, however, the adjustment to life after captivity was primarily a private and personal journey. Family ties had to be renewed, old and new friendships developed, and careers established or re-established. Most importantly, the physical and psychological legacy of captivity had to be managed. These were complex and interconnected problems, and it is impossible to generalise about the ways in which survivors of Gull Force dealt with them. No robust data about the health of Australian prisoners of war, as a cohort, was ever collated after 1945, although many veterans themselves conducted individual negotiations with government agencies, including Repatriation (later Veterans Affairs). We must thus position our understanding of Gull Force's postwar recovery within the wider literature about the return of Australian prisoners of war.[1] We need also to appreciate that it is in the nature of resilience that individuals react to trauma in different ways. Thus, Gull Force survivors coped in ways that were shaped by family circumstances, medical issues, personal skills, employment opportunities, temperament, and even their own childhood. For some, the journey of confronting the traumatic memories of war would never end; for others, it was eased by returning to the site of their captivity, on pilgrimages that continue to this day and remain an enduring legacy of the original veterans.

ADAPTING TO CIVILIAN LIFE

A critical issue for returning prisoners of war was their personal relationships. Most of the men of Gull Force had left their families four years earlier when the 2/21st Battalion had been sent to Darwin. No correspondence had been exchanged with families and friends since February 1942. What reception would the prisoners of war receive? Would they be seen as cowards for surrendering? How had their families changed? Everyone had, of course, aged. 'Baby' brothers, sisters and cousins had grown and were sometimes unrecognisable. Some were in uniform; some married. Bill McGregor and Harold Beamsley were greeted with the news that their fathers had died during their captivity. Bill Chaplin found that his mother had changed from a middle-aged woman to an old one because of the anxiety of the war years. He had been declared missing on Ambon when he was 19 years of age, the same age that his brother had been when he died in an air accident at Point Cook, Victoria.

A further concern for most survivors was their marriage or prospects of marriage. The thought of a fiancée waiting at home had sustained some men throughout captivity – and they married quickly on their return. Tom Pledger and his 'true blue girl', Jessie, married within three months, on 1 December 1945. Clive Newnham's fiancée, Edna, met him at the Albury railway station, the very place they had parted more than four years earlier. We might wonder today at the speed with which these marriages took place, but at the time, few knew about what we would now call post-traumatic stress disorder (PTSD), even though shell shock had been very evident in the interwar years. Moreover, it was widely assumed, by the ex-prisoners, the Australian public and officials alike, that recovery from the trauma of captivity would be aided by a supportive woman, a stable home environment and fulfilling employment.[2] The *Argus*, for example, told Melbourne's women on 1 September 1945 that 'our mission in life is to restore to full fellowship in home and community our boys who suffered imprisonment at the enemy's hands'.[3] In the event, many of the marriages of 1945 and 1946, including Newnham's and Pledger's, would last for decades.[4] Their longevity presumably owed much to the mores of the day, in which marriage was assumed to be for life. But many wives also learnt to accommodate their husband's moods, poor health and troubled behaviour. As Miriam Bodsworth, whose husband had spent the war on Ambon, admitted in 1988, 'It took a lot of sympathy, love and understanding, but we made it.'

The marriages that had been established before Gull Force left Australia faced their own challenges. One was the shock of the husband's physical condition on his return. Although most of the prisoners returned to Australia by ship, and gained some weight on the journey home, some were almost unrecognisable. Bill McGregor knew his wife 'the moment I laid eyes on her' at Spencer Street Station, Melbourne, but she scarcely recognised him: 'this hollow-faced man with haunted blue eyes and hands like claws ... I was 25 years of age and full of hope for our future together.

My husband was a nervous wreck and so unsure of himself.'
Robert Mathews was so ill and thin that his wife and son,
aged five, walked past his bed at Heidelberg hospital. 'I only
recognised him', she later said, 'because Robert had my
name and number on a banner. Then an all-round sobbing
joyously.'

These existing family units had to be recreated and
marital roles redefined. The years of separation had forced
wives to be the head of the family and to develop emotional
and often professional independence. Their husbands, and
the wider Australian society, expected them to revert to
the traditional gendered role of homemaker while the man
resumed the role of breadwinner. In some cases, this was
not possible. Lingering illnesses and major disabilities, such
as blindness or amputation, made men dependent. As Ken
Widmer's wife, Alice, recalled in 1988:

> To be truthful, after five years of marriage I came
> to the conclusion that it was possible that I would
> become an early widow, that I would contemplate
> going into business should the occasion arise. So
> when our youngest child became of school age,
> the opportunity did arise and I took it. This was a
> time when married women just did not go to work.
> Ken was not so keen but when I became successful
> eventually he was a great help in every way.

While spousal relations were renegotiated, so too were
parental roles. Children who had been infants in 1940 had
to accept that the strange man in their home was their father.
Clarrie Hein's daughter, who had been 15 months old when

he left Australia, at least seemed to recognise him. His wife, Dulcie, had ensured that every night for the past four years the girl had said her goodnight prayers to a photograph of Daddy. But Robert Mathews was told by his son soon after his return that he was not the boss: Mum was. Sam Hillian's children declared, when he was trying to discipline them, 'You aren't my mother.' The advice the Australian Army gave such men, in publications meant to help with their adjustment, was that they should resume their place as father gradually, in order to avoid arousing jealousy in the child who might have received 'too much attention and affection' from the mother because of her loneliness.[5]

These domestic problems – and every other challenge the returning prisoners faced – were compounded by their ill health. Many survivors returned with one or more debilitating illnesses: bacterial and parasitical infections of the stomach and bowel; back and other injuries from bashings; irreparable eye and teeth problems; skin diseases and malaria, to name only some of their ailments. Dick Brown's heart was so weakened that he could never resume full-time employment, although with government assistance he developed a nationally recognised expertise in photography. Bob Nowland was incapacitated by the inflammation of his spine after a bashing on Ambon. Sam Hillian had lost 90 per cent of his vision. Walter Hicks' wife, Margaret, recalled decades later:

> His physical health in the early years of our marriage was difficult. He spent long spells ... in hospital at times when I needed his support. For example, during my first pregnancy when I was very sick, and our first

Christmas, and even the days after coming home with Jennifer, our first child, he went into hospital for about six weeks – and then again after the death of our son.

It is not known what struggles, if any, Gull Force survivors had with sexual intimacy. A hospital report immediately after their liberation spoke to 'an evident decline in virilism to which they [the ex-prisoner patients] are acutely sensitive and apprehensive lest it should not return'.[6] Wider evidence suggests that some couples must have grappled with sexual dysfunction.[7]

Beyond physical illness, captivity often left psychological damage. Some Gull Force survivors, it should be stressed, denied that they suffered any emotional scars, although one of these, according to his wife, never let a day pass without mentioning the war or the POW camp. But many survivors suffered from depression, anxiety, the inability to relate to others, restlessness or 'nerves'. They obsessed about not wasting food. They could not sit still for long, nor tolerate the noise of aircraft overhead. War films could trigger the trauma. Walter Hicks jumped to his feet while watching the 1957 movie *The Bridge on the River Kwai* in a public cinema. 'Kill him! Kill him!' he shouted as the film reached its gripping climax. Even men who gave every appearance of having adjusted successfully to civilian life suffered nightmares. As Eddie Gilbert said, 'You can never really push that kind of experience out of one's subconscious.' Colin McCutcheon thought he was being pursued by the Japanese when he was delirious after major heart surgery in 1982.

Yet, the postwar narrative was not unremittingly negative. Despite the long-term impact of captivity on their physical and mental health, many survivors of Gull Force settled back into civilian life, built functioning family units and developed successful careers. My 1988 research found that one in five men surveyed took advantage of government-funded educational schemes offered to ex-servicemen after the war. Most had established themselves in what became their long-term career within 12 months of their return to Australia.[8]

BATTLES WITH GOVERNMENT

The personal struggles of Gull Force survivors were not helped by the ambiguous responses of the Australian Government. It became clear, soon after the war, that prisoners of the Japanese were facing special difficulties in adapting to civilian life. But, while public sympathy was widespread, the Army and the Department of Repatriation were not willing to treat ex-prisoners as a cohort different from other returned soldiers. Rather, their needs and claims were assessed within the established benefits system, on a case-by-case basis.[9] No clear scientific consensus about the effects of prolonged confinement existed at that time, and Australian doctors in the immediate postwar years rejected the idea (developed in an influential British article in 1944) of a 'barbed wire attitude' or 'barbed wire syndrome'; that is, a psychological condition that meant that the depression and irritability of camp life persisted after the prisoners' discharge. While it was known that ex-prisoners of war were manifesting symptoms such as restlessness, violence and cynicism, these were attributed to physical problems such as prolonged nutritional deficiency. Hangovers from past prejudices also linked postwar neurosis to a soldier's pre-existing frailties and suggested that recovery could be impeded, and neurosis aggravated, if pensions were granted too readily.[10]

Successive Australian governments also resisted giving financial compensation to prisoners of the Japanese.[11] From 1946 on, various veterans' associations argued that these men should be paid a subsistence allowance of three shillings for every day of their captivity. The government, it was argued, had saved money by not having to provide rations for these personnel during their years of internment. However, the Labor Chifley government feared the budgetary implications of this claim, which might be extended to include prisoners from European theatres and the First World War. Even frontline troops who, because of logistical problems, had received inadequate rations, might make a subsistence claim. Some of Australia's military leaders also feared that the 'three bob a day' claim might encourage soldiers of the future to surrender and not seek to escape, if captured. The implication that men might prefer captivity to freedom was bizarre and insulting. The president of the NSW branch of the RSL, William Teo, described the suggestion that paying a subsistence allowance might encourage surrender as 'one of the most dastardly allegations' he had ever encountered. The NSW Ex-Prisoners of War Association also protested, with complete justification in Gull Force's case, that it was the 'gross inefficiency and unpreparedness on the part of the higher authorities' that had brought disaster on the prisoners of war, not their own lack of fighting spirit or a willingness to surrender.[12] Still, a 1950 inquiry set up by the newly elected

Liberal government of Robert Menzies rejected the claim for subsistence by a majority vote.[13]

Instead, the Menzies government set up a Prisoner of War Trust Fund. Its initial allocation of £250 000 acknowledged the special hardship suffered by prisoners of war, but their entitlement was not automatic. Veterans had to demonstrate their hardship and prove they suffered a major disability that was not common to other members of the services and was a direct result of their wartime imprisonment. They viewed the application process as intrusive and censorious. Asking for details of family structure, income, assets, mortgages and debts, it smacked of the inquisitorial administration of government and charitable support schemes during the Great Depression years.[14] Still, despite its deficiencies, by the time the Prisoner of War Trust fund finally closed in 1977, it had distributed almost $1 million. About one in three former prisoners of war had applied.[15] How many of these came from Gull Force is unknown. Bob Nowland possibly spoke for many when he said later:

> It soon appeared quite obvious to me that I could, without any trouble at all, become a T&PI [Totally and Permanently Incapacitated] and I was put on a 100 per cent pension straight away. But that wasn't my idea of living. I hadn't come back to be a parasite, dependent on the government, and I was determined to work on my job and get back in the mainstream again.[16]

As the Australian Government saw it, financial compensation for ex-prisoners of war should come from Japan. With the signing of the peace treaty in 1951, Australia gained access to Japanese assets that had been seized during the war, including assets in foreign countries that had been neutral or at war with the Allies. From these funds, each prisoner of the Japanese was allocated a total of £102 across the years 1953 to 1962. But this was approximately half of their original subsistence claim; in Canada, which could access far greater sums from liquidated Japanese assets, ex-prisoners received a considerably larger sum, the equivalent to £650.[17]

We need not trace here the processes whereby official attitudes towards ex-prisoners of the Japanese became more generous in subsequent decades.[18] Suffice to say that by the 1970s, a considerable body of Australian and overseas research had confirmed that, as a cohort, prisoners of the Japanese had suffered disproportionately, and were continuing to suffer ill health as a result. The government of Gough Whitlam (1972–76) extended free medical and hospital treatment to all Australian prisoners of war, whether their condition was war-caused or not. Five years later, widows of former prisoners were automatically granted free medical facilities. Even then, the DVA (as Repatriation was known from 1976) continued to oppose treating prisoners of war as a special cohort, maintaining into the 1990s that to do so would undermine the integrity of the repatriation system by moving away from the principle of 'demonstrated need' by individuals. Yet for all this, it has been concluded that a greater proportion of former prisoners of war received pensions than other veterans and had their claims assessed at a higher rate.[19]

From the 1980s on, the wider public attitudes towards prisoners of war would be transformed, as PSTD became formally diagnosed and Anzacs became widely depicted as victims of war. From around 1990, when the first government-sponsored pilgrimage went to Gallipoli, and a remarkable resurgence in the memory of war swept Australia, prisoners of war were progressively integrated into the mainstream of national remembrance. The Australian War Memorial, the official custodian of war memory, installed its first exhibition to prisoners of war in the mid-1970s. Memorials to the prisoner-of-war experience also sprang up, the most important being the Changi chapel at the Royal Military College Duntroon, Canberra (in 1988); and a new 'national' memorial, naming all prisoners of war across the 20th century, in the Victorian regional town of Ballarat (in 2004).[20] Eight years later, a memorial to the Australian forces on Rabaul, who were sunk when being transported on the Japanese merchant ship *Montevideo Maru* in July 1942, was unveiled in the precinct of the Australian War Memorial.

Prisoners of war were also accorded a prominent place in the year-long commemoration of the 50th anniversary of the end of the Second World War, Australia Remembers, in 1995.[21] In this year, too, 'Weary' Dunlop's translation into an iconic figure, representing all 106 doctors in Japanese captivity, was completed with the issue of a commemorative 50-cent coin bearing his image and the placing of a Peter Corlett sculpture of Dunlop, as an old man wearing a poppy in his lapel, in the precinct of the Australian War Memorial. The culmination of this elevated status of prisoners of war in public memory was confirmed in 2001 when the federal government granted all former prisoners of the Japanese a one-off payment of $25 000. As one of Gull Force noted, it was 'better late than never'.[22]

PILGRIMAGE TO AMBON

Many of these processes of public memory formation, as we will see, did not give especial prominence to Ambon, but Gull Force survivors themselves quickly took the initiative in commemorating their wartime experience. Within weeks of coming home, the survivors created the Gull Force 2/21st Battalion Association.[23] Based in Victoria and with a branch in New South Wales, it provided what Jay Winter has memorably called 'fictive kinship', or adoptive or functional kinship.[24] Linked by experience rather than blood or marriage, the members of the group provided each other and their families with practical and emotional support – critical elements in their postwar recovery. The Association ran a Welfare Fund and when many members of the Association were dying, offered $500 payments to assist families with funeral expenses.[25] In their many exchanges, as noted earlier, they also moulded a collective memory, telling and retelling the stories of trauma that many found impossible to share with their families.

Perhaps most importantly, the Association developed a calendar of commemorative rituals. In Victoria, they met at the 2/21st Battalion memorial tree near the steps of the Melbourne Shrine of Remembrance, the Prisoner of War Memorial Wall in Mornington, Victoria, and, of course, Anzac Day marches. Beyond this, they undertook journeys to Ambon and less often, Hainan. These 'pilgrimages' to what Bruce Scates has described as 'traumascapes of war' – sites of memories that are painful, positive and intense but demand personal and collective remembrance – allowed Gull Force members to come to terms with the memories of their life-transforming experience.[26] Pilgrimages also invested the traumatic past with new, more positive, meanings, by giving Gull Force the opportunity to express their gratitude to the local Ambonese who had supported them during the war at the risk of punishment, even death. These cross-cultural connections, as we shall see, would eventually become as important as the rituals of remembrance.

Personal contacts with Ambon began early. Percy Elsum, for instance, sponsored the migration of the Dutch ex-prisoner major Waaldyk and his Ambonese wife to Australia in the 1950s.[27] But, given the often troubled relations between Australia and Indonesia, the first Gull Force pilgrimage to Ambon did not take place until late 1967.[28] This delegation was led by Ian Macrae and organised by Bill Jinkins, the man who had led the escape to Australia in March 1942. Jinkins had not experienced the worst of Gull Force's captivity on Ambon, but he owed his own debt to the Ambonese. Perhaps, too, he felt some survivor guilt. He had lived when so many others had died, and he had failed in his efforts to persuade the authorities to rescue the men whom he left behind.[29]

The first Gull Force pilgrims received a generous welcome in Ambon. In 1967, they were met by the governor of Maluku and Indonesian military personnel, to whom they presented a bronze plaque, acknowledging the loyalty of the Ambonese to Australian servicemen, and a bronze replica of the badge of the RSL.[30] Ceremonies at sites of war memory followed, together with organised visits to the battlegrounds of 1942 and places of 'general and intimate interest'.[31] When a second delegation attended the dedication of the CWGC cemetery in 1968, the plaque left the previous year was unveiled at Kudamati, on land granted by one of the local families that had assisted Gull Force at great personal cost during the war, the Gasperez family.[32] Kudamati thus joined the Ambon war cemetery as a focal point for the pilgrimage rituals of remembrance. So too, did one of the mass graves at Laha, where the Japanese had been ordered to erect a memorial cairn in September 1945. Degraded over the years by the Ambon climate, it was renovated in 1980 by an Australian Army/RAAF survey group and is maintained to this today with the help of the Ambonese.

This pattern of shared remembrance and local engagement continued to characterise Ambon pilgrimages over subsequent decades. Flags donated by the Beaumaris RSL were presented to the curator of the Ambon war cemetery. RSL tankards and ties were given to the members of the Indonesian Veterans' Association.[33] A statement in Indonesian explaining why the anniversary of Gallipoli mattered to Australians was included in Anzac Day ceremonies at Tan Tui. At the end of the dawn service, the official party moved to the nearby Indonesian Heroes cemetery, laying wreaths in honour of Indonesian military personnel killed in the region, including in the 1950s Moluccan rebellion.[34] The Anzac Day statement continues to this day; the reciprocal honouring of the Indonesian dead does not – though when it stopped, and why, is not known.

This transnational commemoration was given a particular force by virtue of being embedded in an ambitious program of local development aid. The first of Gull Force's initiatives, dating from the late 1960s, was support for the Ambon General Hospital. Project Goodwill, which involved collaboration with a range of organisations – the Queen's

Memorial Infectious Diseases Hospital, Fairfield, Victoria; various Australian medical practitioners and associations, including the Victorian RSL; Caltex; and certain airlines – provided a remarkable array of medical and dental expertise, medicines and equipment.[35] Water reticulation to the hospital was installed and electrical rewiring provided. Beyond this, many other philanthropic programs were introduced: to name only some, visits to Australia for the family of W Gasperez (now a senior government official in the Moluccas), the donation of books to Ambon's educational institutions, the sponsorship of local children in need, and support for those (including Gasperez family members) displaced by the communal violence of 1999.

Gull Force's investment in Ambon was a classic example of how individuals and sub-state organisations, through their 'bottom up' agency, can create opportunities for governments to capitalise on memories of the past. Both the Australian and Indonesian governments came to see the veterans' activism as providing a thread of sub-state goodwill, which continued regardless of the state of the broader diplomatic relationship.[36] Project Goodwill became part of Australia's official aid programs for Indonesia, receiving funding from the Australian Development Assistance Bureau.

The annual rituals of remembrance during Gull Force's pilgrimages meanwhile provided a stage for the performance of transnational amity by senior diplomats and defence personnel. In 1979 Australia's ambassador, Tom Critchley, led an improvised and unaccompanied Australian choir in singing 'Waltzing Matilda'. The local governor and his official party joined in enthusiastically. A cocktail party followed, hosted by the ambassador.[37] The Indonesians, for their part, entertained Australian officials at the nearby naval base at Halong.[38] Everyone enjoyed lunches in the garden of the local caretaker of the CWGC war cemetery, Oscar Simona.

Australian government support also extended in the early years of the pilgrimages to providing RAAF aircraft and RAN vessels to transport the delegations and their supplies to Ambon. This was not without its political sensitivities. The pilgrimage coordinator after Jinkins, Rod Gabriel, was ever the intelligence officer, and told the 1983 delegation:

> You are specially asked NOT to publicise the Service Assistance, particularly as regards Movement, as we do NOT want the future jeopardised. Photographing in Ambon is generally permissible, but do NOT photograph defence establishments or personnel, wharfs or shipping or other 'sensitive' areas, without prior approval.[39]

No official from the Department of Defence, of course, recalled the flawed strategic planning that had contributed to Gull Force's disaster in 1942. Gone, too, was any hint that prisoners of war might be tainted by surrender. Instead, in a message provided for the 1983 Anzac Day ceremony, the Chief of Army, Lieutenant-General Sir Phillip Bennett, spoke of 'sacrifice', using the term, as is so often done, reflexively: the soldiers sacrificed themselves; they were not sacrificed by the Australian state.

> The purpose of the pilgrimage is to honour all those who died in the defence of Ambon – the Dutch, Indonesian and Australian soldiers who sacrificed their

> lives in the pursuit of freedom … the story of Gull
> Force is a proud one, reflecting great honour on all
> those who participated in the fight for Ambon. …
> I urge you to temper your sadness with the memories
> of comradeship and gallantry of years past.[40]

This was high diction worthy of General Archibald Wavell in 1942.

Like all memory processes, the Gull Force pilgrimages evolved over time. By the mid-1980s, the association of no. 13 RAAF squadron – some of its pilots were buried in the Ambon war cemetery – was invited to join, as were representatives of the four corvettes that rescued the prisoners of war in 1945.[41] Notably, as the ex-prisoners of war aged and died, the pilgrimage circle widened to include sons of the veterans, then daughters, and finally, other relatives, descendants and friends. In Ambon, a nearby school took responsibility for the Kudamati memorial, with annual donations from the Office of Australian War Graves. The managers of hotels and local guides who supported the pilgrimages also became part of the fictive kinship network, being greeted with warm embraces as new pilgrimages arrived.

RETURN TO HAINAN

While all these energies were invested in pilgrimages to Ambon, Hainan remained in the wings of commemoration, even for those who had spent much of the war there. This was not only because Hainan was inaccessible at the height of the Cold War, but also because the camp site disappeared with postwar economic development. Even more, the men who died at Hainan had been buried in Yokohama. As the son of a Hainan prisoner said in 2024, 'Perhaps if there was a cemetery there it would have been different.'[42]

That said, the mystery of what had happened to the men captured during the 1944 Hoban ambush troubled Hainan survivors. Eventually, their chance to resolve this seemed to come. As China opened to the West, the New South Wales government established in 1979 a sister-state relationship with Guangdong province, the southern region of China that includes Hainan Island.[43] A team from the New South Wales Department of Agriculture was sent to Hainan to assist Chinese authorities in establishing a cattle farm, which happened to be near the site of the wartime POW camp at Basuo. Through the contacts that the agricultural team and, in turn, the Gull Force Association, established with Chinese authorities, a delegation of ten members of Gull Force was able to go to Hainan in March 1985. The Australia–China Council provided a grant of $5000.

Throughout their trip the delegation met with 'wonderful co-operation' from Chinese authorities, and the Red Cross Society of China, who lauded them as former 'comrades in arms'. The changes to the landscape around Basuo since 1945 – a new road system, buildings, and a pine plantation – made it difficult to identify the former POW camp area and the wartime cemetery. All that remained was 'a fairly narrow track' where the main road outside the camp had once been, and another road built by the prisoners of war. As for the ten missing men, interviews with several elderly villagers who had lived in the Basuo region in 1944 and with veterans who had fought against the Japanese, suggested strongly that the graves of two men at a small village, Lao Ou, were those of two Australians wounded at Hoban. They had died soon after the ambush and been buried by local villagers. Chinese authorities had exhumed and reburied the remains in 1984 and affirmed that men had had big bones and were of apparently European origin. There were, however, no identity discs with the bodies. So far as the other eight missing Australians were concerned, the delegation made little progress, although two reports suggested that they had fought and died with the Chinese. The visit to Hainan concluded with a 'splendid, convivial dinner'.

> In the curious belief that Ron Green had a passable singing voice, the hosts insisted that he give a rendition, so, with devout apologies to his comrades he rasped out what else but 'Waltzing Matilda', ably supported by the rest of the Delegation. Ian Macrae then salvaged the soloist reputation of the Delegation with a fine rendition of 'A wee deoch 'n doris'. This was followed by all linking hands, and 'Auld Lang Syne'.

The Gull Force delegation urged Australian authorities to identify the men buried at Lao Ou and transfer them to an Australian war cemetery. Five years later, the graves were exhumed and the remains re-interred in the CWGC cemetery at Yokohama.[44] 'It must have been a lonely death, far from home and no mates around,' said Captain Ian Pfennigwerth, Australia's Beijing defence attaché at the time, as the remains of the two soldiers were unearthed.[45] The mystery of the missing eight will probably never be solved. Their names are recorded on the Singapore memorial at Kranji War Cemetery.

Apart from this, the level of interest in Hainan as a site of remembrance has been limited. The lead in memory making has been taken not so much by Gull Force as by the Darwin City Council. Darwin was not only part of Gull Force's history in 1940–42, but also a transit stop for the early Gull Force pilgrimages to Ambon. In 1988, Darwin formalised a sister-city relationship with Ambon, and then, in 1990, with Haiku. Although Haiku was on the opposite side of Hainan to the site of the wartime camp, now in modern-day Dongfang, the memory of the prisoners of war had the potential to deepen the transnational relationship. In 2003, the Council joined with the Haiku and Dongfang local governments to erect a memorial at Lao Ou.[46] One of a series of plaques designed by the Melbourne periodontist Ross Bastiaan and installed around the world, the memorial was replicated in Bicentennial Park in Darwin. The unveiling in Hainan was attended by a mayoral delegation from Darwin and one Hainan survivor. Since Lao Ou was some distance drive from Dongfang, it was not on any obvious tourist route. The memorial soon degraded, prompting Darwin to offer recurrent funding to maintain and improve the site.[47]

Darwin's focus, however, lies more naturally on Ambon than Hainan. Since 1976 the Cruising Yacht Association of the Northern Territory has run a Darwin to Ambon yacht race – almost a reversal of the escapes of 1942, although much faster and more direct. It was to Ambon that Darwin's lord mayor led a delegation in 2015, the apogee of Australia's centenary war commemoration, while participating in the Ambon City anniversary.

As for the Gull Force Association, it organised no official visits to Hainan after 1985. One informal group, including two descendants of Gull Force, made the journey in 2012, with a local teacher, Brendan Worrell, as their escort and guide. They visited the memorial at Lao Ou but found nothing of the POW camp other than a piece of rusted rail line and the dirt track.[48] Official visits by Australian government officials, too, were irregular. In 2015, Governor-General Peter Cosgrove visited the site as part of a state visit, in a gesture advertised as a sign of China–Australia friendship. In a notably banal speech he said, 'It's one of those great, sad mysteries of World War II [that] the battalion was isolated on the island of Ambon with no real hope of defending itself.' The conditions on Hainan were 'atrocious and, as we know, lots died'. The press reporting on the visit seemed to confuse the men lost in the Hoban ambush with those who escaped with Macrae in April 1945 and, with one exception, survived. Even Cosgrove said, 'The ones who escaped, well, we're sure that they also perished.' Adding his own historical conceit, the local Chinese army commander Major General Liu Xin added, 'But 70 years ago our two countries, our two armies were united in fighting against a foreign invasion.'[49]

Since then, official activities on Hainan have been 'relatively small scale' and, at the time of writing, yet to resume after the COVID-19 pandemic.[50] The memorial at Lao Ou fails to feature in the breathless official promotional material selling Hainan to potential international travellers on the internet. The wasteland of prisoner-of-war memory is now transformed into a paradise of tropical beaches, deep sea diving, mountains, ethnic diversity and modern infrastructure.[51]

PILGRIMAGE IN THE FUTURE?

Given the role the Ambon pilgrimages have played in sustaining the memory of Gull Force, the question arises as to their future. As the veterans have aged and died, regular pilgrimages have been maintained by their children and other descendants, interrupted only by the communal violence after 1999 and the COVID-19 pandemic. Some children have visited Ambon multiple times. But this next generation of pilgrims are themselves no longer young and they might soon be deterred by the long journey to Ambon, its humidity and the perilous footpaths. Will their children and grandchildren continue the pilgrimage tradition in the future?

This question raises a broader one, as to how the memory of war-caused trauma is transmitted across generations. Exploring this, especially in relation to the Holocaust, the American scholar Marianne Hirsch has coined the term 'postmemory'. By this she means the relationship that the 'generation after' bears to the personal, collective and cultural trauma of those who came before, and to experiences they 'remember' only by means of the stories, images and behaviours to which they were exposed as children. As Hirsch sees it, such experiences are transmitted to younger generations so deeply and effectively as to seem to constitute memories in their own right.[52]

Postmemory arguably goes some way to explain why the families of Gull Force undertook pilgrimages to Ambon from the 1980s on. If their fathers or relatives had died on Ambon, or if they had lived but remained silent about their trauma, the memory of captivity still infused family life: a memory elephant in the room, so to speak. As the daughter of one prisoner explained, after reading the 1988 version of this book:

> I suppose the whole business of [my father's] capture
> and imprisonment was mysterious and bewildering
> to me because of the fact that none of the men who
> went through this horrific time ever talked about it.
> So those of us who loved them had to be content with
> these stray pieces of information and mute every time
> we saw evidence of torture. I can still remember seeing
> Dad's fingernails and toenails – a total mess and grisly
> reminder of this grim secret time in his life … I lost
> my darling father when I was 14 due to his being
> incarcerated.[53]

Pilgrimages to Ambon, especially if undertaken in the company of fathers, gave the next generation a deeper understanding of the way in which captivity had affected their family dynamics. As the memory 'boom' conferred a new status on prisoners of war, they could also position their family history within the wider national narrative of war. WR (Bill) Plunkett died in Ambon in May 1945, and his brother explained in 1988:

> My brother's death, after so many years, had become
> for me until recently but just a residual sad memory,
> but two years ago, it suddenly became very important
> to me to visit Ambon and pay my own personal dues,
> not only for my brother's sacrifice but that of the others
> who died there on our behalf.[54]

However, in the case of the generations after Gull Force children, it is arguable whether postmemory is as useful as an explanatory device. Grandchildren, great-nephews and great-nieces have had far less direct exposure to Gull Force survivors. They might not even have known them. Can we say that they, too, inherited cross-generational trauma?

The 2024 pilgrimage of the Gull Force Association to Ambon, which this author joined as an observer, seems to suggest that postmemory is only part of the story of today's pilgrimages.[55] Almost all of the 2024 group had a family connection with the original Gull Force, but none were direct descendants of prisoners who died during captivity. This is hardly surprising given that three-quarters of Gull Force were unmarried when they enlisted and had not started family formation before they left Australia. Four of the 2024 group journeyed to Ambon to remember uncles or great-uncles who had been executed at Laha. One married couple were continuing a long search for the burial site of the wife's uncle, who had been killed in the 1942 fighting on Mount Nona. However, more than half of the group were remembering not the wartime dead but men who had survived, either on Hainan or by escaping in 1942. As the families of the latter said, they owed their existence to these escapes.

For some of the group, the commemorative rituals in Ambon certainly evoked an emotional response that we would expect of postmemory. The laying of a wreath and Flanders poppies on the small memorial at Tawiri brought tears to the eyes of at least one of those whose uncles were among the Laha victims. The nephew of another of the dead of Laha read a poem (written by another nephew):

Reginald Wade Monk was the uncle that I did not
    meet
I never got to shake his hand or with his children greet
No I never knew my uncle …

Clearly Uncle Reg had remained 'present' in the memory of
his family across the generations. The journey to Ambon, I
was told, would bring some sense of 'closure' to the surviving
members of his extended family. But still, the nephew reading
the poem noted, the ceremony at Tawiri did not have quite
the emotional force he anticipated.[56]

Visits to the Ambon war cemetery, too, aroused only
muted responses within the group. Tan Tui is now a
tranquil garden paradise, with towering moss-covered trees
and terraced rows of graves laid out between immaculately
maintained beds of tropical flowers and bushes. It is hard
to imagine it as the place where hundreds of Australians
starved in abject squalor. A large mosque now covers the
ground over which the men of Gull Force made their way so
regularly to the 'bridge of sighs' on the bay. On our first visit
(the second was the more formal Anzac Day dawn service),
the 2024 group sought out the grave of a family member and
tried to make sense of the rows upon rows of headstones. The
grandson of one of Gull Force who escaped concluded that
this site was significant – but he doubted that his children
would make the journey to see it.

At the third site of memory, Kudamati, the sentiment
was more akin to pride in family history. This site now
hosts a second memorial, additional to the one installed in
1968. Erected in 2013 by the Gull Force Association, with
the financial help of DVA, it is a memorial to the living

rather than dead. Inscribed with the names of all the men of Gull Force who survived the war, it sits firmly within the tradition of Australian war memorials to the Great War that often listed all men who served. Their very volunteering was worthy of honour, given the bitterness of the debates about conscription in 1916–17. So, at Kudamati, the families attached poppies with Blu-Tack to the names engraved on the memorial. 'Was not the poppy for the dead?' I asked. No, came the answer, 'it is for remembrance'. 'Somewhere,' the pilgrimage leader said, 'we wanted our fathers' names to be seen – a place where we could commemorate those who returned home.'

Perhaps most intriguingly, the 2024 remembrance was largely devoid of historical context. Except for the commemoration at the three memorial sites, the Second World War hardly featured in the program. Few of the group seemed interested in the details of the 1942 battles or the struggles of Australians in captivity. Only one family chose to visit the site where their father/grandfather, Arthur Cofield, had escaped in the aftermath of battle. Here, at the small fishing village of Seri on the southern tip of the Laitimor Peninsula, the story handed down to them surely became real. The hills above were so rugged and the village so small, even today, that it must have been hard to find in 1942. Darwin seemed a long way away across the glittering sea. You could only feel awe for the young men who took the huge risk of eluding the Japanese. That said, the spell of the past was fragile. The son of the escaper quipped that the rubbish on the beach would not have been there in 1942. Nor, I thought, would the chapel, replete with a large face of Jesus, and blasting what seemed to be Ambonese Hillsong at the foreign invaders. One of the grandsons thought he might be stabbed.

For most of the 2024 group, then, the focus was not so much on the war, but on the other tradition inherited from their forebears: philanthropy. The pilgrimage, I was told, was 'not about the war, it's about the people'. Friendships and longstanding contacts were joyously renewed as we visited a local school and orphanage, which the Gull Force Association and Rotary supports in cash and kind. Food was donated, ball games played, Australian kitsch distributed liberally, and musical items performed. The tour leader delighted all at another school with his ukulele playing. At the more sombre Tawiri memorial, too, the service, cut short by rain, was quickly followed by a flurry of gift giving to the local children draped over the fence of the memorial space. 'These are the good days,' one of the group later said, 'when you're welcomed to their villages.'

From all this, it seems that the Ambon pilgrimage, with its mix of war remembrance, philanthropy and personal relationships, has become a site of memory in its own right. It might be thought that this term applies only to physical sites and material objects – the battle sites, cemeteries and memorials of Ambon – but, as the French scholar Pierre Nora, who coined the influential term *lieux de memoire*, has argued, 'sites of memory' can include events, commemorative dates, ritual practices; even 'the products of reflection, such as the concept of a historical generation'.[57] These non-physical sites become invested over the years with their own meanings, symbolism and metaphorical representation of values. Take the concept of the returned soldier that is so powerful in Australian discourse about war. It means much more than the individual veteran. It conveys the notion of a consolidated and unified collective and a figurative and metaphorical representation of loyalty, service, citizenship and nationhood.

The 'pilgrimage as site of memory' helps explain the choice of the two-star hotel at which the 2024 delegation stayed. With no Wi-Fi, no hot water in the showers, and no coffee-making facilities in the room, it was basic. The occasional cockroach wandered across the bathroom floor. But comfort was not the point. The hotel is invested with meaning because Gull Force veterans stayed here decades ago. Their host was the mother of the current owner. Today's pilgrims find a welcoming Gull Force banner draped across the hotel exterior, while Australian flags bedeck the bar.

The emergence of the pilgrimage as its own site of memory might seem to compromise a historically informed memory of Gull Force, but it might also be a guarantee of its future. To judge by the 2024 pilgrimage, government interest in the commemoration of war in Ambon has ebbed. The dinners with local officials, the parties at Halong, the socialising with the cemetery curator and the wreath laying at the Indonesian Heroes cemetery are, it seems, things of the past. Australian government representation in 2024 was at the level of the counsellor from Makassar. More senior Australian officials were reportedly attending ceremonies at another site of Second World War memory, Balikpapan. Other elements of Australian government support, including the provision of Defence transport and government funding for development projects, ceased years ago. Gull Force's aid programs have long been privately funded by Association members and other organisations such as Rotary.[58]

However, if the Ambon pilgrimages no longer play the role in bilateral memorial diplomacy that they once did, the commitment of some – we know not how many – within the Gull Force Association to the pilgrimage remains strong. But many of these pilgrims are now in their 70s or 80s and will soon be unable to cope with the rigours of the long journey via Jakarta. For the grandchildren and great-grandchildren, the cross-generational memory of the war will become attenuated and devoid of emotional power. Who really cares, after all, about the men who fought in the Boer War, let alone at Waterloo?

However, the pilgrimage to Ambon might well continue, given that it has become its own site of memory.[59] The philanthropic activities and longstanding friendships with Ambonese – and the values of cross-cultural understanding and generosity that these represent – do not yet eclipse the rituals of remembrance, but they are a powerful parallel legacy that the descendants of Gull Force will inherit. They might well perpetuate it, even when they know little about why and how the war cemetery at Tan Tui and the Ambon pilgrimage came into being. In so doing, they might also help secure the future of the Ambon war cemetery. Around the world something of a hierarchy exists in the CWGC cemeteries. Some are visited by hordes of tourists, others rarely so. A demand-driven model of economics would sit uneasily with remembrance, but at some time in the future, when the wars of the 20th century are in the distant past, the Commonwealth governments that form the CWGC might choose to privilege those cemeteries that have a high number of visitors. Ambon, with its rich history of regular pilgrimages, local aid and shared commemoration, could mount a strong claim for having the precedence needed to survive in any future functionalist environment.

14
GULL FORCE IN NATIONAL MEMORY

To return to our starting point: the place of Ambon in the wider public memory of war in Australia. As mentioned in chapter 1, it seems that over the years, Ambon and Hainan have failed to gain the traction that other narratives of captivity, such as the Thailand–Burma railway and Changi, have done; this, despite the death toll on Ambon being 77 per cent, one of the highest of any group of Australian prisoners of the Japanese. The death toll on Hainan was 32 per cent, comparable to the worst figures from the Thai–Burma railway. The railway, of course, acquired an almost mythic status with the release of the Oscar-winning film *The Bridge on the River Kwai* in 1957. Semi-fictional though much of this was, it secured for the steel bridge in Kanchanaburi and the remains of the railway in Thailand an enduring place in popular memory and Thai tourism: this, despite the fact that the bridge is not the one featured in the film and no Australians worked on this section of the railway.[1] The 1990 film about Ambon, *Blood Oath*, in contrast, received less critical acclaim and, in any case, focused on the war crimes trials of the Japanese held responsible for the execution of Allied airmen, and the Cold War politics supposedly distorting justice, more than the experiences of Australian prisoners on Ambon.[2] The press commentary that accompanied the release of this film said little about Gull Force's captivity, and lapsed into egregious historical inaccuracies, such as that half of the men of Gull Force had been bayoneted or beheaded (it was about a fifth).[3]

Importantly, as prisoners of war were 'discovered' during the memory boom, it was Hellfire Pass on the railway that was chosen by the Australian Government of Paul Keating for an official memorial museum to prisoners of war, in the mid-1990s. The dramatic appeal of the site (25 metres deep with handmade incisions still visible in the rock face) lent itself to such status, as did the fact that the building of the 415-kilometre railway by the Allied prisoners, Asian forced labourers and Japanese engineers was a remarkable achievement. Whatever its terrible cost in lives, it had a logic that the manual work extracted from prisoners on, for example, Ambon, rarely had. The already mentioned Australia Remembers campaign of 1995 gave prominence, so far as prisoners of the Japanese were concerned, to the railway, the death marches of Sandakan and the fall of Singapore, where more than 15 000 Australians had been captured. A four-page feature in the *Canberra Times* on 15 February 1995, marking the anniversary of Singapore's surrender, made no reference to Ambon other than a captionless photograph of emaciated survivors of Gull Force reading newspapers on board a ship after their liberation. The *Age* (the major masthead in Victoria from where the 2/21st Battalion had been drawn) ran a three-part article on the survivors of Sandakan.[4] Six years later, the ABC miniseries *Changi* helped reinforce the popular perception that this camp was synonymous with the horrors of captivity and the lasting trauma of survivors – although this production attracted mixed reviews, for its historical inaccuracies and its sentimentality.[5]

If the author's personal experience is any guide, few Australians today know anything of the tragedy of Gull Force, or even where Ambon and Hainan are. This ignorance inspired composer Lloyd Swanton to write his mixed-media suite *Ambon* in 2015 (Appendix VI). But he, too, concluded, almost a decade later, that his hopes for a 'groundswell of chatter' – including about the nefarious circumstances in which Gull Force had been deployed by the 'top brass' – were not fulfilled. Perhaps the centenary of Gallipoli had induced commemoration fatigue so far as some memories of war were concerned.

This is not to say that Ambon has been overlooked by the official custodian of the national memory of war, the Australian War Memorial. As mentioned, prisoners of war have formed part of the Memorial's gallery displays for some decades, starting with a 1976 exhibition, Barbed Wire and Bamboo.[6] This was intended to be temporary, but it was eventually followed, in 1989, by a more permanent gallery.[7] The Memorial's curatorial approach was to exploit their collections of material objects that might generate an emotional response. Keen to avoid duplication and strike an appropriate balance, they chose themes that were common across different experiences of captivity, from the South African war of 1899–1902 to Korea. These themes included work, brutality, lack of food, disease and death, survival and improvisation, and passing the time.[8] This approach still allowed the Memorial to assign more of its gallery space to prisoners of the Japanese, but it diminished the importance of specific narratives and camps such as Tan Tui. However, Sandakan was accorded a separate annex with a memorial wall of the faces of the 1787 Australians lost in the 1945 death marches, a display that positioned this site as the greatest trauma of captivity – as indeed it was.

At the time of writing, Ambon is allocated a dedicated display case, in which Doolan's last stand at Kudamati, and the poem that immortalises this, is accorded a prominent place. The massacre at Laha takes up about half of the Ambon display, featuring items from the mass graves discovered in 1945, such as the signal wire that bound victims' wrists, metal badges, tobacco tins and a water bottle. In the more general display on prisoners of the Japanese, which covers Changi, the Thailand–Burma railway, the Netherlands East Indies and Japan, Ambon is described as 'one of the most terrible camps in the Dutch East Indies ... 405 of the 528 Australians held there died'. This is accompanied by an image of an emaciated prisoner, HA (Henry) Purvis, a photo of the Galala cemetery, a cross from a grave and a club. The caption reads, 'The club used by Japanese guards to bash prisoners and the grave cross of Private DR (David) Munnerley of the 2/21st Battalion are stark reminders of Gull Force's ordeal.'[9]

Notably, Hainan rates no mention. Nor do the tensions within the camps in Ambon and Hainan. None of the building of the cage, the resort to handing men over to the Japanese, the impact of rank on survival, and the Allied bombing raids that had such a devastating impact on the prisoners of Ambon rates a mention. The narrative is one of victimhood, atrocity and loss. This is, of course, more than appropriate, given Gull Force's calamity, but it reduces the story of survival to the traditional and morally uncomplicated battle between Australians and their enemy.

All memory is selective but the silences in Ambon's case are telling. It seems that there is no place in the national memory of war for the complexities that are integral to the history of Gull Force. Possibly this is because the strategic planning that consigned the force to captivity remains a matter of some sensitivity, even eight decades later. Any narrative that valorises service in defence of the nation, as Anzac still does, has little place within it for a profligate waste of young men's lives by their political and military leaders. Even more importantly, the division, dissension and failures of leadership that were part of captivity on Ambon and Hainan are presumably thought to unsettle, even transgress, key elements of the Anzac legend that so much of the popular discourse about prisoners of war is intent on reinforcing.

However, the story of Gull Force should not been seen in this way. The Anzac legend is precisely that: a mythic articulation of ideals and values that even the soldiers that CEW Bean, the war correspondent and official historian of the war of 1914–18, originally lionised could not always aspire to. The legend provides the standards of behaviour by which Australian soldiers are judged, but it should come as no surprise if men fall short of these ideals in times of acute physical and emotional stress. It should be remembered, too, that the values of courage, sacrifice, endurance and mateship that are core to today's version of the Anzac legend – as the 2002 memorial at Isurava on the Kokoda Track, for one, shows – are not fixed or absolute. They present themselves in different ways in different settings.

The tragic story of Gull Force, in all its complexity, attests to this. Undeniably, there was resentment, anger, division, bitterness and, at times, rank selfishness within the POW camps on Ambon and Hainan. But the immense challenges of surviving and retaining one's personal humanity in these situations also demanded heroism, endurance and mateship – of a different kind to that needed in combat and battle, but no less for that.

APPENDIX I
GULL FORCE STATISTICS

Gull Force numbered 1131 when the Japanese attacked Ambon.

Killed in action	54
Massacred at Laha, Ambon	229
Executed (POW camp, Ambon)	17
Killed by Allied bombing (POW camp, Ambon)	13
Died (POW camp Ambon)	378
Died (POW camp, Hainan)	66
Killed in ambush (Hainan)	9
Missing in ambush (Hainan)	10
Died immediately after liberation	3 (Ambon, 2; Hainan, 1)
TOTAL DEATHS	**779**
Escaped (before and after capture)	52
Repatriated from Ambon	119
Repatriated from Hainan	181
TOTAL GULL FORCE	**1131**

SOURCE Gull Force (2/21 Bn.) Assoc., Report of the Delegation of members of the Gull Force (2/21 Bn.) Assoc. to the People's Republic of China, including Hainan Island, and to Japan, 3rd. to 31st. March 1985, AWM 1067.

APPENDIX II
ORAL SOURCES

This list includes members of Gull Force who were interviewed or responded to questionnaires, 1983–87. It does not include those men and women contacted in 1988 for research on the homecoming of Gull Force. These interviews are referenced in the main text.

	Rank in 1942	Place of internment after October 1942
KR Adamson	Sergeant	Ambon
RK Allen	Private	Hainan
B Amor	Lance Corporal	Escaped
S Anderson	Lieutenant	Hainan
VC Ball	Private	Ambon
L Benvie	Corporal	Hainan
F Biddiscombe	Private	Hainan
JPG Billing	Warrant Officer II	Ambon
S Bodsworth	Private	Ambon
H Braeter	Private	Ambon
R Brassey	Private	Ambon
R (Dick) Brown	Private	Ambon
S Campbell	Private	Hainan
WJ Cook	Private	Hainan

	Rank in 1942	Place of internment after October 1942
C Crouch	Lance Sergeant	Ambon
W Dahlberg	Private	Escaped
A Deakin	Private	Ambon
RT Dean	Private	Ambon
J Devenish	Private	Hainan
L Edwards	Private	Ambon
D Findlay	Private	Hainan
V Findlay	Private	Hainan
IR Fishwick	Private	Hainan
R Gabriel	Captain	Ambon
MJ Gilbert	Private	Ambon
R Godfrey	Lieutenant	Ambon
B Gordon	Private	Hainan
A Grady	Private	Escaped
R Green	Lieutenant	Hainan
DL Griffin	Private	Hainan
C Harrison	Private	Hainan
A Hawkins	Private	Escaped
C Hein	Private	Ambon
W Hicks	Private	Ambon
S Hillian	Corporal	Ambon
WT Jinkins	Lieutenant	Escaped
W Johnson	Private	Hainan
JG Julian	Private	Ambon
E Kelly	Staff Sergeant	Ambon
G Kent	Private	Ambon
GH Kissick	Private	Hainan
WS Knuckey	Private	Hainan
B Larkin	Private	Hainan

	Rank in 1942	Place of internment after October 1942
JD Larkins	Private	Hainan
RJ Leech	Sergeant	Hainan
KE Lupson	Sergeant	Hainan
I McBride	Lieutenant	Escaped
F McCormack	Private	Ambon
J McDougall	Private	Hainan
W McGregor	Corporal	Ambon
D McIntosh	Private	Escaped
I Macrae	Major	Hainan
L Manning (Ayres)	Private	Ambon
A Mason	Private	Ambon
RJ Matthews	Lieutenant	Ambon
K Mellor	Lieutenant	Ambon
PP Miskin	Captain	Hainan
C Newnham	Captain	Hainan
RH Nowland	Lieutenant	Ambon
J O'Brien	Sergeant	Ambon
C O'Bryan	Private	Hainan
MF (Frank) Osborne	Corporal	Haman
WJ Page	Private	Ambon
T Phillips	Private	Haman
WJ Phillips	Private	Hainan
AT Pledger	Corporal	Hainan
AJ Rogers	Private	Ambon
S Rose	Captain	Ambon
L Ryan	Private	Hainan
S Shaw	Private	Escaped
VL Stewart	Lieutenant	Ambon
R Thomas	Corporal	Ambon

	Rank in 1942	Place of internment after October 1942
JM Turner	Captain	Hainan
B Tymms	Private	Hainan
CE Usher	Lieutenant	Hainan
J van Nooten	Lieutenant	Ambon
G de V Westley	Major	Ambon
K Widmer	Lance Corporal	Ambon
H Williams	Private	Ambon
G Williamson	Private	Ambon
J Wilson	Private	Ambon
ET Winnell	Corporal	Ambon
C Woodward	Private	Hainan

APPENDIX III
INQUIRY INVESTIGATING THE AUSTRALIAN ADMINISTRATION OF TAN TUI CAMP, 17–25 SEPTEMBER 1945

An inquiry into the Australian administration of Tan Tui camp was held on Morotai almost immediately after the Australians were liberated from Ambon. The inquiry was set up in response to serious allegations made to US naval interrogation officers by two of the American prisoners who had been interned with the Australians: Ensign John D Carson and Chief Quartermaster Earl D Hunter. These allegations were levelled against 'the camp HQ staff', by which was meant (Major) G de V Westley, (Lieutenant) John van Nooten, (WO I) J Billing, (WO II) M Ryan, (WO II) KR Adamson, (S/Sgt) E Kelly, (Sgt) LA Gray, (S/Sgt) EJ Nugent, (Sgt) JA McMahon and the leading cook.

These were the most serious of the allegations:

1   The camp staff was a 'closed corporation', whose primary purpose was their own welfare and saving their own skins.
2   The constant concern of the camp staff was meeting the daily demands of the Japanese for working parties, irrespective of the physical condition of the men. The

adjutant and the Regimental Sergeant Major (RSM) frequently pulled Australians who were too ill to go on working parties out of their bunks and compelled them to go on working parties, using physical violence where necessary to achieve this purpose.

3   The camp staff did not give the men their full share of the rations.

4   On two cited occasions Australians who had committed offences were severely beaten by way of punishment by other Australian prisoners, in one case the adjutant and RSM participating.

5   The camp staff, and Westley in particular, would never make complaints to the Japanese on behalf of the prisoners for fear of making them angry, and only under the greatest pressure would Westley file requisitions for food and medical supplies.

6   On occasions, Westley threatened to hand offenders, when caught, over to the Japanese for punishment and on one occasion this was done.

When the inquiry convened, Carson and Hunter proved unwilling to stand by much of what they had said previously. They retracted certain parts of the above allegations, modified other charges and failed to produce any substantive evidence to support their case. This, together with the testimony presented by Australian personnel such as van Nooten and Adamson, led the inquiry to dismiss almost all the allegations.

In detail, the inquiry decided the following:

1   Westley and his staff did all that was within their power to prevent the ill treatment of the prisoners and to obtain adequate food and medicines from the Japanese.

2   The actions taken by Westley and his staff to provide working parties for the Japanese were in the interests of the prisoners. Even though there were times when, of necessity, sick men had to work in order to spare men who were even more ill, and the occasional 'bludger' had to be coerced into going out on working parties, the camp staff constantly tried to ensure that the fittest men were allocated to the harshest tasks and that the lighter jobs were reserved for the weak. The doctor of the Royal East Indies Medical Services, (Captain) JHQ Ehlhart, was always the final arbiter as to which men should be allocated to the various working parties.

3   Any allegations as to the unequal distribution of food received from the Japanese were unfounded. Even though the officers and NCOs did maintain separate gardens from those of the men and benefited from the food these produced, so far as Japanese rations were concerned, all food was distributed fairly and equitably among the prisoners. Ryan introduced flat cooking trays that allowed the cooks to produce meals in easily divisible segments or, if food had to be served otherwise, it was ladled out in visibly equal portions.

4   Westley never handed men over to the Japanese for punishment but instead instigated the 'boob'.

Although the inquiry exonerated the Australian camp staff – and commended van Nooten and Ryan especially for their efforts in defence of the prisoners – it was critical of certain aspects of Westley's management of the camp. Westley was judged to have acted with less vigour than he might have in his relations with the Japanese, and he was considered to have displayed a lack of leadership so far as the Australian prisoners were concerned.

Westley, and the Australian prisoners generally, were also criticised for their failure to establish an effective system of producing food communally within the camp and pooling the produce of gardens. The individualistic attitudes manifested towards gardening were deemed by the inquiry to be evidence of a lack of esprit de corps in the 2/21st Battalion.

When interviews for this book were conducted in the 1980s, a copy of the allegations considered by the inquiry were shown to the ex-prisoners from Ambon. Reactions covered a spectrum, from outraged refutation to almost complete endorsement. Certain allegations were dismissed universally; for example, that van Nooten used physical violence to get prisoners to go on working parties and that Australians beat each other as punishment. On other questions opinion was divided and the judgments of the survivors were often less charitable than those of the inquiry.

SOURCE The files on the preliminaries to the inquiry are found in NAA MP729/8 44/431/63 and AWM54 229/27/1; the report of the inquiry, NAA B3856 146/1/14. The members of the inquiry were Colonel JM Kinlay, Lieutenant-Colonels VJ Schofield and L Byrne.

APPENDIX IV
THE PROFILE OF GULL FORCE

These tables were compiled for the first edition of this book. Data were taken from the attestation forms filled out by members of Gull Force when they volunteered for the AIF, and their personal records, held in the National Archives of Australia. The data on attestation forms was not always complete and the accuracy of the information provided by men when they enlisted cannot be taken for granted. The data below thus should be viewed as indicative.

State of residence of 2/21st Battalion and Gull Force at time of enlistment (%)

	VIC	NSW	QLD	SA	WA	TAS	ACT	Other
2/21st	93.6	5.7	–	0.3	0.2	0.2	–	–
Gull Force	78.6	15.3	5.0	0.3	0.4	0.2	0.1	0.2

Age of 2/21st Battalion and Gull Force
at time of enlistment (%)

	Under 21	21–25	26–30	31–35	36–40	41–45	Over 45
2/21st	4.6	43.9	23.4	13.8	12.0	1.9	0.3
Gull Force	4.4	41.8	23.5	14.9	13.3	1.8	0.3

NOTE Since these figures are based on the attestation forms filled out by recruits as they enlisted, there is obviously some inaccuracy in the lower and higher age brackets, where recruits may have given false ages. However, since men were unlikely to have raised or lowered their ages by more than a few years, the age profile of the battalion and Gull Force was presumably much as shown here.

Marital status of 2/21st Battalion and Gull Force (%)

	Single	Married	Divorced	Separated	Widowed	Unknown
2/21st	78.8	20.4	0.1	0.1	0.4	0.1
Gull Force	75.5	23.5	0.3	0.1	0.5	0.2

Religion of 2/21st Battalion and Gull Force (%)

	Church of England	Catholic	Non-conformist
2/21st	43.0	18.6	36.7
Gull Force	43.6	18.6	36.3
1933 census (Victoria)	34.4	18.4	31.2

NOTE Census figures relate to men aged 20–39, the age bracket from which approximately 93 per cent of the 2/21st Battalion came at the time of enlistment. Both the battalion and Gull Force included a very small proportion of Jewish men and men who named no religion.

Residence of 2/21st Battalion and Gull Force
(by region) at time of enlistment (%)

	Capital city	Non-metropolitan
2/21st	52.4	47.3
Gull Force	49.8	49.7
1933 census (Victoria)	51.6	48.1

NOTE Information about place of residence was lacking for a small number of both the 2/21st Battalion and Gull Force.

Prewar professions of officers and other ranks,
Gull Force (%)

	Officers	All other ranks	NCOs	Privates
Professionally qualified and high administrative	14.8	0.7	1.4	0.4
Managerial and executive	14.8	2.7	2.0	3.2
Inspectional, supervisory and other non-manual	59.3	12.0	23.6	8.6
Routine and manual	1.9	6.0	7.4	5.7
Semi-skilled manual	1.9	13.1	14.9	11.5
Unskilled manual	–	42.6	29.1	47.7
Unemployed	–	1.1	2.0	0.7
Unknown	–	0.6	0.7	0.6

NOTE The occupational categories used were adapted from the Hall-Jones Scale of Occupational Prestige for Males, in AN Oppenheim, *Questionnaire Design and Attitude Measurement*, Heinemann, London, 1968, chosen because of its relative proximity to the war years. 'Managerial and executive' included those with some responsibility for initiating and directing policy.

Residence of officers and other ranks, Gull Force, at time of enlistment (%)

	Capital city	Non-metropolitan	Unknown	N/A
Officers	81.5	16.7	1.9	–
Other ranks	48.3	51.3	0.3	0.2

APPENDIX V

PERSONNEL IN UNDERGROUND DRUG ORGANISATION ON HAINAN ISLAND, 1943-45

Within the camp
(Captain) W Aitken
(Captain) PP Miskin
(Sergeant) Ron Leech
(Lance Sergeant) DG Foley
D Griffin

Outside in officers' gardens and village area
(Major) Ian Macrae
(Captain) W Aitken
(Captain) PP Miskin
(Captain) ES Tanner
(Chaplain) VE Cochrane

Outside camp in working parties
(Sergeant) FS Bates
(Sergeant) JW Brown
(Sergeant) RH Brown
SD Campbell
(Corporal) AG Cole

DC Gaunt
D Griffin
M Higgins
(Sergeant) Ron Leech
(Sergeant) KE Lupson
(Sergeant) RA McCallum
(Corporal) RP McDonald
CG McDougall
AJ McCoomb
AG Perrin
CE Rivett
KJ Thatcher
SJ Vaughan
RC Woodman

SOURCE Combined medical and Q report by W Aitken and PP Miskin, appendix 22 to Scott's report A, pt II, AWM54 573/6/1A, duplicate at AWM54 481/12/174.

LLOYD SWANTON'S *AMBON*

The memory of Stuart Swanton, whose diary of captivity on Ambon has been quoted in this book, had a powerful presence in his family across the decades. Stuart's brother, Howell, who spent the war heading the War Damage Commission, frequently referenced Stuart's death. With a ghastly irony, this occurred on 14 August 1945, a day before the Pacific war ended. For the surviving brother, the account in Stuart's diary of his birthday gift of two fried eggs spoke poignantly to the hardships of captivity. The lesson, so Howell told his children, was to appreciate their blissful lives, to never waste any of life's opportunities, and to remember that what might ordinarily be seen as the humblest of gestures could mean a great deal more when circumstances are grim.

It was not until one of these children, Stuart's nephew Lloyd, stumbled upon a copy of the 1988 edition of this book that this memory of Ambon moved from family into public commemoration. Lloyd, a jazz double bass player, decided to honour his lost uncle by composing a mixed-media concert suite. He was inspired by the many references in Stuart's diary to the role that music played in the prisoners' morale and struggle for survival. There was, Lloyd thought, beauty in the prisoners' lives as well as horror.

Ambon, first performed in 2015, is an eclectic work of 14 pieces scored for double bass, bass clarinet, saxophones, recorder, brass, ukulele, guitar, slide guitar, percussion, drums and Stuart's own viola, which had not been used since the 1930s. The music is accompanied by readings from the wartime diary and projections of visual images of Stuart's artefacts. The melodies for some of the pieces are taken from hymns that Stuart himself had composed before the war; others draw on his diary. For example, 'Top brass' references an entry mentioning the Japanese giving the prisoners some brass instruments left behind by a Dutch band. None of them were complete, forcing the Australians to improvise, not all that successfully. 'Top brass' is then an improvised performance in which the players of various instruments swap instrument parts in something akin to a slapstick comedy. Another piece, drawing on Stuart's diary reference to a 'coconut band', evokes a concert at Tan Tui by creating Pacific-island-style music, complete with a ukulele, a slide guitar and the viola that Stuart left in Melbourne. 'The Long Carry', as its title suggests, uses a work song to recall the murderous working party of 1944.

Ambon was performed five times, in New South Wales, Victoria and Canberra in 2015–16, to very positive receptions. The CD release of a studio recording of the suite also sold out. But a decade later it seems that the composer's aspiration 'to bring the story back to life because it was in danger of fading into the mists of history' was not fully realised. The hoped-for 'groundswell of chatter' – the secondary discussion about the nefarious circumstances in which Gull Force had been deployed by the 'top brass' –

did not eventuate. The Australian War Memorial library declined to accept the donation of a copy of the Ambon album. They claimed they took items only from soldiers or veterans. Local libraries were more receptive.

SOURCE Interview, Lloyd Swanton and author, 4 April 2024.

NOTES

Chapter 1: An attempt to understand

1   Gavin Long, *The Final Campaigns*, vol. VII, series 1, *Australia in the War of 1939–1945*, Australian War Memorial, Canberra, 1963, pp. 633–4.

2   For the evolution of Anzac across recent decades, see Joan Beaumont. 'Remembering the heroes of Australia's Wars: From heroic to post-heroic memory', in Sibylle Scheipers (ed.), *Heroism and the Changing Character of War: Towards Post-Heroic Warfare?* Palgrave Macmillan, Hants, UK, 2014, pp. 334–48.

3   Christina Twomey, 'Trauma and the reinvigoration of Anzac: An argument', *History Australia*, vol. 10, issue 3, 2013, pp. 85–108.

4   No Australians were taken prisoner in the Vietnam War.

5   For detail on the historiography and memory of Australian prisoners of war, see Joan Beaumont, Lachlan Grant and Aaron Pegram, 'Remembering and rethinking captivity', in Joan Beaumont, Lachlan Grant and Aaron Pegram (eds), *Beyond Surrender: Australian Prisoners of War in the Twentieth Century*, Melbourne University Press, Melbourne, 2015, pp. 1–17.

6   Figures used here and below are taken from Gull Force Association's calculations, compiled by its former intelligence officer, RC Gabriel: see E499-3-3-8 pt 2, National Archives of Australia (NAA). The figure for Ambon excludes those who were killed in action in February 1942, or who escaped. The figure for Hainan excludes those killed in a 1944 ambush by Chinese guerillas.

7   AJ Sweeting, 'Prisoners of the Japanese', in Lionel Wigmore, *The Japanese Thrust*, vol. IV, series 1, *Australia in the War of 1939–1945*, Australian War Memorial, Canberra, 1957 (rep. 1968), p. 604.

8   Hank Nelson, 'Australian prisoners of war 1941–1945', <anzacportal. dva.gov.au/resources/australian-prisoners-war-1941-1945>, accessed 17 September 2024.

9   Sweeting, 1957, pp. 604–11; Courtney Harrison, *Ambon, Island of Mist: 2/21st Battalion AIF (Gull Force) prisoners of war 1941–45*, TW and CT Harrison, North Geelong, 1988; Alisa Rolley, *Survival on Ambon*, A Rolley, Beaudesert, Qld: 1994; Roger Maynard, *Ambon: The Truth about One of the Most Brutal POW Camps in World War II and the Triumph of the Aussie Spirit*, Hachette Australia, Sydney, 2014.

10   See Joan Beaumont, 'Hellfire Pass Memorial Museum', in Martin Wegner and Bart Ziino (eds), *The Heritage of War*, Routledge, New York, 2012, pp. 19–40.

11 For a summary of Gull Force casualties, see Appendix I.

12 For the dangers of travelling by sea, see Lachlan Grant, 'Hellships, prisoner transport, and unrestricted submarine warfare in World War II', in Beaumont, Grant and Pegram, 2015, pp. 196–217.

13 Les Hohl, 5 August 1992, cited in Paul Rosenzweig, '"In Australia Forever": The 2/21st Battalion in defence of Darwin, 1941', *Journal of Northern Territory History*, issue 9, 1998, p. 29.

14 Les Hohl to author, 18 November 1983, in author's possession.

15 This research was published as Joan Beaumont, 'Gull Force comes home: The aftermath of captivity', *Journal of the Australian War Memorial*, no. 14, 1989, pp. 43–52.

16 See Alistair Thomson, *Anzac Memories: Living with the Legend*, Monash University Publishing, Melbourne, 2013, pp. 11–14.

17 Quoted Thomson, 2013, p. xv.

18 Thomson, 2013, p. 14.

19 According to Scott's closest confidant in the camp on Hainan, (Lieutenant) DW (Denis) Smith, officers of Gull Force kept information about Japanese brutality on scraps of paper hidden in their clothing, shoes and other places unlikely to be detected. When, however, the passage of time made these records illegible, he was given responsibility for keeping a secret record: statement by Lieutenant DW Smith, 13 November 1945, (NAA B3856 144/14/77). (Captain) Clive Newnham, who was for a time adjutant on Hainan, denied this vigorously to the author. Since Newnham gave evidence at the war crimes trial of Japanese personnel in 1947, and since certain aspects of Smith's account seem implausible, I have preferred Newnham's account.

20 The main extant diary of Ambon is that kept, in code, by Stuart Swanton, a digitised copy of which is found at AWM67/3 387, Australian War Memorial (AWM). For Hainan, the most detailed diaries are those kept by FA Biddiscombe (AWM 3DRL 1763), Austin Carr (AWM PR00304), Alan Murnane (AWM PR 87/006) and Tom Pledger (AWM PR00871).

21 Stan Arneil, *One Man's War,* Alternative Publishing, Sydney, 1980; EE Dunlop, *The War Diaries of Weary Dunlop*, Nelson, Melbourne, 1986.

22 Scott submitted his account of Gull Force on Ambon and Hainan in two reports, one of which was official, one unofficial. The official Report on Ambon and Hainan by Lieutenant-Colonel WJR Scott of May 1946 (AWM 54, 573/6/lA), on which Sweeting's account of Gull Force's captivity in the official history was very heavily dependent, was open for a number of years before the unofficial, and much more contentious, part of the report written in April 1946 (AWM 54 573/6/1B) was released. In the notes for following chapters, the above reports will be referred to as Scott's report A (which itself consists of parts II and II) and Scott's report B. Until 1984, the contents of part B of Scott's report were not known to the survivors of Gull Force. After being alerted to the report, several officers of the 2/21st submitted rebuttals to the author and then deposited them with the Australian War Memorial (AWM PR86/2).

Chapter 2: Waiting to fight, 1940–41

1   Much has been written about the evolution of the Anzac legend, but a
    key overview is Carolyn Holbrook, *Anzac: The Unauthorised Biography*,
    NewSouth, Sydney 2014. See also Beaumont, 2014. A classic early study
    is KS Inglis, 'The Anzac tradition', *Meanjin Quarterly*, 1965, republished
    in John Lack, *Anzac Remembered: Selected Writings of K.S. Inglis*,
    Melbourne University Press, Melbourne, 1998, pp. 18–42.

2   See, for example, CEW Bean, *The Story of Anzac from the Outbreak of War
    to the End of the First Phase of the Gallipoli Campaign, May 4, 1915*, vol.
    1, *The Official History of Australia in the War of 1914–1918*, Australian
    War Memorial, Canberra, 11th edn, 1941 (first published, 1921), pp. 46,
    126; and CEW Bean, 'Sidelights of the War on the Australian Character',
    Journal of the Royal Australian Historical Society, vol. XII, no. IV, 1927,
    pp. 218–20.

3   Bean, 1941, p. 5.

4   Bean, 1941, p. 550.

5   General Sir John Monash, *The Australian Victories in France in 1918*,
    Hutchinson, London, 1920, p. 294.

6   For problems with discipline, see: Bill Gammage, *The Broken Years:
    Australian Soldiers in the Great War*, Penguin, Melbourne, 1975 (first
    published in 1974), pp. 37–40; Suzanne Brugger, *Australians and Egypt:
    1914–1919*, Melbourne University Press, Melbourne, 1980, pp. 61–4;
    Peter Stanley, *Bad Characters: Sex, Crime, Mutiny and Murder and the
    Australian Imperial Force*, Pier 9, Millers Point, NSW, 2010; Ashley Ekins,
    'Fighting to exhaustion: Morale, discipline and combat effectiveness in
    the armies of 1918', in Ashley Ekins (ed.), *1918: Year of Victory*, Exisle,
    Auckland, 2010, pp. 112–13.

7   Jean Bou and Peter Dennis, *The Australian Imperial Force*, vol. 5, *The
    Centenary History of Australia and the Great War*, Oxford University Press,
    Melbourne, 2016, p. 174.

8   CEW Bean, *Anzac to Amiens: A Shorter History of the Australian Fighting
    Services in the First World War*, Australian War Memorial, Canberra, 1961
    (first published in 1946), p. 538.

9   Monash, 1920, p. 293.

10 Bean, 1941, p. 6.

11 Bean, 1941, p. 607.

12 LL Robson, 'The origin and character of the First AIF, 1914–18: some
    statistical evidence', *Historical Studies*, vol. 15, issue 61, 1973, p. 748.

13 Bou and Dennis, 2016, p. 174.

14 T Inglis Moore, 'The meanings of mateship', *Meanjin Quarterly*, vol. 24,
    issue 1, 1965, pp. 52–3; Jane Ross, *The Myth of the Digger: The Australian
    Soldier in the Two World Wars*, Hale & Iremonger, Sydney, 1985, p. 73.

15 Paul Hasluck, *The Government and the People 1939–1941*, vol. I, series 4,
    Australia in the War of 1939–1945, Australian War Memorial, Canberra,
    1952, appendix 8.

16 Gavin Long, *To Benghazi*, vol. I, series 1, *Australia in the War of 1939–
    1945*, Australian War Memorial, Canberra, 1952 (reprinted 1961),
    p. 87.

17 Unless otherwise stated, details about the battalion's time in Australia are taken from its war diary, AWM52 8/3/21.

18 *Australasian*, 28 September 1940.

19 'AIF on the March', *The Age*, 2 October 1940.

20 'AIF March', *The Age*, 26 September 1940.

21 For photos, see especially *Sun News Pictorial*, 25 September 1940; *Leader*, 5 October 1940.

22 Lionel Wigmore, *The Japanese Thrust*, vol. IV, series 1, *Australia in the War of 1939–1945*, Australian War Memorial, Canberra, 1957 (reprinted 1968), pp. 56–9, 76.

23 Herman Bussemaker, 'Australian–Dutch defence co-operation, 1940–1941', *Journal of the Australian War Memorial*, issue 29, 1996, <www.awm.gov.au/articles/journal/j29>, accessed 8 February 2024.

24 I have developed this argument in greater detail using the theories about two modes of cognition, System 1 and System 2, developed by the late Nobel-prize-winning behavioural psychologist, Daniel Kahneman, in his bestseller, *Thinking Fast and Slow*, Farrar, Straus and Giroux, New York, 2011: see Joan Beaumont, 'The psychology of military decision making', in Joan Beaumont and Garth Pratten (eds), *Military History Supremo: Essays in Honour of David Horner*, ANU Press, Canberra, in press. 2025.

25 Norman Dixon, *On the Psychology of Military Incompetence*, Jonathan Cape, London, 1976, pp. 152–3.

26 Letter to Mainie, 2 May 1941, AWM PR05233.

27 MJ (Eddie) Gilbert; T (Tommie) Phillips.

28 A good account of the 2/21st's time in Darwin is Rosenzweig, 1998, pp. 29–42. For the 2/40th in Darwin, see Peter Henning, *Doomed Battalion: Mateship & Leadership in War & Captivity: The Australian 2/40 Battalion, 1940–45*, Allen & Unwin, Sydney, 1995, ch. 2.

29 Report by Major Macrae – 2 i/c – on History of Unit up to Arrival at Ambon, appendix A to Scott's report B, pp. 3–4.

30 ET (Ted) Winnell, Gordon Kent, Brian Tymms.

31 Report by Macrae, p. 4.

32 Information confirmed by R Ashton, RSL, Feb. 1986.

33 Letter to Mainie, 2 May 1941, AWM PR05233.

34 Biddiscombe diary, AWM 3DRL 1763.

35 'Medical report POW camp Hashio (Bakli Bay) Hainan Island', appendix 22, Scott's report A, pt II, p. 2.

36 Weekly intelligence and security report, no. 11, 28 November 1941, AWM 52 8/3/21.

37 'Riot at Darwin', *Border Morning Mail* (Albury), 2 September 1941; 'AIF in Darwin riot', *Examiner* (Launceston), 3 September 1941.

38 Scott's report B, pp. 5–7.

39 Typical examples of suppositions lacking supporting evidence can be found on pp. 11 and 17 of the report (for example, 'In any case I doubt very much that strong representation was made to visiting officers'). Scott contradicted himself by criticising the battalion's leadership for allowing good officers to be transferred to other units because 'they were not in favour as were those remaining', while at the same time, accusing the

leaders of providing 'men who company commanders were anxious to be rid of' for the drafts sent south from Darwin (pp. 8–9).
40   Scott's report B, p. 5.
41   Comments by Lieutenant-Colonel RJ Green, AWM PR86/2, p. 12.
42   War diary entries for July-October 1941, AWM52 8/3/21.
43   Cited in Rosenzweig, 1998, p. 34.
44   Scott's report B.
45   Report by Macrae, p. 3. A number of men interviewed in 1983–84 denied categorically that there was any decline in morale or discipline in Darwin, but Macrae's report, written much closer to the event, together with his later comments, provide a convincing case for some deterioration in morale.
46   Report by Macrae; comments to author by Green, 25 June 1984; John van Nooten, 29 May 1984.
47   AWM52 8/3/21. See also press telegrams in Miscellaneous file dealing with the behaviour of Australian personnel while on leave, AWM54 233/4/3.
48   Arneil, 1980, p. 3.
49   Roach, Leonard Nairn, Service record, NAA B883.
50   I am grateful to Peter Stanley and Richard Gehrmann for information about the Indian Army.
51   Richard Gehrmann, 'Service Personnel: Australian experiences of interculturality and violence in British India', in Robert Mason (ed.), *Legacies of Violence: Rendering the unspeakable past in modern Australia*, Berghahn, New York, 2017, p. 202.
52   'Mesopotamia', *Register* (Adelaide), 1 September 1920.
53   Letter, Macrae to author, 13 March 1986. Macrae mistakenly thought Roach served in Dunster Force, established in December 1917 and intended to organise local units in northern Iran (Persia) and South Caucasus, to replace the Tsarist army that had fought the Ottoman armies in Armenia.
54   Michael Cathcart, *Defending the National Tuckshop: Australia's Secret Army Intrigue of 1931*, McPhee Gribble/Penguin, Melbourne, 1988, p. 56.
55   Geoffrey Serle, *John Monash: A Biography*, Melbourne University Press, Melbourne, 1982 (1985 reprint), p. 518.
56   Roach to Monash, 12 November 1930, Box 47, Monash Papers, National Library of Australia (NLA), MS1884.
57   Adjutant-General to Secretary Military Board, c. 11 March 1942, NAA MP742/1 R/2/1803; Garth Pratten, *Australian Commanders in the Second World War*, Cambridge University Press, Melbourne, 2009, p. 316.
58   Ian Macrae, Walter Hicks.
59   Scott's report B, pp. 8, 15–17.
60   Order of Ceremony at the Dedication of the Ambon War Cemetery and Memorial, Ambon, Indonesia, 2 April 1968, NAA E203 161-3-D1.
61   LN Roach, Visit to NEI, 26 May 1941, Memo to 23 Aust Inf Bde, 27 July 1941, 13 October 1941; Gavin Long, Papers of the Official Historian, Lt-Colonel Roach file, AWM67; Reconnaissance Reports,

Timor and Ambon, by Brigadier EF Lind, 6–12 Oct 1941, AWM54
573/6/4.

62   For further details see DM Horner, *High Command: Australia and Allied Strategy, 1939–1945*, Australian War Memorial, Canberra, and George Allen & Unwin, Sydney, 1982, pp. 142–3.

63   Horner, 1982, p. 143.

64   Chiefs of Staff Appreciation–Defence of Australia and Adjacent Areas, 15 December 1941, War Cabinet Agendum, NAA A2671 418/1941.

65   AHQ Operation Instruction no. 15, 6 December 1941, AWM54 573/6/3.

66   Diary of James Frederick Armstrong, AWM PR89/16/51.

67   A nominal roll of Gull Force can be found in Maynard, 2014, pp. 279–303.

Chapter 3: Crisis of command, 1941–42

1   ES De Klerck, *History of the Netherlands East Indies*, vol. 1, BM Israel NV, Amsterdam, 1975, p. 122.

2   The account that follows draws on the Dutch official history of the campaign on Ambon (C van Hoogenband and L Schotborgh, *Nederlands-Indië Contra Japan deel VI: De Strijd op Ambon, Timor en Sumatra*, Staatsdrukkerij-en Uitgeverijbedrijf, 's-Gravenhage, 1959; Wigmore, 1957, pp. 418–41; and cited archival records and oral history.

3   Dutch sources use several terms, such as 'Home Guard', 'Militia', 'Territorials', without the distinction between these forces being made clear.

4   Report by Lieutenant GL Snell, 'De Strijd op Het Vliegterrein Laha (Amboina)', 8 May 1942, p. 2, document 9/35, Department of Military History of the Netherlands Army, 's-Gravenhage. Snell escaped from Ambon at the end of the campaign and made his way to Australia where he made this report.

5   Details of Dutch artillery can be found in Hoogenband and Schotborgh, 1959, pp. 11–12. There is some disparity between this account and the Australian reports, so far as details of the positioning and calibre of the artillery are concerned. Presumably the Dutch report is the more reliable.

6   There seem to have been six Lockheeds also on the island at one time but details as to their deployment are lacking: Major IF Macrae, Action of the Gull Force on Amboina, December 1941–43, February 1942, appendix A, Scott's report A, pt I, p. 4. Macrae's report was written ten months after the campaign while he was in captivity.

7   Hoogenband and Schotborgh, 1959, p. 8; Kenneth Munson, *Aircraft of World War II*, Ian Allen, London, 1962 (reprinted 1973), p. 180.

8   Roach to Scott, 13 December 1941, AWM54 573/6/10.

9   Macrae, Action of the Gull Force, p. 3.

10   Kapitz did not anticipate landings directly behind Paso from Baguala Bay, which was mined: Memorandum by Lieutenant BJ Huizing, 20 February 1946, document 9/42, p. 4, Department of Military History of the Netherlands Army, 's-Gravenhage; Report by Captain AGM Schouten, 10 March 1945, appendix G, Scott's report A, pt I.

11   Macrae, Action of the Gull Force, pp. 2–3.

12   Memorandum by Huizing, p. 2.

13   MJ (Eddie) Gilbert, Ambon, 1941–1945: *Recollections of a Survivor*, p. 2, AWM PR03121.
14   Walter Hicks, RJ Matthews, L Ryan, Keith Mellor; MS by A (Bert) Grady, PR88.092.
15   Roach to AHQ Melbourne, Gull Force at Action Stations, 24 December 1941, AWM 67 3/328 pt 1.
16   Roach to Scott, 13 December 1941, AWM67 3/328 pt 1.
17   AHQ Operation Instruction no. 15, 6 December 1941, AWM 67 3/328 pt 1.
18   Gull Force to AHQ, 24 December 1941, AWM 67 3/328 pt 1.
19   Roach to AHQ Melbourne, Disposition Gull and NEI Forces, 27 December 1941, AWM67 3/328 pt 1.
20   DCGS to CO Gull Force, 26 December 1941, AWM67 3/328 pt 1.
21   Gull Force to Army Melbourne, [29 December], AWM67 3/328 pt 1. According to Roger Maynard (2014, p. xvi), Sturdee 'deliberately withheld arms and other military support to avoid them falling into the hands of the enemy' but this claim is not substantiated by archival evidence.
22   Rod Gabriel to author, February 1986.
23   Roach to Scott, 1 January 1942, AWM54 573/6/10.
24   Wigmore, 1957, p. 423.
25   Gull Force to Army Melbourne, AWM67 3/328 pt 1.
26   Roach to Scott, 13 December 1941, AWM54 573/6/3; Macrae, Action of the Gull Force, p. 5.
27   See Roach to AHQ, Melbourne, 4 May 1942, NAA MP742/1 R/2/1803.
28   Macrae to Scott, 1 January 1942, Tanner to Chief of General Staff Army Melbourne, 13 January 1942, AWM 67 3/328 pt 1.
29   Wigmore, 1957, pp. 423–4.
30   Wigmore, 1957, p. 424.
31   Rowell to Roach, AHQ Operation Instruction no. 29, 14 January 1942, AWM 67 3/328 pt 1.
32   Roach to AHQ, Melbourne, 26 January 1942, NAA MP742/1 R/2/1803.
33   Sturdee's memorandum to minister for the army, AWM54 573/6/10.
34   Introduction, pp. 1–2, Scott's report A.
35   Draft memo, Chief of the General Staff to Minister, January 1942, AWM54 573/6/10B.
36   Sturdee to Wavell, 14 January 1942, to den Poorten, AWM54 573/6/10.
37   Wigmore, 1957, p. 424.
38   General Wavell's Despatch on Operations in South-West Pacific, 15 January – 25 February 1942, National Archives, London, WO10/2556.
39   Kahneman, 2011, p. 71.
49   For 'high diction', see Paul Fussell, *The Great War and Modern Memory*, Oxford University Paperback, London, 1977, esp. pp. 21–2.
41   Lieutenant-General Vernon Sturdee, AWM67 3/384.
42   Scott to Wigmore, 15 June 1954, AWM67 3/353.
43   The description of Scott that follows is based on Robert Darroch 'The man behind Australia's secret army', *Bulletin*, 20 May 1980, pp. 58–70; Andrew Moore, *The Secret Army and the Premier: Conservative Paramilitary*

Organisations in New South Wales 1930–32, UNSW Press, Sydney, 1989; and Moore, 'Scott, William John (1888–1956)', *Australian Dictionary of Biography*, ANU Press, Canberra, online edition, <adb.anu.edu.au/biography/scott-william-john-8373>, accessed 12 December 2023. Details of Scott's military career are taken from his personal record held at 'Scott, WJR', NAA B2455.

44   Eric Campbell, *The Rallying Point: My Story of the New Guard*, Melbourne University Press, Melbourne, 1965, p. 27.
45   Robert Darroch, *DH Lawrence in Australia*, Macmillan, London, 1981.
46   Campbell, 1965, p. 16.
47   *Sydney Morning Herald*, 9 May 1921.
48   Darroch, 1980, p. 66.
49   See, for example, *Sydney Morning Herald*, 14 November, 29 December 1932, 18, 23 February 1933.
50   Drew Cottle, quoted in Andrew Moore, 'Guns across the Yarra', in Sydney Labour History Group, *What Rough Beast?; The State and Social Order in Australian History*, Allen & Unwin, Sydney, 1982, p. 232.
51   Darroch, 1980, p. 66.
52   Scott to DMOP, 11 January 1942, AWM54 573/6/10.
53   Annotation on Roach telegram, Gull [sic] 'G' & 'I' matters, 24 December 1941, AWM54 573/6/3.
54   Preamble, Scott's report B.
55   Scott, Alan Humphrey, NAA B2455.
56   CEW Bean, *The AIF in France, 1917*, vol. IV, *The Official History of Australia in the War of 1914–1918*, Angus & Robertson, Sydney, 1933, p. 836n.
57   Scott, William John Rendel, NAA B883.
58   Roach to AHQ, Melbourne, 19 November 1945, NAA MP742/1 R/2/1803.
59   Roach to AHQ, Melbourne, 9 February 1942, NAA MP742/1 R/2/1803.
60   Roach to AHQ Melbourne, 4 May 1942, NAA MP742/1 R/2/1803.
61   'Grave injustice', Roach to AHQ, Melbourne, 10 March 1942, NAA MP742/1 R/2/1803. On 10 September 1942 Lind submitted a summary of events to GOC Melbourne saying that events at Ambon had 'made clear the justice and wisdom of the representations of [Roach]', AWM52, AIF and Militia unit war diaries (1939–1945), item 8/2/23, 23rd Brigade, appendix K.
62   Judge Advocate General to FM Forde, Minister for Army, 26 February 1943, NAA MP742/1 R/2/1803.
63   Lieutenant-Colonel KE Wheeler to Roach, 16 January 1946, containing an extract from the HQ AMF memo 387, of 14 January 1946, NAA MP742/1 R/2/1803.
64   Letter, CEM Lloyd to Roach, 25 November 1943, AWM54 573/6/10.
65   Roach to AHQ, Melbourne, 28 February 1946, NAA MP742/1 R/2/1803.
66   Note for AHQ Southern Command, various dates stamped, NAA MP742/1 R/2/1803.

Chapter 4: Battle and defeat, February 1942

1 Unless otherwise stated, the account of the campaign which follows is based on the following sources: Hoogenband and Schotborgh, 1959; Macrae, Action of the Gull Force, appendix A, Scott's report A, pt I; and Wigmore, 1957, pp. 427–36. Where the evidence about Dutch operations differed between Dutch and Australian sources, the Dutch was preferred, as the Australians had only incomplete knowledge of events in the Dutch-controlled areas of Ambon. Macrae's report was preferred to Scott's, as it was written only ten months after the event. Scott's report would seem to have relied heavily on Macrae's.
2 Cited by Rod Gabriel, 3 February 1982.
3 Macrae, Action of the Gull Force, pp. 4–5.
4 Memorandum by Lieutenant BJ Huizing, pp. 4–5.
5 Lieutenant IH McBride, Report on the Japanese invasion of Ambon, 1 April 1942, p. 1, NAA MP729/7 35/421/67.
6 Papers of Thomas W Clark, AWM PR89/091.
7 Macrae, Action of the Gull Force, pp. 4, 9; McBride, Report, p. 2.
8 Macrae, Action of the Gull Force, p. 8.
9 Macrae, Action of the Gull Force, pp. 7–8.
10 Scott to Mrs Newbury, 21 November 1945, given to author during 1980s research.
11 Wigmore, 1957, p. 427.
12 Report on 'Amboina' (based on diary by Lieutenant GL Snell), 2 April 1942, p. 2, document 9/35, Department of Military History of the Netherlands Army.
13 Diary of Alan Thomas Murnane, AWM PR87/006.
14 B Larkin, AT (Tom) Pledger, CE Usher.
15 Hoogenband and Schotborgh, 1959, p. 9.
16 According to the Dutch official history, Kapitz asked Scott to help stem the Japanese advance across the Laitimor Peninsula by deploying some Australian troops to counterattack, but Scott refused on the grounds that the terrain was impassable. The Australian records make no mention of such a request.
17 Interview with author.
18 Statement on Laha battle by Takada Haruo, 13 November 1945, appendix 20, Scott's report A, pt II.
19 Memorandum by Huizing, pp. 8, 16–17.
20 Memorandum by Huizing, p. 17.
21 Maynard, 2014, p. 51.
22 WT Jinkins, Report on Japanese attack on Ambon, AWM54 573/6/12.
23 Wigmore, 1957, pp. 434–5.
24 Thomas Clark, AWM PR 89.091.
25 AWM PR89.091.
26 According to Geoff Cookesly (AWMPR00567), 30 or 40 men went to Regimental Aid Post without arms.
27 Clark, AWM 89.091.
28 Scott's report B, p. 16.
29 Macrae, Action of the Gull Force, p. 15.

30   Wigmore, 1957, pp. 434–5.
31   Clark, AWM PR89.091.
32   James Frederick Armstrong, Diary, AWM PR89.165.
33   Japanese sources are the statement by Takada Haruo, 13 November
       1945, appendix 20, Scott's report A, pt II; and Shinichi Ichise, Report
       concerning Laha battles, 26 October 1945, NAA MP742/1 336/1/1956,
       pt 1. The main Australian written source is the McBride Report. The
       Dutch officer, Snell, also gave details of the Laha battle in his report.
34   McBride, Report, p. 3.
35   A useful source on events at Laha is Kathryn Boin, 'The massacres of
       1942', 1997, AWM MSS2068.
36   Appendix 20, Scott's report A, pt II.
37   Ichise, Report, NAA MP742/1; statement on Laha battle by Hamanishi
       Shiego, 16 November 1945, appendix 21, Scott's report A, pt II; evidence
       by Lieutenant-Commander Kenichi Nakagawa in Prosecution Court of
       Tokyo Naval General Court Martial, 8 November 1945, and in Tokyo
       General Demobilisation Court, 22 and 19 December 1945 (provided to
       author by John van Nooten). One report suggested that some prisoners
       perished when the ship that was taking them across the bay to Ambon
       was sunk by a mine (Report concerning Australian POWs captured in
       Ambon, by Major HS Williams, 3 November 1945, AWM 226 72 pt 1).
38   Boin, 1997, pp. 16–17.
39   Hamanishi Shigeo statement.
40   Boin, 1997, pp. 17–18.
41   Boin 1997, p. 16.
42   Hamanishi, Takada and Nakagawa all said this. See also Oka Mitsujiro,
       interrogated 12 December 1945, AWM 1010/9/121; and examination of
       Akiyama Kumaichi, 24 January 1946, AMW 226 71 pt 1.
43   Hamanishi is the only one to suggest this (p. 5).
44   Court of Inquiry with reference to Landing of Japanese forces in New
       Britain, Ambon and Timor, vol. 1, 8 July 1942, AWM226 1/2.
45   Doolan's story has been covered extensively in newspaper accounts of Gull
       Force. His daughters, June Treadwell and Wendy Twigg, had an extensive
       collection of these, which the author accessed in the 1980s.
46   'Inquiry on A.I.F. Island Forces Urged', Herald, 4 October 1945.
47   'Epic stand held Japs', Herald, 3 October 1945; 'Grave Ambon charges',
       Herald, 5 October 1945. Politicians supporting the call for an inquiry
       were Larry Anthony (Liberal) and Senator George McLeay (Liberal).
       For examples of letters to the press requesting an inquiry see Sun News-
       Pictorial, 5 October 1945, 26 October 1945; Age, 5 October 1945,
       25 September; Argus, 5 October 1945.
48   L Ryan, I Fishwick, Arthur Deakin.
49   Murnane diary, 12 March 1942.
50   Scott's report B.
51   HE Jessup, Changi Diary, Mitchell Library, NSW, ML MSS 2799.
       See also Wigmore, 1957, p. 511.
52   Introduction, p. 1, Scott's report A.

Chapter 5: Escape from Ambon, 1942

1   The following account of Lieutenant WAM Chapman's escape party is based on several sources: diaries kept during the escape by Chapman himself (AWM54 573/6/17) and Corporal JW Chugg (loaned to author by his family); a diary kept by A (Bert) Grady (AWM PR88/092); an audiocassette response to my questionnaire in the early 1980s by Alex Hawkins; an interview with Doug McIntosh, and the testimonies of various members of the escape party to the courts of inquiry held in Australia on 1 April 1942 and 28–30 May 1942 to investigate the circumstances in which the members of Gull Force had escaped (NAA MP729/7 38/421/222). The Chapman escape party originally included himself, W/O LC Warren, Sgt F Anderson, Cpl JW Chugg, K Ashton, G Ashton, AH Ault, JL Cassidy, TW Clark, AT Cofield, JF Cookesly, A Grady, ER Hansen, AS Hawkins, FG Hobbs, W Johnson, AD McIntosh, A Palmer, PH Palmer, RA Warren and F White.

2   Chugg's diary.

3   Personnel ex-Ambon – Court of Inquiry, 23 June 1942, NAA MP729/7 38/421/222.

4   Alex Hawkins.

5   Alex Hawkins.

6   Twenty-one men initially left Laha with Lieutenant Ian McBride: including W/O II HF Drane, NT Dengate, HJ Devers, H Digney, JT Drummy, NE Ellis, JW Fincher, GA Hawkins, AE Howe, HS Kitson, JL McMahon, F Ogilvie, BR Mackieson, AJ Keenan and SL Shaw (Evidence by IH McBride, Report on Proceedings of Court of Enquiry, 4 June 1942, NAA MP729/7 38/421/222). The following account of the escape from Laha is based on testimonies to the inquiry and on the author's interviews with Ian McBride and Stan Shaw.

7   Court of Inquiry with reference to Landing of Japanese forces in New Britain, Ambon and Timor vol. 1, convened 13 May 1942, AWM 226 1/2.

8   S Shaw.

9   S Shaw.

10   Maynard, 2014, p. 78 attributes the story to Leslie Hopkins.

11   Benjamin Amor, To Put the Record Straight, AWM PR03/10; Ben Amor, Don and Vic Findlay.

12   Amor, To Put the Record Straight, p. 15.

13   Evidence of WC Dahlberg, RB Goodall, D Johnson and FA Redhead to Court of Inquiry, 28–30 May 1942, NAA MP 729/7 38/421/222.

14   The account of Jinkins' escape is based on author's interviews with him and on the log of his party's escape kept by one of its members, Arthur Young (supplied to author by Doug Allen).

15   Scott's report A, pt II, p. 5.

16   '1500 more bravery awards to Australians', *Herald* (Melbourne), 6 March 1947.

17   According to Jinkins, and Amor (p. 16), the Dutch families at Saumlaki were rescued by Australian corvettes.

18   Alan Powell, *War by Stealth: Australians and the Allied Intelligence Bureau 1942–1945*, Melbourne University Press, Melbourne, 1996, p. 17.

19 Scott's report A, pt II, pp. 6–7.
20 Forde to Sturdee, 19 May 1942, NAA MP1217 Box 532.
21 Report by HC Wright, 1 June 1942, NAA MP 1587/1 115C.
22 Report by Wright.
23 G Herman Gill, *Royal Australian Navy 1942–1945*, vol. II, series 2.
    Australia in the War of 1939–1945, Australian War Memorial, Canberra,
    1968, p. 211–12; Jinkins interview.
24 Leary, Memorandum, 3 June 1942, NAA B6121 115C.
25 Maynard, 2014, p. 103.
26 Jinkins interview.
27 See *The Official History of the Operations and Administration of Special
    Operations (Australia)* vol. 2, *Operations*, 1946, pp. 3, 15, pt 3, pp. 61–5,
    pt 5, pp. 17–22, NAA A3269 08/A; Powell, 1996, pp. 63, 170–8, 271–3,
    292–3, 302.
28 WT Jinkins, NAA B883; AWM, <www.awm.gov.au/collection/
    R1561868), accessed 17 December 2023.
29 This information has been researched using the names and army numbers
    listed in the files of the 1942 court of enquiry into the escapes, and the
    details contained in individual service records in NAA B883.

Chapter 6: First months, to October 1942

1   See AL Cochrane, 'Notes on the psychology of prisoners of war', *British
    Medical Journal*, vol. 23, 1946, p. 282; Walter A Lunden, 'Captivity
    psychoses among prisoners of war', *Journal of Criminal Law and
    Criminology*, vol. 39, 1949, p. 725.
2   Charles A Stenger, 'Life style shock: The psychological experience of
    being an American prisoner of war in the Vietnam conflict', *Newsletter for
    Research in Mental Health and Behavioural Sciences*, vol. 15, no. 2, 1973,
    pp. 1–2.
3   Cochrane, 1946, p. 283; PH Newman, 'The prisoner-of-war mentality:
    Its effect after repatriation', *British Medical Journal*, 1 January 1944,
    pp. 8–9, <www.bmj.com/content/1/4330/8>, accessed 23 December
    2023.
4   Cochrane, 1946, p. 284.
5   C Crouch, Ron Green, Gordon Kent, T Phillips, L Ryan.
6   H Braeter, Eddie Gilbert, Gordon Kent, W Knuckey, RH (Bob)
    Nowland, WJ Page, J Julian, AJ Rogers, Ken Widmer.
7   See AE Field, 'Prisoners of the Germans and Italians', in Barton
    Maughan, *Tobruk and El Alamein*, vol. III, series 1, *Australia in the War
    of 1939–1945*, Australian War Memorial, Canberra, 1966, pp. 756, 761,
    773–7; Bob Moore, *Prisoners of War: Europe: 1939–1956*, Oxford, Oxford
    University Press, 2022, pp. 214–25. The precise number who died on
    the Bataan death march is impossible to determine but of the 11 796
    American and 66 304 Filipino troops on the Bataan Peninsula at the
    time of the US surrender, 650 Americans and between 5000 and 10 000
    Filipino troops died (Tom Lansford, 'Bataan Death March', in Stanley
    Sandler (ed.), *World War II in the Pacific: An Encyclopedia*, Garland,
    New York, 2001, p. 160).

8   Scott's report A, pt II, p. 3; Evidence by John van Nooten to Australian War Crimes Board of Inquiry, 23 October 1945 (hereafter referred to as 'van Nooten, War Crimes'), p. 15, AWM54 1010/4/143.

9   Notes on Ambon Island, based on questions to Captain Ehlhart, Dutch medical officer, and Lieutenant van Est, 23 September 1945, NAA A471 81709, pt 4.

10   Van Nooten, War Crimes, p. 8.

11   Report by WT Jinkins on Prisoner of War Camp, 'Tan Toey', Ambon, AWM54 573/6/12.

12   Court of Inquiry, appointed to inquire into facts and circumstances associated with the landing of Japanese Forces, and events subsequent thereto, in Ambon, held in Melbourne, 1 July 1942, AWM54 573/6/9.

13   Jinkins report, AWM54 573/6/12.

14   Keith Mellor; van Nooten, War Crimes, p. 15.

15   Report by Australian naval intelligence on AIF and Dutch escapees from Ambon (based on interviews with eleven escapees), 7 May 1942, document 9/22, Department of Military History of the Netherlands Army; FA Redhead, D Johnson, RB Goodall; Jinkins report, AWM54 573/6/12.

16   Van Nooten, War Crimes, p. 8.

17   Diary kept by van Nooten, POW camp, Ambon, February 1942 – September 1945 (hereafter referred to as 'van Nooten diary') (in possession of family; used by permission of Betty van Nooten), p. 7; Notes on Ambon island (Ehlhart and Est).

18   Van Nooten, War Crimes, p. 6.

19   Clarrie Hein, Bob Nowland.

20   Rod Gabriel, RJ Matthews; Murnane diary, 8 April 1942.

21   Walter Hicks.

22   Van Nooten, War Crimes, p. 16.

23   Reg Brassey, Dick Brown, Eddie Gilbert, Gordon Kent, William Page, Ken Widmer, George Williamson.

24   Murnane diary, 9 July 1942.

25   George Williamson.

26   Maynard, 2014, p. 147.

27   Of all the ex-POWs interviewed, only one said that he had operated on his own in the camp.

28   Stewart Wolf and Herbert Ripley, 'Reactions among Allied prisoners of war subjected to three years of imprisonment and torture by the Japanese', *American Journal of Psychiatry*, vol. 104, 1947, p. 185; Lavinia Warner and John Sandilands, *Women Beyond the Wire*, Hamlyn Paperbacks, Feltham, Middlesex, 1983, p. 185; William H McDougall, *By Eastern Windows: The Story of a Battle of Souls and Minds in the Prison Camps of Sumatra*, Arthur Baker, London, 1951, p. 82.

29   There is some disagreement on this question. According to van Nooten's diary (p. 15) and Westley's evidence to the War Crimes Board of Inquiry (AWM54 1010/4/146) (hereafter referred to as 'Westley, War Crimes'), in the latter period of their captivity officers were forced to do manual work, but it is not clear whether by this they meant camp

chores, or other tasks within Tan Tui camp, or going out with working parties. The overwhelming impression gained from interviews with the other ranks is that the officers did not do manual work on the working parties.

30   Redhead's evidence to Court of Inquiry, AWM54 573/6/9.
31   Murnane diary, 22 June 1942; van Nooten diary, p. 22; van Nooten, War Crimes, p. 12.
32   Commandant, Tan Toey POW Camp to Scott, 29 June 1942, appendix 1, Scott's report A, pt II.
33   Van Nooten, War Crimes, p. 14; Westley, War Crimes, p. 9. For payment in other camps in the Far East see, for example, A Coates and N Rosenthal, *The Albert Coates Story: The Will that Found a Way*, Hyland House, Melbourne, 1977 (Burma); Sweeting, in Wigmore, 1957, pp. 519, 531–2 (Changi), 537 (Bandung), 543, 548, 559, 566 (Burma and Thailand); MS by Captain HB Toothill, Imperial War Museum, London, 77/153/1 (Rangoon jail).
34   Van Nooten, War Crimes, p. 14.
35   Van Nooten, War Crimes, pp. 5–6; van Nooten diary, p. 28; Redhead's evidence to Court of Inquiry, AWM54 573/6/9; Jinkins report, AWM54 573/6/12.
36   Ken Widmer.
37   Ken Widmer, Eddie Gilbert.
38   Murnane diary, 8 June 1942; van Nooten diary, p. 5.
39   Van Nooten diary, p. 4.
40   Scott's report A, pt II, p. 8.
41   Sworn statement by AJ McCoomb, 28 August 1945, NAA B3856 144/14/77, B336/1/1956 pt 1; Scott's report A, pt II, p. 8; sworn statement by CE Rivett, 26 August 1945, NAA B3856 144/14/77.
42   Sworn statement by Captain JM Turner, 27 August 1945, NAA B3856 144/14/77, also at B336/1/1956, pt 1.
43   Van Nooten diary, p. 37.
44   Scott's report A, pt II, p. 9. Memories of the Japanese reaction to the 'garden party' vary, some ex-prisoners saying that the Japanese gave flowers to the Dutch widows (Keith Mellor, Reg Brassey), but the essentials of the story remain common.
45   Sworn statement by Lance Sergeant WD Harries, 27 August 1945, NAA MP742/1 336/1/1956, pt 1. See also sworn statement by Captain ES Tanner and Lieutenant CE Usher, 28 August 1945, NAA B3856 144/14/77.
46   Sworn statement by Turner, 27 August 1945, NAA B3856 144/14/ 77; sworn statement by Acting Sergeant KE Lupson, 26 August 1945, NAA MP742/1 336/1/1956, pt 1.
47   Personal authority is sometimes described in the scholarship as 'referent power', and competent authority as 'expert power'. See, for example, Ralph M Stogdill, *Handbook of Leadership; A Survey of Theory and Research*, Free Press, New York, 1974, pp. 284–5. Dennis Wrong (*Power: Its Forms, Bases and Uses*, Basil Blackwell, Oxford, 1979, ch. 3) uses the terms 'legitimate authority' (which depends upon the power holder's

acknowledged right to command) and 'coercive authority' (which depends upon the ability to obtain compliance from subordinates by threats of force).

48   David R Segal, 'Leadership and management: Organization theory', in James H Buck and Lawrence J Korb (eds), *Military Leadership*, Sage Publications, Beverly Hills, 1981, p. 42; Wrong, 1979, p. 48.

49   Scott's report A, pt II, p. 7.

50   Rod Gabriel was the only source for this information, but since he was the officer who reported the prisoner concerned to Scott, there seems no reason to doubt his evidence.

51   Scott's report A, pt II, p. 11.

52   Letter, C Varkevisser to author, nd 1988?, in author's possession.

53   Van Nooten, War Crimes, p. 2.

54   Scott's report A, pt II, p. 11.

55   Scott's report A, pt II, p. 11.

Chapter 7: Surviving, 1943–44

1   This account is based on van Nooten, War Crimes, pp. 17–20, and evidence presented by other members of Gull Force to the Australian War Crimes Commission: Sergeant NE Balcam, 6 October 1945; VC Ball and Sergeant EJ Nugent, 25 September 1945, NAA A471 81709, pt 2. Ball was himself a victim of the beating. The evidence of J Joseph, a resident of Galala, Ambon, presented to the war crimes trial was also considered.

2   Eric Kelly, Arthur Deakin.

3   Van Nooten, War Crimes, p. 19. A Japanese source for these events is found at War Criminals Ambon, p. 5, NAA A471 81068.

4   Van Nooten, War Crimes, p. 20.

5   Ball's evidence, NAA A471 81709, pt 2.

6   Evidence of Captain Gordon Marshall, 25 September 1945, NAA A471 81709 pt 2.

7   Those executed were RA Bennett, GW Brown, AJ Collins, DA Evans, JF Kelly, AW King, NG Leary, PJ O'Donoghue, S Rainsbury, W Ripper and CE Tucker (AWM54 1010/9/2).

8   Van Nooten diary, pp. 9–10.

9   Statement by the counsel for the accused at the Ambon war crimes trial, p. 2, NAA A471 81709 pt 1.

10   Van Nooten diary, p. 10.

11   Statement by the counsel for the accused, p. 3; handwritten note on letter Westley to commanding officer, Japanese forces, B336/1/1956, pt 1.

12   Van Nooten diary, p. 11; van Nooten, War Crimes, pp. 8–9.

13   The Writings of Pte Walter D Hicks, p. 4, AWM PR MSS1547.

14   Westley, War Crimes, p. 6.

15   Van Nooten diary, p 9.

16   Diary of Sergeant Stuart Mill Swanton, 4 March 1943, AWM 67 3/387, <https://www.awm.gov.au/collection/C2674606>, accessed 29 December 2023; Jim Wilson.

17   Van Nooten diary, p. 12.

18   Van Nooten diary, pp. 12–13.

19   'Troops sing in the rain', *Herald*, 27 September 1940.

20 Van Nooten diary, p. 11; Report of Court of Inquiry – Tan Toey Camp, Ambon, 2–4 October 1945 (hereafter referred to as 'Inquiry report'), p. 7, NAA B3856 146/1/14. Those killed in the bomb blast were PE Boreham, (Lieutenant) EP Campbell, (Captain) P Davidson, (Captain) J Hooke, (Lieutenant) IG Jaffrey, RA Leishman, Chaplain C Patmore, JG Sargent, (Staff Sergeant) WWG Stanbridge and (Sergeant) CM Wilson (Jinkins' stand-in).

21 On the role of doctors in POW camps, see Rosalind Hearder, *Keep the Men Alive: Australian POW Doctors in Japanese Captivity*, Routledge, Oxford, 2009.

22 Walter Hicks.

23 I base this conclusion, in part, on comments made to me by Westley in an interview in 1983.

24 Van Nooten diary, p. 11; Reg Brassey, Charles Crouch, Arthur Deakin, Bob Nowland, Ken Widmer.

25 Letter C Varkevisser, Mount Martha, to author, nd, 1988?; letter, J vd Oudenhoven, The Hague, to author, 23 March 1989; both in author's possession.

26 In his long letter to the author, Oudenhoven included a summary of a diary entry about the bomb blast from a Dutch prisoner at Tan Tui, Sergeant C Varkevisser. This, if anything, confirms the Australian impressions. It read: 'I have respect for the women. The men [the Dutch civilians] were worthless and completely blank. [One Dutch officer] was sitting behind a big rock with some other officers … doing nothing. The Aussies tried with buckets [of] water to kill the fires.' One American ex-prisoner's (albeit second-hand) recollections, on the other hand, attested to Dutch men being in the bucket line bringing water up from the beach to quench the fires (CA Rearick, cited in letter from Walter Hicks to author, 13 December 1989).

27 Letter J vd Oudenhoven to author, 10 December 1989.

28 Information from Elsum's son, Ian, May 2024.

29 For examples of Australians being critical of Dutch prisoners, see Russell Braddon, *The Naked Island*, Pan Books, London 1955 (first published 1952), pp. 264–5; ER (Bon) Hall, *The Burma–Thailand Railway of Death*, Graphic Books, Armadale, Vic., 1981, p. 91; Rohan D Rivett, *Behind Bamboo: An Inside Story of the Japanese Prison Camps*, Angus & Robertson, Sydney, 1946, pp. 347–8. *The War Diaries of Weary Dunlop* are not quite as damning of the Dutch but it is clear (pp. 71, 73) that there were tensions between them and the Australians.

30 Eddie Gilbert, Eric Kelly, Bob Nowland.

31 Van Nooten diary, p. 30; Murnane diary, 13 May 1942.

32 The US prisoner Ed Weiss made repeated attempts after the war to investigate the bombing but concluded that 'the complete files from that bombing raid were never recovered' (Maynard, 2014, p. 133).

33 NAA B6121 115C.

34 GP 90-HI, p. 14. Copy supplied by Research Services Division, Department of the Air Force Historical Research Agency (DAFHRA), Alabama, USA.

35 SQ-BOMB-319-SU-OP, 5 February – 23 June 1943. DAFHRA.
36 Operations report, SITREP no. 617, 13 February 1943, AWM66
    2-4-11. The most detailed image of the camp (FEN 11/4 Amboina …
    [15 February 43 1255]) is held in the private papers of Sergeant Percy
    Elsum, held by his son Ian. The Australian War Memorial holds images
    taken from a greater height and different angles, series 11/3, but not series
    11/4 (correspondence author and Stuart Bennington, AWM, 23 May
    2024 and subsequent dates).
37 SITREP no. 626, 16 February 1943, AWM66 2-4-11.
38 FEN-11, Allied air attack on Ambon, 15 February 1943, AWM66 2-1-4.
39 Joe Zobel of the MacArthur Memorial, Norfolk, Virginia, who explored
    the question on the author's behalf, advised: 'There is a record of the raid
    on Ambon in Sutherland's papers, 9 B-24s from the 319th hitting the
    island. [General Richard Sutherland was General Douglas MacArthur's
    Chief of Staff]. That is it. There is nothing in the Kenney diaries [General
    George Kenney was commanding officer of Allied Air Forces in the South-
    West Pacific]. There is nothing in RG-4, Official Correspondence with
    the Australian government. I went through War Department message
    traffic through October 1943 and there was nothing about it in there
    either. Most of our stuff is catalogued in the computer and could find
    no reference or mention of Tan Toey.' (Email to author, 11 April 2024.)
40 531st Bombardment Squadron, Report no. 13, 5 September 1943; Report
    no. 9, 19 September 1943, A00636, DAFHRA.
41 380th Bombardment Group, Report no. 19, 20 September 1943, A0636,
    DAFHRA.
42 Report on that Portion of Gull Force remaining on Amboina from
    26 Oct. 42 to 10 Sep. 45, by Major G de V Westley (hereafter referred
    to as 'Westley's report'), pp. 5–6; appendix 2, Scott's report A, pt II.
43 War Criminals – Ikeuchi Masakiyo, 10 February 1947, MP742/1
    336/1/1153.
44 Record of Military Court (Japanese War Criminals), appendix B,
    NAA MP742/1 336/1/1956, pt 2.
45 Westley, War Crimes, p. 8; van Nooten, War Crimes, p. 3.
46 Australian Headquarters, Tan Toey, To all Ranks, 3 March 1944,
    NAA MP742/1 336/1/1956, pt 1.
47 Amendment to Japanese regulations, 13 September 1944, NAA MP742/1
    336/1/1956, pt 1.
48 Japanese Headquarters, Tan Toey, Summary of Japanese regulations,
    5 November 1943, AWM54 1010/6/64: Aust. HQ, To all Ranks.
49 Swanton diary, 29 April 1943, 21 March 1944.
50 AHQ, To all Ranks.
51 Swanton diary, 28, 31 March 1943, 17 March 1944; RJ Matthews,
    Jim Wilson.
52 Swanton diary, 3 April 1944.
53 Swanton diary, 26 February 1944; van Nooten diary, p. 17; Reg Brassey,
    Bob Nowland.
54 According to Walter Hicks, the bags were 100 kilograms at first, and later
    120 kilograms.

55 Quoted in Hank Nelson *POW: Australians under Nippon*, Australian Broadcasting Corporation, Sydney, 1985, pp. 89–90.
56 Van Nooten diary, pp. 16–17; Reg Brassey, Arthur Deakin, George Williamson.
57 Swanton diary, 8 March 1944.
58 Van Nooten diary, p. 23; van Nooten, War Crimes, p. 11.
59 Van Nooten diary, p. 24.
60 Sworn statement by RW Bryans, NAA MP742/1 336/1/1956, pt 1.
61 Sworn statement by AR Grimison, NAA MP742/1 336/1/1956, pt 1.
62 Sworn statement by S Hillian, NAA MP742/1 336/1/1956, pt 1.
63 Van Nooten, War Crimes, p. 12. The Australians killed were FB Hackett, KE Pitman, TR Noble and CP Scott.
64 AHQ, To all Ranks.
65 Westley explained Japanese behaviour in these terms (War Crimes, pp. 13–14), as did the Japanese defence counsel at the Ambon war crimes trial.
66 Sworn statement by N (Noel) Carter, 20 September 1945, AWM54 1010/9/113.
67 Sworn statement by VC (Verdun) Ball, 25 September 1945, NAA A471 81709, pt 2.
68 Sworn statement by Ted Winnell, 1 October 1945, AWM54 1010/9/113.
69 Sworn statement by John Culton, 6 October 1945, NAA A471 81709, pt 2.
70 Van Nooten, War Crimes, p. 4. (Captain) Rod Gabriel was adjutant for a short time before van Nooten.
71 Van Nooten, War Crimes, p. 27; van Nooten diary, p. 30.
72 Sworn statement by Winnell, AWM54 1010/9/113; evidence by Sergeant Major FH Waaldyk to Ambon war crimes trial, NAA A471 81709, pt 1.
73 Van Nooten, War Crimes, p. 3; Waaldyk evidence, p. 74; Reg Brassey, Arthur Deakin, Walter Hicks, Bob Nowland, Harry Williams.
74 Eric Kelly, Keith Mellor.
75 Van Nooten.
76 Swanton diary, 4 August 1943.
77 Summary of Japanese regulations, 5 November 1943, AWM54 1010/6/64; Inquiry report.
78 Swanton diary, 27 April 1943.
79 Inquiry report, p. 4.
80 Dick Brown, Clarrie Hein, Bob Nowland. Details of trading appear throughout Swanton's diary. For the American prisoners making salt, see Edward W Weiss, *Under the Rising Sun*, Edward W Weiss, Pennsylvania, 1946, 1992, pp. 258–9.
81 Swanton diary, 12 April 1944.
82 Swanton diary, 6 October 1943; Reg Brassey, Charles Crouch, Arthur Deakin, R Godfrey, Eric Kelly, AJ Rogers, Sam Rose.
83 J Julian, Sam Hillian, B Thomas, Jim Wilson.
84 Inquiry report, pp. 7–8.
85 Van Nooten, Details of instructions from Japanese Headquarters, 3 March 1944, NAA MP742/1 336/1/1956, pt 1.

86   Swanton dates the ban on private cooking as 21 April 1944.
87   Summary of Japanese regulations, 5 November 1943, AWM54 1010/6/64.
88   See Richard Chauvel, *The Rising Sun in the Spice Islands: A History of Ambon during the Japanese Occupation,* Centre of Southeast Asian Studies, Working Paper no. 37, Melbourne, 1985.
89   Van Nooten diary, pp. 41–2.
90   Swanton diary, 13 March 1944.
91   Summary of Japanese regulations.
92   AJ Rogers, Jim Wilson.
93   Eric Kelly.
94   Jim Wilson, Clarrie Hein, Bill McGregor.
95   Swanton diary, 26 April 1944.
96   Weiss, 1992, p. 252.
97   Swanton diary, 26 August 1943; Clarrie Hein.
98   Arthur Deakin, Jim Wilson.
99   Amendment to Japanese regulations, 13 September 1944, NAA MP742/1 336/1/1956, pt 1.
100   Reg Brassey, Charles Crouch, Arthur Deakin, George Williamson.
101   Van Nooten, War Crimes, p. 9.
102   Eric Kelly.
103   Van Nooten, War Crimes, p. 9; Westley, War Crimes, p. 7.
104   Van Nooten, War Crimes, p. 9.
105   For example, 14 April, 4 July, 29 September 1943.
106   Swanton diary, 20 April, 23 August, 7 September 1943, 3 February 1944; for concerts, various dates.
107   Swanton diary, 19, 23 March, 20 April, 18 May, 17 July 1943, 3 February 1944.
108   Clarrie Hein, Keith Mellor. Harold Beamsley collected recipes given by fellow servicemen, and additional culinary tips, in one of the notebooks he kept while a prisoner (AWM PR05146).
109   Van Nooten diary, pp. 21–2, Swanton diary, 7 January 1944.
110   Westley's report, p. 4.
111   Ted Winnell, Swanton diary, various dates.
112   Bob Nowland, Keith Mellor.
113   Westley, War Crimes, p. 6.
114   Van Nooten, War Crimes, p. 5.
115   Summary of Japanese regulations, 5 November 1943; AHQ, To all Ranks.
116   Designation Sheet for 530 Bomb Sqn of 380 Bomb Group for August 1944, A0636, DAFHRA.
117   Allied Air Operations, SITREP no. 443, 28 August1944, AWM66 2/4/59.
118   Van Nooten diary, pp. 40–1.
119   Weiss, 1992, pp. 263–4.
120   Allied Air Operations, SITREP no. 443, 28 August1944, AWM66 2/4/59.
121   Van Nooten diary, p. 13. Those killed in the raid were RE Beattie, HE Maile and LS Matthews.

122 George Odgers, *Air War Against Japan, 1943–1945*, vol. II, series 3, *Australia in the War of 1939–1945*, Australian War Memorial, Canberra, 1957, p. 246.

Chapter 8: Catastrophe, 1944–45

1 Daily death rates, Tantoei PW camp 1945, NAA A471 81709 pt 3. This is the source for other mortality figures cited later in this chapter.
2 Swanton diary, 1–2 July 1943.
3 Van Nooten diary, p. 16; Inquiry report, p. 4, NAA B3856 146/1/14.
4 Report on medical conditions of POW camp, Ambon, by Captain GC Marshall (hereafter referred to as 'Marshall report'), appendix 3, Scott's report A, pt II; Notes on Ambon island, based on questions to Ehlhart and Lt van Est, 23 September 1945, NAA A471 81709 pt 4. Unless otherwise stated, Marshall's report is the source for information in the following account of health and medical conditions.
5 Swanton diary, 5 July 1943.
6 Van Nooten diary, p. 17.
7 Van Nooten, War Crimes, p. 10; van Nooten diary, p. 16.
8 Van Nooten diary, pp. 16–17.
9 Waaldyk evidence, examined by the prosecuting officer, p. 12, NAA 471 81709 pt 1.
10 Van Nooten, War Crimes, p. 10; Marshall report, p. 2; Inquiry report, p. 6.
11 Van Nooten diary, p. 17.
12 Swanton diary, 16 February, 21 February 1944.
13 Arthur Deakin, Ken Widmer.
14 Swanton diary, 26 April 1944; van Nooten, War Crimes, p. 6.
15 Marshall report, p. 1; Waaldyk evidence, p. 12, NAA A471 81709, pt 1.
16 Notes on Ambon island (Ehlhart and van Est).
17 Swanton diary, 25 September 1943.
18 Van Nooten, War Crimes, p. 11.
19 Marshall report, p. 5.
20 Statement by Marshall, NAA A471 81709, pt 2.
21 Notes on Ambon island (Ehlhart and van Est).
22 Van Nooten, War Crimes, p. 10; van Nooten diary, p. 12; Notes on Ambon island (Ehlhart and van Est).
23 Marshall report, p. 2.
24 Marshall report, pp. 3–4; van Nooten diary, pp. 12–13.
25 Marshall report, p. 6.
26 Marshall report, p. 5.
27 Marshall report, p. 4.
28 Interrogation of Surgeon Lt-Commander Nakamura, 5 December 1945, NAA A471 81709 pt 4. Although there are differing accounts of what the injections consisted of, the commanding officer of the 10th Australian Field Ambulance, Lt-Colonel Palmer, who interrogated Nakamura, thought that his evidence seemed 'quite consistent and credible' from a medical point of view (NAA A471 81709, pt 4).
29 Van Nooten diary, pp. 18–19.

30   Comment by CO, 10th Australian Field Ambulance, NAA A471 81709 pt 4.
31   The account that follows is taken from van Nooten diary, pp. 24–6; van Nooten, War Crimes, pp. 12–13; Westley, War Crimes, p. 4.
32   The Contention and Proof of the Counsel for the Accused, p. 2, NAA A471 81709, pt 1.
33   Quoted in Nelson, 1985, p. 95.
34   Inquiry report, p. 5, NAA B3856 146/1/14.
35   Nelson, 1985, pp. 84 ff.
36   Van Nooten diary, p. 27.
37   Sworn statement by Verdun Ball, 25 September 1945, NAA A471 81709, pt 2.
38   Van Nooten diary, p. 35.
39   Letter from MA Schaefer, 16 September 1945, Schaefer, Frederick Norman, NAA B883.
40   Van Nooten diary, pp. 35–6; Minister assisting the Minister of Defence to (sister) Mrs Weir, 21 August 1975, Elmore, James Frederick, B883. For the trial relating to Schaefer's murder see AWM54 1010/6/80.
41   Van Nooten diary, p. 36.
42   Statement by Naval Lieutenant Kawahara Kiyomune, AWM 54 1010/9/2.
43   Georgina Fitzpatrick, Tim McCormack and Narelle Morris, *Australia's War Crimes Trials*, Brill Nijhoff, Leiden, 2016, pp. 191, 341n.
44   Van Nooten, War Crimes, p. 24. See also van Nooten diary, p. 27.
45   Statement by Petty Officer (2nd class) Kakuda, NAA MP742/1 336/1/1956.
46   Fitzpatrick, McCormack and Morris, 2016, pp. 190–1. Shimakawa's description of the execution can be found in Boyce's personnel file in B883.
47   Daily death rates, Tanteoi PW camp, NAA A471 81709, pt 3.
48   Contention and Proof of the Counsel for the Accused, pp. 4–5, NAA A471 81709 pt 1; petition by Shirozu Wadami, 31 May 1947, AWM54 1010/6/32.
49   Chauvel, 1985, pp. 12–13.
50   Van Nooten, War Crimes, p. 7.
51   Record of Military Court, 15 May 1946, A471 81068.
52   Van Nooten, War Crimes, p. 6.
53   Van Nooten War Crimes, p. 6.
54   Answers to questions put by I McLoy, 63 Aust Inf Bn to Elhart and Lt van Est, 22 September 1945, MP742/1 336/1/395.
55   Marshall report, p. 5.
56   Marshall report, p. 2.
57   Nominal roll, 26 Oct 42, NAA A471 81709 pt 3.
58   Extract from war crimes questionnaire completed by Marshall, AWM54 1010/9/113.
59   Marshall report, p. 3.
60   Van Nooten diary, p. 21.
61   Sworn statement by John Culton, 6 October 1945, NAA A471 81709 pt 2.

62 Sworn statement by FH Waaldyk, 10 November 1945, MP 742/1 336/1/395.

63 Van Nooten diary, p. 22.

64 Letter, VC Ball to author, 15 December 1983.

65 Marshall report, p. 6.

66 Marshall report, p. 2.

67 Quoted in Nelson, 1985, p. 96.

68 Walter Hicks.

69 There is some dispute at to who among the prisoners finally confronted the Japanese and forced them to acknowledge that the war had ended. van Nooten claimed he did so (Nelson, 1985, p. 97), but some of the Americans interned with the Australians in Tan Tui asserted that they were the ones who took the initiative, because Westley and van Nooten were too intimidated by the Japanese (memorandum by Lieutenant TR Drake, USNR, 14 September 1945, AWM 54 229/27/1). See also Weiss, 1992, pp. 292–6.

70 Westley's report, p. 3; extract from Marshall's war crimes questionnaire, AWM54 1010/9/113.

71 Van Nooten, War Crimes, pp. 14–15.

72 Letter by A Smith, HMAS *La Trobe*, 11 September 1945, supplied to author by Keith Mellor; account by Peter Walker, c. 1947, in author's possession.

73 Peter Walker account; letter Tom Davies to parents, 14 September 1945, copy supplied to author.

74 Letter, Audrey Prince (sister) to author, 29 May 1990.

75 Letter, Peter Walker to author, 27 February 1984.

76 ML Powell, 2/5 Aust Gen. Hospital, Report on Recovered PWs. Ex Amboina, 14 September 1945, NAA 471 81709 pt 4.

77 Commanding Officer HMAS *Glenelg*, Evacuation of Allied POW's from Ambon, 12 September 1945, AWM 41/4/15.

78 IC Galbraith, Surgeon Lieutenant RANR, Report on Reception and Treatment of Prisoners of War at Ambon, AWM 54 779/12/5.

79 Extract from contemporary letter by Peter Walker, provided to author.

80 In the discussion that follows, opinions expressed during interviews are not attributed to individuals, in view of the sensitivity of some of the issues.

81 Arneil, 1980, introduction, n. p.

82 See Nelson, 1985, pp. 66–7.

83 Inquiry report, p. 9.

84 Van Nooten.

85 Westley's report, p. 5.

86 Information about officers' work and conditions supplied in a letter from R Godfrey to author, 10 July 1988.

87 The battalion tailor, EN Kelly, wrote to the author after reading the first edition of this book, expressing the view that the reason he survived, when stronger men did not, was because, as the tailor, he was in the position of continuing to do the work he had always done: 'it helped me mentally to accept the situation. Also the fact that I did not have to do much of the

heavy work as well as being in the position of being able to [gain] "extras" from the guards for doing tailoring for them'. (Letter to author, nd 1988?)

88 These figures have been calculated from nominal rolls given to the author during interviews in the 1980s; copies are still in the author's possession. The men substituting for the officers who escaped in March 1942 have been counted as officers for this purpose, as they enjoyed that status throughout captivity.

89 For an analysis of deaths on the Thailand–Burma railway, see Joan Beaumont, 'Officers and men: Rank and survival on the Thai–Burma railway', in Beaumont, Grant and Pegram (eds), 2015, pp. 174–95. For a wider study of the impact of rank on captivity see Joan Beaumont, 'Rank, privilege and prisoners of war', *War and Society*, vol. 1, no. 1, 1983, pp. 67–94.

90 Letter, R Godfrey to author, 10 July 1988.

91 Memo by Lieutenant-General FH Berryman, chief of staff, Advanced Land Headquarters, Southwest Pacific Area, 19 September 1945, NAA MP 729/8 44/431/63.

92 Inquiry report, pp. 1, 3.

93 Inquiry report, pp. 6, 10–11.

94 Inquiry report, p. 9.

95 This description and the following paragraph are based on the Inquiry report, pp. 9–10.

96 Roger Maynard, 2014, pp. xii–xii, gives a much more lurid description of the cage: 'encased in barbed wire, its metal tentacles and sharp spikes capable of drawing blood at every turn … One ill-judged stretch or repositioning of the body could leave a painful and potentially fatal gash in the flesh.' But no sources are cited for this, nor for the claim on p. 176 that a night spent in the cage was 'sheer torture'.

97 Given that Westley's memory seemed so vague on the question of the cage, and that he delegated so much responsibility within the prison camp, it may be speculated as to whether the initiative for the cage came from some other Australian officer or officers. To judge by the Inquiry report, however, Westley accepted full responsibility for it.

98 Inquiry report, p. 10.

99 Coates and Rosenthal, 1977, p. 136.

100 McDougall, 1951, p. 197.

101 One Australian, Lance Corporal B Porter, was located at a Japanese listening station on Ceram. His physical condition at the end of the war, and his own admission of better treatment, indicated that he was 'obviously rendering the enemy valuable aid' (Report regarding Treatment by Japanese at Amboina of Two Allied PWs', 13 November 1945, NAA B3856 144/1/356). But AHQ decided that there was insufficient evidence to warrant disciplinary action (Director of Personal Services to Officer in Charge, Second Echelon, nd, ibid).

Chapter 9: Crisis on Hainan, 1942–43

1 The following account of the journey to Hainan is based on JM Turner, Report on Year Oct 1942 – Oct 1943, appendix 4, Scott's report A, pt II

(hereafter referred to as 'Turner report'); and information from interviews with Sam Anderson, Laurie Benvie, Stuart Campbell, Vic Findlay, I Fishwick, Ron Green, B Larkin, JE McDougall, WJ (Jim) Phillips and L Ryan.

2   Bob Allen.
3   For 'hell ships' statistics, see Grant, 2015, pp. 204–5.
4   Joan Beaumont, 'Victims of war: The allies and the transport of prisoners-of-war by sea, 1939–45', *Journal of the Australian War Memorial*, no. 2, 1983, pp. 1–7.
5   Scott's report A, pt II, p. 13.
6   Scott (ibid.) gives the distance as 6.5 kilometres, but Tahara Susumu, one of the defendants at the war crimes trial in January 1948, estimated it as only 2.4 kilometres (Proceedings of the Australian Military Court, Hong Kong, AWM54 1010/3/111).
7   Scott's report A, pt II, p. 13.
8   G Kissick, Laurie Benvie, JE McDougall, Jim Phillips.
9   The following account of the camp is taken from Scott's report A, pt II, p. 13; Turner report; evidence by CS McCutcheon to the Australian Military Court, Hong Kong (hereafter referred to as 'McCutcheon evidence'), AWM54 1010/3/111; report by EB Bailey on POWs recovered on Hainan, NAA B3856 144/1/400; and the Combined medical and Q report by W Aitken and PP Miskin (hereafter referred to as 'Combined med. & Q report'), appendix 22, Scott's report A, pt II.
10 Pledger diary, end August 1943, AWM PR00871. Pledger's diary did not always give precise dates.
11 Pledger diary, 9 December 1944.
12 Statement by the prosecution and evidence by CF Newnham to the Australian Military Court, Hong Kong (hereafter referred to as 'Newnham evidence'), AWM54 1010/3/111. Newnham was adjutant from 16 October 1943 to 6 June 1945, replacing Turner who had a severe attack of malaria in October 1943.
13 B Larkin.
14 Scott's report A, pt II, p. 13.
15 Scott to camp commandant, 23 January 1943, 5 May 1945, appendix 26, Scott's report A, pt II.
16 The following description is based on RT Phillips, 'The Japanese Occupation of Hainan', *Modern Asian Studies*, vol. 14, no. 1, 1980, pp. 93–109.
17 Prosecution and defence statements, Australian Military Court, Hong Kong, AWM54 1010/3/111.
18 Declaration, appendix 5, Scott's report A, pt II.
19 Scott's report A, pt II, p. 15; Turner report. For the declaration they were meant to sign, see appendix 8, Scott's report A, pt II.
20 Turner report; Newnham evidence.
21 Newnham evidence.
22 Turner report.
23 Don Findlay.
24 Scott's report A, pt II, p. 14.

25   Evidence by Scott to Australian War Crimes Board of Inquiry (hereafter referred to as 'Scott, War Crimes'), 24 October 1947, AWM54 1010/4/127; affidavit by C. S. McCutcheon, 18 August 1947, AWM54 1010/4/99; Turner report.

26   Scott, War Crimes.

27   Sworn statements by IF Macrae, 20 September 1945, NAA B3856 144/14/77.

28   Scott's report A, pt II, p. 17.

29   Sworn statements by RJ Green, 28 August 1945, NAA B3856 144/14/77.

30   Affidavit by Green, 6 June 1947, AWM54 1010/4/62.

31   Newnham's evidence to the Australian Military Court confirms this.

32   Turner report; Combined med. & Q report.

33   Pledger diary, nd, mid-1943.

34   Combined med. & Q report.

35   Turner report; Newnham evidence.

36   Sworn statement by PP Miskin, 28 August 1945, NAA B3856 144/14/77.

37   Miskin to author, 9 January 1987.

38   Turner report.

39   Newnham evidence; Laurie Benvie, Don Findlay, Vic Findlay, Ron Green, KE Lupson, T Phillips, L Ryan.

40   McCutcheon evidence; Don Findlay, KE Lupson, JE McDougall.

41   Frank Biddiscombe, Don Findlay, Vic Findlay, Courtney Harrison, Tom Pledger.

42   McCutcheon evidence; Vic Findlay, Ron Green, B Larkin, PP Miskin.

43   Murnane diary, 22 August 1943; Stuart Campbell, Don Findlay, Vic Findlay, I Fishwick, T Phillips, L Ryan, Charlie Woodward.

44   Murnane diary, 8 January 1944.

45   Combined med. & Q report.

46   Scott's report A, pt II, p. 17.

47   Pledger diary, late August 1943.

48   Murnane diary, 27 August 1943.

49   Bob Allen, Sam Anderson, Laurie Benvie, KE Lupson, IF Macrae.

50   Scott's report A, pt II, p. 17.

51   Laurie Benvie, Stuart Campbell, Charlie Woodward.

52   Don Findlay, T Phillips, L Ryan.

53   The following account is compiled from W Aitken's Medical report POW Camp (Hasio) [sic] Bakli Bay Hainan island, appendix 22, Scott's report A, pt II; and Aitken's affidavit of 4 July 1946, AWM54 1010/4/2. Unless otherwise stated, these two documents are the source for all information concerning the Australians' medical conditions contained in this chapter.

54   Turner report; Scott's report A, pt II, pp. 18–19.

55   Aitken Medical report, p. 3.

56   McCutcheon affidavit, AWM54 1010/4/99.

57   ibid.; Newnham evidence.

58   Diary by JE McDougall (in private hands), 17 August 1943; Murnane diary, 15 August, 1, 3 September 1943.

59   Scott's report A, pt II, p. 19; Newnham evidence.

60   Newnham evidence; evidence by AT Pledger to Australian Military Court, Hong Kong (hereafter referred to as 'Pledger evidence'), AWM54 1010/3/111.
61   Pledger diary, end September 1943.
62   Murnane diary, 4 March 1943, 14 October 1943.
63   Murnane diary, 10 December 1943; G Kissick.
64   Scott's report A, pt II, p. 20; McDougall diary, 11 December 1943; PP Miskin.
65   Newnham and McCutcheon evidence; Scott's report A, pt II, pp. 19–20. The diary written by L/Sgt DGP Foley (AWM54 253-1-4) lists the issues of cigarettes from the Japanese. These feature regularly in Frank Biddiscombe's dairy (AWM 3DRL 1763.)
66   Scott's report A, pt II, pp. 19–20.
67   Murnane diary, 22 December 1943.
68   Scott's report A, pt II, p. 16.
69   Pledger diary, 4 December 1943. See also McDougall diary, 25 December 1943.
70   Scott's report A, pt II, p. 15.
71   Scott's report A, pt II, p. 15. Scott chose to describe himself in the third person in his postwar reports.
72   Macrae interview, 23 September 1983.
73   Very few of those interviewed knew anything of the situation as Scott described it in his report.
74   Frank Biddiscombe, B Larkin, I Fishwick, G Kissick, Clive Newnham, T Phillips, Tom Pledger, L Ryan, Brian Tymms, Charlie Woodward.
75   Johnson interview, 14 November 1983.
76   Scott's report A, pt II, pp. 15-16.
77   Scott's report A, pt II, p. 17.
78   Details of the offences for which men were punished in 1943–44 and the punishments they received were listed in a report prepared by the Australian adjutants, the original of which was held by Clive Newnham and shared with the author in 1983. Descriptions of the electric-shock punishment are from Scott's report A, pt II, p. 17 and conversation with WJ Cook, 27 May 1987. Murnane's diary mentions the use of electric shocks on men handed over to the Japanese for punishment (6 June 1943). Macrae in interview denied that punishments were so severe.
79   Bob Allen, WJ Cook, Don Findlay, Vic Findlay, Ron Green, Courtney Harrison, B Larkin, Ron Leech, JE McDougall, Frank Osborne, Tom Pledger, T Phillips, Jim Phillips, L Ryan, JM Turner, Charlie Woodward.

Chapter 10: Violence, ambush and division, 1944
1   Newnham evidence; McCutcheon evidence; Scott's report A, pt II, p. 20.
2   Newnham evidence; Scott's report A, pt II, p. 22.
3   Pledger diary, 28 March 1944; B Larkin. Austin Carr's 1944 diary (AWM PR00304) is replete with references to the supplementation of his diet through the gardening of tomatoes, pumpkins, onions etc.

4   Bob Allen, Laurie Benvie, Don Findlay, Vic Findlay, Ron Green,
     Courtney Harrison, JE McDougall, T Phillips.
5   The account of the trading organisation is based on Aitken's medical
     report, the Combined med. & Q report, McCutcheon evidence, and an
     interview of the author with PP Miskin, 9 January 1987. Miskin shared
     original copies of correspondence between himself and Scott in December
     1943, setting up the system for auditing Q supplies. For some details of
     how exchanges were managed within the camp, see the diary written by
     L/Sgt DGP Foley (AWM54 253/1/4).
6   Handwritten report by Aitken and Miskin, copy given to author by
     Miskin, in author's possession,
7   Scott's report A, pt II, p. 18.
8   Scott, War Crimes; Newnham evidence; sworn statement by AG Cole,
     1 September 1945, NAA B3856 144/14/77.
9   Frontispiece to McDougall diary.
10   Scott, War Crimes.
11   Murnane diary, 13, 14, 24 February 1944. Murnane's dates for the start of
     Allied raids are confirmed by McDougall's and Pledger's diaries. See also
     McCutcheon evidence.
12   Pledger diary, mid-February 1943; Scott's report A, pt II, p. 21;
     McCutcheon evidence.
13   McCutcheon evidence.
14   Newnham evidence.
15   Sworn statement by ES Tanner, 28 August 1945, NAA B3856 144/14/77.
16   McCutcheon evidence.
17   Sworn statement by RF Long, 26 August 1945, NAA B3856 144/14/77.
18   McCutcheon affidavit, AWM54 1010/4/99; I Fishwick.
19   Sworn statement by K Lupson, 26 August 1945, AWM54 1010/4/93.
20   Sworn statement by F Elliot, 27 August 1945, NAA B3856 144/14/77.
21   Murnane diary, 15, 24 March 1944.
22   Murnane diary, 2, 15 November 1943; McDougall diary, 5 October,
     2 November, 6 December 1943.
23   The following account of the Hoban ambush is based on evidence given
     under oath soon after the event (and repeated in September 1945) by:
     W Aitken, WJ Cook, RJ Green, FA Hillier, JV McMahon, AT Murnane,
     JH Nelson, CF Newnham, CG O'Donnell, FL Taylor (statements found
     at NAA B3856 144/14/177).
24   Statement by RJ Green, 28 September 1945, NAA 3856 144/14/77.
25   Statement by JV McMahon, 27 September 1945, NAA 3856 144/14/77.
26   Statement by FA Hiller, 28 September 1945, NAA 3856 144/14/77.
27   Murnane diary, 8 April 1944.
28   Statement by W Aitken, 6 June 1944, NAA B3856 144/14/77.
29   Statement by RO Smith, 27 September 1945, NAA B3856 144/14/77.
30   Those killed in the ambush were JF Armstrong, VG Claxton,
     LG Cornell, CF Dyer, (Cpl) KR Gilder, RS Hynes, CG McKenzie,
     HER Russell-Talbot, RS Wharton. Taken prisoner by the Chinese were
     AH Chenoweth, AN Haines, AA Hawking, WS Lynch, EM Ratcliffe,

LA Shiells, ETG Stafford, FH Stokes, HA Struhs, HC Youngberry (Scott, Ambush of Australian Work Party, 7 January 1946, appendix 11, Scott's report A, pt II).

31 Maynard, 2014, p. 169.

32 Green evidence.

33 Newnham evidence.

34 Greg Foley listed details of all the personal articles the missing men had left behind (diary written by VX 23913 L/Sgt DGP Foley, AWM54 253-1-4). Frank Biddiscombe kept graphic notes of the injuries the men had suffered in the ambush (Biddiscombe diary AWM 3DRL 1783). Austin Carr's diary, which usually focused on food and work, also listed details of the ambush (AWM PR00304).

35 Scott's report A, pt II, p. 16.

36 Medical report POW Camp, Hashio (Bakli Bay), Hainan Island, appendix 22, Scott's report A, pt II, p. 2.

37 Newnham evidence; Murnane and McDougall diaries, 17 June 1944; Scott to camp commandant, 10 January 1945, appendix 25, Scott's report A, pt II.

38 Reports by VE Cochrane, Chaplain, MP 742/1 336/1/1956.

39 Medical report, p. 2.

40 Bob Allen, Sam Anderson, Laurie Benvie, Stuart Campbell, I Fishwick, Tom Pledger, L Ryan, Brian Tymms, CE Usher.

41 Murnane diary, 24 September 1944; Pledger diary, end September 1943.

42 Maynard, 2014, p. 171 cites Roy Harris, Roy's mate, as the source. Biddiscombe's diary entry for 31 October 1944 says that Roy spoke 'a few home truths' (AWM 3DRL 1763).

43 Scott's report A, pt II, p. 23. The section of the report dealing with Roy's punishment was written by Smith.

44 Newnham, McCutcheon and Pledger evidence.

45 Roy, Lewis Harrison George, NAA B883.

46 NAA A8321 32 Roy Lewis Harrison George.

47 Scott's report A, pt II, p. 23.

48 Letter by John Larkins to his brother, October 1945 (in Larkins' possession).

49 Typescript statement given to author in 1980s by PP Miskin, copy in author's possession. It is not known what circulation this document had.

50 PP Miskin.

51 Miskin, typescript statement.

52 Scott's report A, pt II, p. 16.

53 Scott's report A, pt II, p. 24.

54 D Griffin, PP Miskin. Apart from these two interviewees, a number of other interviewees made veiled references to this incident.

55 Report by VX 44787 – Major IF Macrae, 24 September 1945, appendix 28, Scott's report A, pt II; Macrae interview.

56 Scott's report, A, pt II, p. 23.

57 Sam Anderson, WJ Cook, Don Findlay, Vic Findlay, I Fishwick, Ron Leech, Frank Osborne, L Ryan, Brian Tymms.

58 The Dutch prisoners on Hainan, with whom the Australians appear to have had little close contact, also resorted to punishing thieves with a walking stick: McDougall diary, 26 March 1945.

59 Ron Leech, who was a key member of the vigilance committee, maintained that it was set up as a response to Scott's request to him and that it was confirmed by a meeting of Australian prisoners. Cook, who was also on the committee, had no recollection of a popular vote. Macrae's report of 24 September 1945 says that Scott approved of the committee, but whether this was in advance or in retrospect is not clear.

60 Vic Findlay, I Fishwick, KE Lupson, JE McDougall, Tom Pledger, Jim Phillips, CE Usher.

61 Don Findlay, I Fishwick, Courtney Harrison, John Larkins, CE Usher, Charlie Woodward.

62 For Green's beating, see his statement, 6 June 1947, AWM54 1010/4/62.

63 For violence directed against Anderson, see his affidavit, 3 June 1947, AWM54 1010/4/5.

Chapter 11: Surviving to the end, 1945

1 Newnham evidence.

2 Sworn statements by HW Beamsley, KC Alder, M Higgins, CF Newnham, 23 March 1945, NAA B3856 144/14/77. This file also contains details of the other acts of violence on the beach party in March 1945.

3 Scott's report A, pt II, p. 26; Newnham evidence.

4 According to Newnham's evidence and Ron Green, there was the occasional small working party required to gather wood for the camp.

5 Newnham evidence; Murnane diary, 17 March 1945.

6 Scott's report A, pt II, p. 27.

7 Scott's report A, pt II, p. 17.

8 Murnane diary, 23 February 1943.

9 Scott's report A, pt II, p. 19; Murnane diary, 4 June 1944; Bob Allen, T Phillips.

10 Scott's report A, pt II, p. 25.

11 McCutcheon evidence, Scott's report A, pt II, p. 25.

12 Ron Green, 10 November 1983.

13 The following account, with the exception of some details provided by Ron Leech, is taken from a description of the escape written by Macrae in October 1983 (shared with author). Those who escaped were Macrae, Leech, Stuart Campbell, M Higgins, T Lockwood and A Perrin (report by Macrae, NAA B3856 144/1/400).

14 Scott's report A, pt II, p. 27; Newnham evidence.

15 Scott's report A, pt II, pp. 24–5.

16 Details of the food situation in early 1945 are taken from the Combined med. & Q report, Newnham and McCutcheon evidence, and a letter and notes that Scott prepared for a conference with the Japanese camp commandant early in May 1945 (appendix 14, Scott's report A, pt II).

17 Combined med. & Q report; sworn statement by Miskin, 28 August 1945, NAA B3856 144/14/77.

18   Scott's notes for Japanese commandant; McCutcheon evidence; Frank Biddiscombe, Ron Green.

19   Pledger diary, 3 May 1945; Pledger and McCutcheon evidence; JE McDougall.

20   This account is based on discussions with PP Miskin and original documents that were in his possession when interviewed by the author, detailing the instructions he issued for cooking food and the confrontation between him and Scott late in May 1945. The document describing the confrontation was witnessed by Newnham and Aitken, both of whom were present.

21   Scott's report A, pt II, p. 29. Scott's account of this issue is extremely brief and uninformative.

22   Scott's report A, pt II, pp. 28–9; Scott's notes for Japanese commandant; Aitken's medical report; Newnham and McCutcheon evidence; Pledger diary, 20 June, 24 July 1945; letter from Scott to Japanese commandant, 5 June 1945, appendix 15, Scott's report A, pt II.

23   Aitken's medical report is the source for the following paragraphs.

24   Statement by Aitken, 4 July 1946, AWM54 1010/4/2.

25   Newnham evidence; Ron Green.

26   Aitken's medical report, p. 5.

27   Green affidavit, AWM54 1010/4/62; Newnham evidence.

28   This account is based on Aitken's medical report and Pledger's evidence.

29   Aitken singled out for his highest praise BH Gordon, WJ Phillips and Pledger, all of whom he recommended for promotion.

30   McCutcheon evidence; sworn statement by ES Tanner and VE Cochrane, 28 August 1945, NAA B3856 144/14/77.

31   Scott's report A, pt II, p. 29.

32   Scott's report A, pt II. p. 30.

33   The following account is based on Scott's report A, II, pp. 29–33; report by EB Bailey on POWs recovered on Hainan, NAA B3856 144/1/400; Ron Green.

34   Scott's report says that they were taken to Hasho but Green and Newnham were both certain this was not the case.

35   Sworn statement by PP Miskin, 14 September 1945, appendix 12 to Scott's report A, pt II.

36   Letter, Pledger to Jessie, 18 September 1945, AWM PR00871.

37   See Joan Beaumont, 'The long silence: Australian prisoners of the Japanese', in Peter Dean (ed.), *Australia 1944–45: Victory in the Pacific*, Cambridge University Press, Melbourne, 2016, pp. 88–9.

38   Letter, BJ Plunkett, writing of his brother WR (Bill Plunkett), to author, 13 July 1988, in author's possession.

39   For the lack of communication between families and Australian prisoners of war, see Beaumont, 2016, pp. 88–9.

40   Letter, Jill James to author, 7 June 1994, in author's possession.

41   Janette Bomford, Fractured lives: Australian prisoners of war of the Japanese and their families, PhD thesis, Deakin University, 2001, p. 122.

42   This excludes the 19 killed in the Hoban ambush.

43   Vast though the literature on prisoners of war is, very little of it deals

explicitly with the question of the factors determining individual survival, as opposed to differences between cohorts of prisoners (by location, captor, nationality). Among those authors who do are: AJ Barker, *Behind Barbed Wire*, Batsford, London, 1974, pp. 198–200; JE Nardini, 'Survival factors in American prisoners of war of the Japanese', *American Journal of Psychiatry*, vol. 109, issue 4, 1952, pp. 241–8; Wolf and Ripley, 1947, pp. 180–93. A topic that seems to have preoccupied scholars more than the reasons for survival is the related, but separate, question of the prisoners' psychological adjustment to captivity.

44   A medical prisoner of war from Malaya, who agreed that married men had advantages over single, was Stanley S Pavillard, *Bamboo Doctor*, Pan Books, London, 1962 (first published, 1960), p. 99.

45   Nardini, 1952, p. 246.

46   Aitken's medical report.

47   For comments about the importance of will, see Nardini, 1952, pp. 244–5; Pavillard, 1962, p. 81, and Warner and Sandilands, 1983, pp. 227–8.

48   For further analysis of attestation forms, see Beaumont, 1988, pp. 209–11.

49   Sergeant Wilson, who was the substitute for Jinkins, is counted as an officer for this purpose.

50   See Beaumont, 1983 ('Rank'), particularly pp. 76–81.

51   Reviewed petition for commutation, 10 October 1946, NAA MP742/1 336/1/1153. For Shirozu, see Petition by Capt Shirozu Wadami, 15 May 1947, AWM1010/6/32.

Chapter 12: Justice and burials

1   This is the title of Michael McKernan's 2001 study, *This War Never Ends*. He took the phrase from an interview with a former prisoner of war of the Japanese (email communication with author, 10 April 2024).

2   The account of the Ambon war crimes trials that follows draws on Fitzpatrick et al., 2016, pp. 374–5, 384–401.

3   NAA MP742/1 336/1/1956, pt 3.

4   Director of Prisoners of War and Internees, 'War Crimes – Laha Massacre', 12 June 1946, NAA MP742/1 336/1/1587 pt 2. A decision on Recommendation of reduction of sentence, re Hatakeyama Kunito, NAA 16 April 1954, B4166 763.

5   Sgt Winnell – Informant, Ambon Tan Toey Galala Camp, B336/1/1956, pt 1.

6   'Ill-treatment toward Japanese POWs at Morotai camp committed by Australians', NAA MP742/1 336/1/1153.

7   Fitzpatrick et al., 2016, p. 398.

8   'Ill-treatment toward Japanese POWs'.

9   'Ill-treatment toward Japanese POWs'.

10   '"Renamed" by AIF', *Sun News-Pictorial*, 4 January 1946.

11   Investigating Officer's Report, Alleged Ill-treatment of Navy Civilian Ikeuchi Masakiyo, NAA MP742/1 336/1/1153.

12   John Ellis, RMO Eighth Military District, 'Medical examination of Ikeuchi Masakiyo', 20 January 1947, NAA MP742/1 336/1/1153.

13   The analysis that follows relies on Fitzpatrick et al., 2016, pp. 781–809.
      See Gavan McCormack, 'Apportioning the blame: Australian trials
      for railway crimes' in Hank Nelson and Gavin McCormack (eds),
      The Burma–Thailand Railway: Memory and History, Allen & Unwin,
      St Leonards, NSW, 1993, p. 86 for Japanese historians unanimously
      depicting trials as victors' justice.
14   See Sandra Wilson, Robert Cribb, Beatrice Trefault and Dean
      Aszkielowicz, *Japanese War Criminals: The Politics of Justice after the Second
      World War*, Columbia University Press, New York, 2017, p. 6.
15   '290 murdered on Ambon in 8 months', (Melbourne) *Herald*, 3 January
      1946; 'Ambon prison regulations provided execution for excitement', *Sun*,
      7 January 1946; 'Sadism of enemy in POW camp', *Argus*, 9 January 1946;
      'Jap "villain" denies part in 400 deaths', *Herald*, 7 February 1946.
16   Wilson et al., 2017, p. 68, say 92 defendants.
17   Wilson et al., 2017, p. 81.
18   Fitzpatrick et al., 2016, p. 809; Wilson et al., 2017, p. 5.
19   The records of the trials relating to Ambon are held in the Australian
      War Memorial, under AWM54 1010/6/[various numbers]. Given how
      extensive they are, they are best searched by the location of the crime
      (e.g. Laha), the victim/s (e.g. Schaeffer, Boyce) or name of Japanese
      defendant (e.g. Ikeuchi Masakiyo, Shirozu Wadami).
20   Ikeuchi's petition of 10 October 1946 is found in NAA MP742/1
      336/1/1153. Letter to Rearick, 7 December 1946, ibid.
21   Letter to my wife, NAA MP742/1/ 336/1/1153.
22   Kotoko Ikeuchi to Commanding General, Australian Army, Rabaul,
      Petition for Re-Trial of Ikeuchi, Masakiyo, 15 December 1946, NAA
      MP742/1 336/1/1153.
23   Kiki Kimura, to Confirming Authority, Australian War Criminal
      Tribunal, 6 December 1946, NAA MP742/1/ 336/1/1153.
24   Masaharu Mochizuki and Hajime Ode, To Commanding General,
      Australian Army Rabaul, re Ikeuchi Masakiyo, 10 December 1946,
      NAA MP742/1/ 336/1/1153.
25   Fitzpatrick et al., 2016, p. 341n.
26   L Barham, Adjutant-General, Japanese War Criminals sentenced by
      Australian military courts, 11 May 1956, Decision of recommendation
      re reduction of sentence, 16 April 1954, NAA B4166 763.
27   The proceedings of the Hainan trials are found at NAA 871 81590
      pts 1–6, replicated AWM54 1010/3/111. See also Fitzpatrick et al.,
      2016, pp. 606–46.
28   For sentences, see AWM 226 17.
29   W Anderson, Adjutant-General, 'Hainan Island Trial – Trial by Military
      Court Capt Tahara Susumu and others', 15 October 1948, NAA A471
      81950, pt 1.
30   War crimes – Supplications and petitions, NAA MP742/1 B336/1/1593,
      pt 2.
31   For further discussion of the reasons for this, see Joan Beaumont,
      'The Yokohama war cemetery, Japan: imperial, national and local
      remembrance', in Patrick Finney (ed.), *Remembering the Second World*

War, Routledge, London, 2018, pp. 159–60. The governments on the IWGC were Britain, Australia, Canada, India, New Zealand, Pakistan and South Africa.

32 The following account is based on reports by Major HW Jackson, Hainan Search Detachment, 3 Australian PW Contact and Enquiry Unit, 3 May, 19 August, 26 October 1946, NAA CRS B3856 144/1/400.

33 Adjutant-General, 'Transfer of Australian remains from Hainan to Yokohama', 8 October 1946, NAA MP 742/ 132/1/496.

34 GHQ SEALF, Quarterly Historical Report, Graves, 1 Oct–31 Dec 1946, WO 268/109, National Archives, London.

35 Adjutant-General, 'Transfer of Australian remains from Hainan to Yokohama'.

36 Cyril Chambers, Minister for the Army, to Colonel RS Ryan, Parliament House, no date; Cyril Chambers, Minister for the Army to Prime Minister Chifley, no date, NAA MP742/1 132/1/496.

37 The figure for Germany is taken from cemeteries with more than 200 war dead, <www.dva.gov.au/recognition/office-australian-war-graves/war-cemeteries-and-gardens-remembrance/war-cemeteries-overseas#war-cemeteries-overseas-with-more-than-200-australian-war-dead>, accessed 23 September 2024.

38 'Gull Force played epic part in delaying Jap advance', *Argus*, 28 September 1946.

39 Parliament of Australia, House of Representatives, Question, Thomas White, 8 November 1946, <parlinfo.aph.gov.au>.

40 WG Farrell to Colonel RS Ryan, Parliament House, 1 November 1946, NAA MP742/1 132/1/496.

41 EE Dunlop, President, Australian Prisoners of War Relatives' Association, to Prime Minister (Chifley), 11 October 1946, NAA MP 742/1 132/1/496.

42 Letter, Roland A Newton, Honorary Secretary RSS & AILA, 18 October 1946, 132/1/461, NAA MP742/1 132/1/496.

43 FM Forde to Prime Minister Chifley, 30 October 1946, NAA A705/2 95/1/29. Forde recommended this, despite the problematic issue of what to do with the ashes of Australian prisoners who had died while in camps in Japan and whose remains had been mixed with those of the dead of other nationalities.

44 F Strahan, Secretary to Cabinet to Cyril Chambers, Minister for the Army, 7 November 1946, NAA A705/2 95/1/29.

45 Parliament of Australia, House of Representatives, Question, Cyril Chambers, 8 November 1946, <parlinfo.aph.gov.au>.

46 'War graves in Japan', *Sydney Morning Herald*, 9 November 1946; 'Burial of soldiers in Japan deplored', *Canberra Times*, 9 November 1946; 'Australian war graves to remain in Japan', *Argus*, 24 December 1946.

47 Parliament of Australia, House of Representatives, Question, Cyril Chambers, 8 November 1946, <parlinfo.aph.gov.au>.

48 Boin, 1997, p. 18.

49 Lim to H Wrigley, Command Australian Forces Ambon, 12 January 1946, NAA A431 1946-679.

50 Departmental despatch no. 10 from Australian Embassy Djakarta. By
    JDL Hood, nd 1950?, NAA A4367 252-7; 'Political developments
    relating to the provinces', 3 January 1951, NAA 11838 403-5-1-1-2 pt 3.
51 Departmental despatch NAA A4367 252–7.
52 LR McIntyre, ambassador, Jakarta, to Secretary Department of External
    Affairs, Canberra, 31 January 1959, LJ Lawrey, counsellor, Australian
    embassy, Jakarta, to Secretary Department of External Affairs, Canberra,
    3 January 1959, NAA 3211 1973-3004.
53 AE Brown (Secretary-General for Commonwealth War Graves, South-
    East Asia) to W Wynne Mason, IWGC, 7 August 1958, NAA 3211
    1973-3004.
54 Memo, Commonwealth–Indonesian War Graves Agreement, Letter KCO
    Shann, Djakarta, to Sir S Gilchrist, British ambassador, Djakarta, 5 April
    1965, NAA A1838 1510-3-24-1 pt 4.
55 TK Lim to 15th 'Pattimura' Military Command, Ambon, 30 September
    1965, NAA 1838 1510-2-24 pt 4.
56 CWGC, 'Ambon war cemetery', <www.cwgc.org/visit-us/find-cemeteries-
    memorials/cemetery-details/2015000/ambon-war-cemetery> accessed
    10 April 2024.
57 Letter WJ Chalmers (CWGC) to FC Boyle, Australia House, London,
    19 April 1968, NAA A1838 1510-3-24-1 pt 3.
58 The order of service can be found at NAA E203 161-3-D1.
59 Australian Government, Department of Foreign Affairs and Trade, <www.
    dfat.gov.au/news/media/Pages/australian-aid-to-help-victims-of-violence-
    in-maluku-indonesia>, accessed 12 November 2024.
60 Conversation with John McCarthy, Australian ambassador to Jakarta
    1997–2001, 23 October 2023.
61 Email, Kenneth Brownrigg (former defence attaché, Jakarta) to author,
    29 October 2023.
62 Email, Commonwealth War Graves Commission to author, 27 October
    2023. The CWGC did not grant the author access to files relating to this
    decision.

Chapter 13: Living with the memory
1   The only studies of Gull Force's homecoming are my own 1989 article;
    and Bomford, 2001. Both studies drew on interviews with Gull Force
    survivors and their families; in the case of my 1989 article, 48 former
    members of Gull Force and 31 of their wives and widows were surveyed.
    Unless otherwise stated, all biographical details about and quotations
    from Gull Force survivors and families are taken from this article. For
    wider studies of the return of prisoners of war, see Stephen Garton, *The
    Cost of War: Australians Return*, Oxford University Press, Melbourne,
    1996, ch. 7; McKernan, 2001; and Christina Twomey, *The Battle Within:
    POWs in Postwar Australia*, NewSouth Publishing, Sydney, 2018.
2   Bomford, 2001, pp. 137–8.
3   'Smooth their way back', *Argus*, 1 September 1945.
4   See Bomford, 2001, pp. 158–9.
5   *Going Home*, cited in Bomford, 2001, p. 156.

6   ML Powell, Report on Recovered Prisoners of war – 2/5 Aus Gen Hosp, AWM54 481/12/174.
7   For a discussion of POW impotence, see Twomey, 2018, pp. 134–6.
8   Beaumont, 1989, p. 47.
9   For further detail, see Garton, 1996, pp. 219–21; McKernan, 2001, pp. 94–5. For press coverage, see McKernan, pp. 114–16, 122, 127–8.
10 See Twomey, 2018, ch. 2 for extensive discussion of the ambiguity in official attitudes towards ex-prisoners of war.
11 For a synthesis of the history of compensation, see Christina Twomey, 'Compensating prisoners of war of Japan in post-war Australia', in Beaumont, Grant and Pegram, 2015, pp. 254–75.
12 Twomey, 2018, pp. 72, 61.
13 The decision of the so-called Owen Committee to refuse the ex-prisoners a subsistence allowance was not unanimous. Ted Fisher, who had been a doctor on the Thai–Burma railway and was now president of the Council of the 8th Division, submitted a dissenting report (Twomey, 2018, pp. 69–70).
14 Twomey, 2018, pp. 77, 82–8.
15 The original allocation of 1952 was supplemented by further government grants in the 1960s and 1970s: Twomey, 2018, p. 77. Garton (1996, p. 224) concludes that a greater proportion of former prisoners of war received government pensions than other veterans. Moreover, they were likely to have their pensions assessed at a higher rate and have their pension rate increase over time.
16 Cited in Beaumont, 1989, p. 46. Rowland would progress after the war to hold executive positions in a major insurance company.
17 Twomey, 2018, pp. 74–5.
18 For details see Garton, 1996, pp. 226–7; Twomey, 2018, ch. 9.
19 Garton, 1996, pp. 224–5.
20 For this memorial see Lachlan Grant, 'What makes a "National" War Memorial? The case of the Australian ex-prisoners of war memorial', *Public History Review*, vol. 12, 2006, pp. 99–102.
21 Liz Reed, *Bigger than Gallipoli: War, History and Memory in Australia*, University of Western Australia Press, Crawley, WA, 2004, esp. pp. 83–90. For an accessible survey of POW literature, see Beaumont, Grant and Pegram, 2015, pp. 1–17.
22 Gull Force (2/21 Bn) Association 2001 Newsletter.
23 Gull Force, <www.gullforce.org.au> accessed 30 May 2024.
24 Jay Winter, 'Forms of kinship and remembrance in the aftermath of the Great War', in Jay Winter and Emmanuel Sivan (eds), *War and Remembrance in the Twentieth Century*, Cambridge University Press, Cambridge, 1999, p. 40.
25 Gull Force (2/21 Bn) Association October 199 Newsletter.
26 Bruce Scates, *Anzac Journeys: Returning to the Battlefields of World War II*, Cambridge University Press, Melbourne, 2013, p. 3.
27 Information given to author by Ian Elsum, 20 May 2024.
28 For an overview of pilgrimages see Paul Rosenzweig, 'Anzac on Ambon: 30 years of Gull Force pilgrimages', *Sabretache*, vol. 40, no, 2, 1999, pp. 3–15.

29 Others in the first pilgrimage were Ian Macrae, Laurie Benvie, Walter Hicks, RJ Mathews, AJ Rogers and Ted Winnell, CJ Righetti replacing Rod Gabriel). Three had spent less than a year on Ambon before being transferred to Hainan.

30 'Pilgrimage to Ambon, October 1967', NAA 4359 221-7-19. A good survey of early activities, from which much of the material in this section is taken, can be found in 'Gull Force and Gull Force Association, Ambon Anzac Day visits', NAA E499 3-3-38 pt 2.

31 Project Goodwill, Report, NAA A3808 1974-5393 pt 4.

32 Bill Gasperesz (alternate spelling Gasperez) was the eldest son of the traditional Raja of Nakoe who was living in Galala village near Tan Tui during the war and assisted Jinkins in his escape. His brother was beheaded by the Japanese (Rosenzweig, 1999, p. 8). His memories of the war, and those of his wife, Barbara, can be found in the AWM's sound archive: <www.awm.gov.au/collection/C1202711>, accessed 22 June 2023.

33 Project Goodwill, Report, NAA A3808 1974-5393 pt 4.

34 Order of service Ambon Anzac Day, NAA E499 3-3-8 pt 2. This file contains various detailed reports by Rod Gabriel on Anzac Day pilgrimages.

35 Unless otherwise stated, information about Project Goodwill is taken from RC Gabriel, 'Gull Force and Gull Force Association', NAA E499 3-3-8 pt 2; and correspondence held in NAA 4359 221-7-19. The donated equipment included electrical generators, an operating theatre and laboratory equipment, plumbing and electrical material, three motor launches, dental chairs and equipment, a lawn mower, and many other items. A former prisoner and Melbourne dentist, Geoff Sutcliffe, donated his time and expertise to the hospital dental clinic.

36 For Ambon being more important for Australia than Indonesia, conversation with (former ambassador) John McCarthy, 23 October 2023.

37 Report by Jinkins, NAA A6932-10-02.

38 Gull Force (2/21 Bn) Association reports on 1983 and 1984 pilgrimages, NAA E499 3-3-38 pt 2.

39 Gull Force Association, Gull Force Anzac Day Memorial Service and Pilgrimage, Administrative Instruction no. 1 1983, NAA E499 3-3-38 pt 2.

40 To those attending the Anzac Day Memorial Service at Ambon War Cemetery, NAA E499 3-3-8 pt 2.

41 Letter from Ambon committee to Assistant Chief of the Defence Force (Operations), 27 December 1984, Gabriel to Secretary, Department of Defence, 30 November 1985, NAA E499 3-3-38 pt 2.

42 Rob McDougall, email to author, 17 June 2024.

43 The following account draws on Gull Force (2/21 Bn.) Assoc., Report of the Delegation of members of the Gull Force (2/21 Bn.) Assoc. to the People's Republic of China, including Hainan Island, and to Japan, 3rd. to 31st. March 1985, AWM 1067. The delegation included Rod Gabriel, Clive Newnham*, Walter Hicks, Andy Kirwan, Neil Roach (son of Len),

Stan Vaughan*, Ron Green*, Ian Macrae* and Stuart Campbell*. Five, marked*, had been prisoners on Hainan.

44 'Australian PoW mystery solved', *Age*, 30 March 1990; Gull Force (2/21 Bn.) Association December 1992 Newsletter.

45 'After 46 years, Australian POW mystery solved', *Age*, 30 March 1990, <www.theage.com.au/world/asia/from-the-archives-1990-after-46-years-australian-pow-mystery-solved-20210326-p57eby.html>, accessed 28 June 2024.

46 DVA, Gull Force memorial, <www.dva.gov.au/recognition/commemorating-all-who-served/memorials>, accessed 18 June 2024.

47 Information supplied by Cherry Cai, Manager of Economic Development and International Relations, Darwin City Council, 22 August 2023.

48 Information supplied by Christine Moore, daughter of Stan Vaughan, prisoner on Hainan, 8 July 2024.

49 Stephen McDonell, 'Gull Force monument on China's Hainan Island recognises mystery of Australian prisoners of war who fought alongside Chinese guerillas in WWII', ABC, <www.abc.net.au/news/2015-03-28/wwii-tale-of-cooperation-strengthens-australia-china-relations/6355250>, accessed 22 June 2024.

50 Email Darren Kerr, defence attaché, Australian embassy Beijing, to author, 18 June 2024.

51 The official 2018 Hainan Island Promotional Video, <www.youtube.com/watch?v=nexKvA1fh9E>, accessed 26 June 2024.

52 Marianne Hirsch, 'Postmemory', <postmemory.net>, accessed 18 June 2024.

53 Letter, Jane Washington-Smith to author, 27 June 1988, in author's possession.

54 Letter, BJ Plunkett to author, 13 July 1988, in author's possession.

55 A fuller description of the 2024 pilgrimage can be found in Joan Beaumont, '"I never knew my uncle": The phenomenon of pilgrimages and postmemory', *Australian Book Review*, July 2024, pp. 19–22.

56 Ian Swan, April 2024, who also provided the author with the copy of the poem written by Reginald Monk and agreed to its use.

57 See Pierre Nora, *Realms of Memory: Rethinking the French Past*, Columbia University Press, New York, 1992, pp. 18, 14.

58 Rob McDougall, treasurer of the Gull Force Association since 2001, affirms there has been no government funding in this time: email to author, 22 June 2023.

59 Space precludes a comparison of the Ambon pilgrimages with those to other Second World War sites. For these, see Joan Beaumont, 'The diplomacy of extra-territorial heritage: The Kokoda Track, Papua New Guinea', *International Journal of Heritage Studies*, vol. 22, no. 5, pp. 355–67; and Scates, *Anzac Journeys*.

Chapter 14: Gull Force in national memory

1 For the *Bridge on the River Kwai* and a Changi-based film, see Karl Hack and Kevin Blackburn, 'The *Bridge on the River Kwai* and *King Rat*: Protest and ex-prisoner of war memory in Britain and Australia', in Karl Hack

and Kevin Blackburn (eds), *Forgotten Captives in Japanese-Occupied Asia*, Routledge, London, 2007, pp. 147–71.

2   The film was produced by Brian Williams, son of the war crimes prosecutor John Williams: see Maynard, 2014, pp. 264–6; Hank Nelson, '*Blood Oath*: A reel history', *Australian Historical Studies*, vol. 24, issue 97, 1991, pp. 429–42.

3   'Blood & Bamboo', *Advertiser*, 31 July 1999.

4   John Lahey, 'Of 2500 soldiers, only six survived', 25 January 1995.

5   For a critique see Stephen Garton, 'Changi as television: Myth, memory, narrative and history', *Journal of Australian Studies*, vol. 26, no, 73, pp. 79–88.

6   See AWM315 328/003/017 05 for the Barbed Wire and Bamboo exhibition.

7   A special issue of the *Journal of the Australian War Memorial* (no. 14, 1989) marked the new gallery and included an article ('Showing people captivity', pp. 3–10) by Memorial staff Matthew Higgins, Jane Peek, Ron Gilchrist, Lola Wilkins and Joyce Bradley, on which the following analysis draws. In addition to its own collections, the Memorial used some of the interviews from the ABC series collated by Hank Nelson and Tim Bowden. I am grateful to Peter Stanley for his recollections on gallery development, 24 June 2024.

8   BEW Kelson, Deputy Director, Museum Collections and Services, explained to correspondent L Hudson on 17 July 1989 that given space constraints and 'in the interests of maintaining a balanced presentation, it is not possible to do more than deal with, for example, the general experience of Australians under the Japanese or the Germans in World War Two. The same is true of Australian prisoners of war in World War One and Korea', AWM371 88-0282.

9   Munnerley died on Ambon on 18 May 1945.

INDEX

9 781761 170027